The Present State of Scholarship in Historical and Contemporary Rhetoric

The Present State of Scholarship in Historical and Contemporary Rhetoric

Revised Edition

Edited by Winifred Bryan Horner

University of Missouri Press

Columbia and London

Library of Congress Cataloging-in-Publication Data

The Present state of scholarship in historical and contemporary
rhetoric / edited by Winifred Bryan Horner.—Rev. ed.
     p.   cm.
   Includes bibliographical references and index.
   ISBN 0–8262–0763–4. — ISBN 0–8262–0764–2 (pbk.)
   1. Rhetoric—Historiography.   2. Rhetoric—Bibliography.
I. Horner, Winifred Bryan.
PN183.P7   1990
016.808—dc20   90–45384
                                                        CIP

∞™ This paper meets the requirements of the
American National Standard for Permanence of Paper
for Printed Library Materials, Z39.48, 1984.

Designer: Kristie Lee
Typesetter: Connell-Zeko Type & Graphics
Printer and binder: Thomson-Shore, Inc.
Typeface: Palatino and Engravers Text

Contents

Preface

The first edition of *The Present State of Scholarship in Historical and Contemporary Rhetoric* served to define the field in a way that no other book on rhetoric had done before. It has become a classic for scholars and students alike, but, because of the burgeoning scholarship in rhetorical studies, that first edition quickly became dated. Bibliographies need to be as lively as the field that they document, so it has become necessary to rework this study. Much that is old and still worthwhile is retained, and much that is new and valuable has been added. Some suggestions for future directions included in the first edition have been taken up and pursued, some remain to be explored, and more have been added by the authors, each an active worker in the field of rhetoric. This book is built on the work of scholars in rhetoric, and it is their research that makes this compilation possible. It stands as a tribute to them, and its purpose is to make their work available to scholars in a number of different fields.

This work is an attempt to put together under one cover the wide variety of scholarship in the diverse field of rhetoric. The classical period is included since much that follows is either a reinforcement of or a reaction against the first canon. Rhetoric dominates the life of the middle ages, as is evident in Professors Murphy and Camargo's chapter, and Professor Abbott's study suggests that the reassertion of rhetorical scholarship is making possible and necessary a rewriting of Renaissance literature. In Chapter 4 Professor Barton and I describe the shift in rhetoric's focus in the eighteenth century and trace the decline of the old rhetoric and the emergence of the new in the epistemology of the period. Donald Stewart traces this new rhetoric through the nineteenth century, bringing the present book's historical record to a close.

Finally, James L. Kinneavy concludes with an account of the contemporary concepts that have their roots in this history. In this section he traces the blossoming of the traditional rhetorical concerns as they invade a number of disciplines and theoretical constructs in the modern academy. Kinneavy does not attempt to follow the historical thread set up by the earlier chapters, since narrating a history that is still in the making is an impossible undertaking. Rather he gives an account of the contemporary scene.

One problem evident in all the periods covered in this new edition has been the difficulty of documenting the new awareness of works by women and about women in the history of rhetoric. Much of this material is still unpublished and is best known through papers and lectures at rhetoric conferences. A search through the journals often does not turn up such materials, since, as studies that are still considered marginal, they often find voice only in marginalized publications.

Given the nature and scope of this project, it has been necessary to place some limitations on the reviews of the scholarship for each period. Obviously, it would not be possible thoroughly to cover the rhetoric of any of these periods in the space of just one chapter. Each of the above contributors has attempted to provide information and recommendations about primary and secondary works that should be most beneficial to readers who wish to pursue the study of the rhetoric of one of the periods. It is hoped that readers will continue to use this work as a point of departure for further study; thus, evaluative comments that are offered are with the intent of helping the reader choose those works that most deserve more careful attention.

This book is a gathering of the works of many scholars from a number of fields, but it is finally a collection for those students and scholars who see in rhetoric the core of humanistic studies.

Abbreviations

ABR	*American Benedictine Review*
AFM	*Archivum Franciscanum Historicum*
AJP	*American Journal of Philology*
BCRE	*British and Continental Rhetoric and Elocution Microfilms.* Ann Arbor: Mich.: 1953.
CCC	*College Composition and Communication*
CE	*College English*
CIMAGL	*Cahiers de l'Institut du Moyen-Âge Grec et Latin*
CM	*Communication Monographs* (formerly *Speech Monographs*)
CQ	*Communication Quarterly*
CSSJ	*Central States Speech Journal*
EAI	*Early American Imprints, 1639–1800.* Edited by Clifford K. Shipton. Published for the American Antiquarian Society. Worcester, Mass.: Readex Corporation, 1969.
ECS	*Eighteenth-Century Sources for the Study of English Literature and Culture.* Micrographics, 11. Keswick, Va., 1979.
ECSt	*Eighteenth-Century Studies*
EJ	*English Journal*
HSCP	*Harvard Studies in Classical Philology*
LSE	*Leeds Studies in English*
MÆ	*Medium Ævum*
MARS	*Medieval and Renaissance Studies*
MLR	*Modern Language Review*
MP	*Modern Philology*
MS	*Mediaeval Studies*
NLH	*New Literary History*
PMLA	*Publications of the Modern Language Association of America*
PQ	*Philological Quarterly*
PR	*Philosophy and Rhetoric*
Pre/Text	*Pre/Text: A Journal of Rhetorical Theory*
QJS	*Quarterly Journal of Speech Communication*
RQ	*Renaissance Quarterly*
RR	*Rhetoric Review*
RSQ	*Rhetoric Society Quarterly*
SM	*Speech Monographs* (now *CM, Communication Monographs*)
SMed	*Studi Medievali*
SP	*Studies in Philology*
SSB	*Southern Speech Bulletin* (now *SSJ, Southern Speech Communication Journal*)

SSJ	*Southern Speech Communication Journal* (formerly *SSB, Southern Speech Bulletin*)
SSL	*Studies in Scottish Literature*
WC	*Written Communication*
WJSC	*Western Journal of Speech Communication* (formerly *WS, Western Speech*)
WMQ	*William and Mary Quarterly*
WS	*Western Speech* (now *Western Journal of Speech Communication*)

The Present State of Scholarship in Historical and Contemporary Rhetoric

Foreword
Walter J. Ong, S.J.

The emergence and continued presence of rhetoric as a subject of academic study and as a focal point for academic and para-academic life is one of the central features of Western civilization. Although verbal performance in all cultures across the globe can be highly sophisticated and effective, nothing quite like the rhetoric worked up by the ancient Greeks and their successors developed anyplace else in the world.

Apart from its present specialized reference in the United States to courses in effective writing, the term *rhetoric* commonly suggests to the modern mind, in the United States as elsewhere, verbal profusion calculated to manipulate an audience, an operation whose aims are suspect and whose typical procedures are mostly trivializing. Yet in centuries past *rhetoric* was commonly used in the West to refer to one of the most consequential and serious of all academic subjects and of all human activities. As the art of persuasion, the art of producing genuine conviction in an audience, rhetoric affected the entire range of human action as nothing else in theory or in practice quite did. The study and use of rhetoric enabled one to move others, to get things done.

To many Renaissance humanists, as Jerrold E. Seigel has shown in *Rhetoric and Philosophy in Renaissance Humanism*, by contrast with rhetoric most if not all other academic subjects were trivializing: philosophical and scientific theorizing was utterly inconsequential because it had no effect on events, on the way people actually behaved. The study of rhetoric required engagement in the totality of human affairs, in politics and other decision-making fields, in real life, as the ancient Greeks and Romans had already appreciated. Rhetoric conferred power, and admirably humane power, for its power depended on producing conviction in others, on giving others grounds to act on out of free human decision resulting from deliberation. Such power befitted human beings. It was radically different from the brute power exerted by war and other uses of physical force. Compared to knowledge of rhetoric, with its power to determine the course of history, the rest of knowledge in itself was ineffectual twaddle, unless it could be put to rhetorical use— as any or all of it might be, for, as Cicero insisted, it is the business of the orator or practicing rhetorician, who is the leader in public affairs, to know everything. The demands of rhetoric defined for Cicero what liberal education was.

Yet the ancient and Renaissance worlds also had some misgivings about rhetoric. Socrates and Plato and Aristotle professed to believe that the Sophists of their day generally were dishonest rhetoricians, using their intellectual and verbal skill to trick their audiences and teaching their disciples to do the same. This charge illustrates in another way the power of rhetoric. There are dangers of deception at many levels inherent in its use: if the charge is true, the Sophists were rhetorical deceivers; if it is not, their accusers were guilty of the rhetorical deception of which they accused the Sophists. It seems that honors here were in fact somewhat even. Much modern scholarship has shown that the Sophists were in fact often brilliant and learned men, though more concerned with training for practical life than with theories of "philosophy," and that they did not all profess or teach intellectual or verbal irresponsibility or chicanery.

Aristotle defined the art of rhetoric as the faculty of finding in any given case the available means of persuasion. As this definition astutely indicates, one who wants to persuade needs skills that are essentially heuristic, an art of finding. Rhetoric starts with the conclusion, the position it wants to convince others to take, for which it must find supporting reasons. In this it contrasts with logic. Logic lets premises lead to whatever conclusions they lead to. Rhetoric knows its conclusions in advance, and clings to them. This heuristic nature of rhetoric is what makes it open to charges of opportunism. With its end in view, it will use any means, moral or immoral, that work to achieve that end.

Aristotle notes that the practice of rhetoric grows at first from a natural ability. Most people attempt to support or assess or attack one or another opinion verbally or to defend or attack other persons verbally, and through hit-and-miss experience many eventually develop a certain knack for highly effective procedures. Presumably such was the case from the beginning of humankind in all cultures. Rhetoric remained pretty much in this relatively unreflective state in the West until the effective interiorization of alphabetic writing among the ancient Greeks by the fifth century B.C. Such writing made possible the lengthy, analytic linear organization of thought that we call scientific and that, once it had become more or less a habit of mind, could transform orally composed thought itself into a new literate orality, using thought processes unavailable before writing. Like Plato, Aristotle felt the new drive to the more abstract, logically sequential thought and undertook to investigate and state in abstract scientific form, among other things, how successful speakers in his milieu gained their ends and why. The result was the book we know as his *Art of Rhetoric*. In Pope's words, Aristotle "methodized" what had previously been a "natural" rhetoric into a consciously reflective, analytic "art." Of course, as Pope had perhaps not been entirely aware, developing "nature" into an "art" changes nature a bit. Reflection always entails creation.

Like all developments deeply embedded in human existence, the new "art" of rhetoric faced into the past as well as into the future. On the one hand its development into a scientized "art" depended on the mind's having interiorized writing, which was the wave of the future leading quickly not only to abstractly organized science but also to the foundation of empires. But on the other hand, the subject matter of rhetoric among the ancient Greeks belonged to the past: in Aristotle and elsewhere rhetoric was in fact concerned not with written discourse primarily but with oral discourse, the earlier mode of verbal expression, of course still very much alive. *Rhētōr* in Greek means orator, public speaker, and *technē rhētorikē*, or, more simply, *rhētorikē*, means public speaking. To Aristotle's world, teaching students rhetoric meant teaching them to become orators. Deflection of rhetoric from oral performance to written argumentation as such, vaguely incipient at best in Aristotle, would occur only very slowly and imperceptibly over the centuries. Yet it must be remembered that the oral speeches Aristotle was concerned with were in fact no longer purely oral but were already being shaped by the chirographic milieu to post-oral thought forms. The mental processes of academically educated Greeks in Plato's day and later, as Eric Havelock has shown in *The Greek Concept of Justice*, differed considerably from those of Homer's age, and these processes, though grounded in literacy, showed clearly not only in written treatises such as the *Art of Rhetoric* but also in the oral performance of literates.

Its longstanding commitment to orality over the centuries, a commitment not consciously designed or even adverted to, suggests that the deepest roots of rhetoric are archaic, though now covered by a centuries-old tangle of academic and other cultural growth. Rhetoric plays an important part in the growth of consciousness that marks human psychic and cultural history and that is accelerated vastly as verbal discourse is technologized through writing, then print, and now electronics and as thought processes are transformed while greater and greater stores of knowledge are accumulated. In its overall effect, rhetoric raises consciousness, as Gilbert Durand has shown in *Les Structures anthropologiques de l'imaginaire*, moving thought from the older, more purely imaging stages toward the greater abstractions of logic. Rhetorical antitheses are negotiable: *yes, more or less; no, more or less*. The antitheses of formal logic are typically nonnegotiable, absolute—setting up irreducible binarism that ultimately makes its way into the computer. *It is, or it isn't.*

The patterns whereby consciousness grows out of the unconscious of course differ from culture to culture—indeed, such patterns in the last analysis may constitute the most basic differences between cultures. And rhetoric is of course not the only factor that determines and registers the patterns of growth. But certainly in the West rhetoric is a central determinant and indicator. In other parts of the world, rhetoric was managed differently. In *Polarity and Analogy*, G. E. R. Lloyd has shown how ancient Greek thought generally specialized in differences (polarities) as against likenesses (analogies) more than any of the many other cultures that he examines from across the globe. Greek rhetoric, specifically, certainly specialized in antitheses, and out of this specialization, as I. M. Bochenski has shown in *A History of Formal Logic*, grew the logic that underlay Greek analytic thinking and that underlies modern science and the changes in human life that science has wrought. In *Communication and Culture in Ancient India and China*, where of course rhetoric was practiced, as it has been everywhere, Robert T. Oliver reports no interest in formalized rhetoric comparable to that of ancient Greece. (Formal logic came into being also in India, as Bochenski points out—perhaps independently of the Greek invention—but some five hundred years later than in Greece.)

The centrality of rhetoric in the West is tied in largely with its conspicuous academic and para-academic presence. But academic rhetoric has led no eremetical existence. From the ancient Greeks to the present, the teaching of rhetoric has affected and been affected by political and other social institutions, philosophical theories (themselves often partly rhetorical in origin), educational practices and aims, the growth of science, and much else.

From patristic times and earlier, rhetoric has also much affected and been much affected by the Judeo-Christian ethos—a fact more taken for granted than discussed by historians of rhetoric. Judeo-Christian teaching sets up a kind of rhetorical situation between human beings and God. Job argued with God. He argued with utter reverence—observed decorum, as a later rhetoric would put it—but unabashedly, for the relationship of each human being to God in faith is personal and personally interactive. Christian teaching regarding the Incarnation intensified the interaction. The Word himself became flesh, the Word who is also the Son, the Second Person of the Trinity of Father, Son, and Holy Spirit. The Word or Son is the communication of the Father—Son inasmuch as he is Word, and Word inasmuch as he is Son (*eo verbum quo filius*, as the succinct Latin logion puts it), and he came as a human being to announce the Good News, the Gospel, the *kerygma*. Human speaking and persuasion are of the essence of Christianity, though

Christian faith as such transcends the human action with which it meshes. *Pistis*, the Greek term for faith among the early Christians, which Paul says "comes from hearing" (Romans 10:17), is the same word that occurs in rhetoric texts for the conviction that the public speaker undertakes to establish in his hearers. Moreover, the Word, the Son, brings human beings to the Father, and Christians plead rhetorically with the Father "through him, with him, and in him." The Holy Spirit, who enables the faithful to pray, is identified by Jesus as the *Paraklētos*, the "advocate," one who pleads another's case as in court. In this protreptic milieu, it is little wonder that the liturgy of the Christian Church, Eastern and Western, is shot through with highly self-conscious rhetoric: the hundreds of opening prayers at Mass in the Latin Liturgy, for example, and comparable prayers in other liturgies, Protestant as well as Catholic, are rhetorical showpieces, as are also countless homilies.

As the studies in this book make abundantly clear, rhetoric as an academic subject persisted, with varied fortunes and intensities, from classical antiquity through the Middle Ages, the Renaissance, and intervening centuries down to the present. Drilled into students in the earlier years of the curriculum, rhetoric inevitably extended itself with greater or lesser force far beyond the classroom, for rhetorical skills were supposed to be applied everywhere: in law and politics, in public celebrations marked by the florid oratory that into the present century bears the mark of academic rhetorical (oratorical) training, in preaching, in medicine (before the present century, physician-patient relationships often depended more upon vocal exchange promoting trust than on precisely targeted pharmaceuticals), in letter-writing and in poetry and fiction (novelists such as Hawthorne and Melville clearly show speechifying tendencies in their prose), and in general through all affective human relations.

The persistent presence of rhetoric as a recognized force in Western culture can be seen in the number of major intellectual figures known today chiefly for their work in a variety of other subjects who at one time or another taught rhetoric or wrote about it. In the recent English-speaking world alone one finds, for example, the scientist Joseph Priestley, the economist Adam Smith, the political scientist and diplomat and sixth president of the United States of America John Quincy Adams, who became professor of rhetoric and belles-lettres at Harvard after being in the United States Senate, the physician James Rush, the litterateur Thomas De Quincey, and the engineer cum physical scientist cum philosopher Herbert Spencer—all noted, along with others, in the present book.

Perhaps partly because of the very pervasiveness of rhetoric, the history of rhetoric has only begun to shape up effectively in recent times. Early histories of the subject, even as late as John Quincy Adams's brief account, could not achieve the distance required for historical effectiveness. As Donald C. Stewart indicates in his chapter here, Adams did not at all understand the complex relationship of rhetoric to cultural history and assimilated rhetoric in his own day uncritically to that of ancient Greece. The period between ancient Greece and Adams's own time he felt was nonexistent.

In recent times rhetoric has become more vigorous and more protean than ever before. The modern world has found new ways of exercising the persuasion that used to be practiced chiefly through verbal performance. Rhetoric has spread from its original habitat in the world of direct vocal exchange into newly created arenas, first to the written page, then to the printed page, with its charts and diagrams and illustrations—presenting the reader with what William M. Ivans, Jr., in *Prints and Visual Communication*, has called "exactly repeatable visual statements"—then to display advertising, a quite new development that utilizes dramatic arrangements of variously printed words as well as illustrations, on to skywriting, television, and all the rest. The present human lifeworld is saturated with rhetoric. Concern with various kinds of human interaction has alerted the present age, perhaps more in the United States than elsewhere, to the precise rhetorical elements in business transactions, in storytelling, in professedly objective reporting, in documentary films, and in philosophy and science, to name only a few of rhetoric's domains. Suddenly, rhetoric, the art of persuasion originally connected chiefly with oratory, has become totally amoeban, surrounding and consuming our entire lifeworld. The reason for this is essentially simple, although it is unfashionable to note it: paradoxically, in our technological world interpersonal relations have become more frequent and more complex in many ways than before. In his chapter here on Contemporary Rhetoric, James L. Kinneavy lists some of the specialized kinds of rhetoric he might have treated but, if only for want of space, could not: the rhetoric governing marketing, managerial science, interviewing, oral interpretation, film and radio and television production (he does treat rhetoric in the mass media), rhetoric as viewed in general semantics, literary criticism, theory of description (the old rhetoric had ample room for persuasive description, no room at all for exact visual description of a clinical sort), axiology, learning theory, cognitive sciences, and much else.

The recent foundation of the International Society for the History of Rhetoric registers the growing scholarly interest in the provenience and significance of this massive and pervasive subject that has meant so much in the history of Western culture, as well as other cultures in our now one world. The need is obvious for a book such as the present one, which undertakes to sum up the state of scholarship today and to suggest lines of study for the future, providing both discussion and invaluable bibliographic guides for each period it treats. The book concerns itself chiefly with verbal rhetoric, basically as represented in the academic teaching of rhetoric in the West. It starts with the ancient tradition, in Greek originally and then more and more in Latin, that underlies all Western academic rhetoric; then, in its later chapters, dealing with the vernacularized academic world that took shape gradually after the Renaissance, it narrows its focus to the history of rhetoric in the English-speaking world of the British Isles and the United States of America.

Richard Leo Enos, with the help of Ann M. Blakeslee, begins the book where one must begin the study of all academic and para-academic life in the West, with the ancient Greeks and then the Romans. James J. Murphy provides an exhaustive account of scholarship concerned with medieval rhetoric, a subject to which he has given his superabundant energies for many years. He is aided by Martin Camargo. Don Paul Abbott treats the complexities of the Renaissance, where a turnaround took place, largely under the influence of Peter Ramus, that signaled the beginning of a new rhetorical era marked by the subtle and pervasive effects of print. Winifred Bryan Horner, to whom credit and gratitude go for the conception of this book, shows that what we already know of rhetorical history in the eighteenth century makes this century one of the most fascinating of all. She is assisted by Kerri Barton. Donald C. Stewart shows how much has been done to provide modern editions of the rhetorical writings of the nineteenth century that have so much influenced the teaching of written composition in our own day, and James L. Kinneavy discusses work on the manifold shapes that rhetoric has taken in our own time and reviews the vast literature on the relationship of various kinds of rhetoric and rhetorical theories to the teaching of writing.

In the historiography of rhetoric in the West, it appears that a disproportionate amount of work has been done by United States scholars. The reasons for this are various, but the fact itself suggests that rhetoric relates to social structures and to psychic life in the United States somewhat differently than it does in the other parts of the Western world. It is sometimes said that Europeans and Latin Americans learn how to practice rhetoric and United States scholars study it. The rhetorical heritage is a part of the ethos of Europe. It is less familiar, more distanced, and more intellectually interesting to scholars in the United States. Whatever the case, this book should be of great practical value to scholars around the world and of special value to those teaching writing as well as to those interested in many areas of literary study not often associated with rhetoric, such as reader-oriented criticism and speech-act theory, structuralism, textualism, deconstructionism, and much else. It is a book for all seasons.

THE CLASSICAL PERIOD

Richard Leo Enos
and Ann M. Blakeslee

Primary Works

Pre-Socratic Philosophers and Sophists:
Homeric to ca. the Peloponnesian War

The discovery, publication, and translation of primary works offer
ever-increasing evidence for rhetoric's early evolution to a discipline.
Often, notions about the suasory power of discourse, and techniques
of articulating thoughts and sentiments, are revealed indirectly in such
literary works as Homer's *Iliad* and *Odyssey* and Hesiod's *Works and
Days*. Yet, explicit attention to concepts that would become subsumed
under rhetoric is evident in the fragments of pre-Socratic thinkers. The
most comprehensive collections of this material are *Die Fragmente der
Vorsokratiker* (ed. Hermann Diels and Walther Kranz, 1972) and *Artium scriptores: Reste der voraristotelischen Rhetorik* (ed. Ludwig Radermacher, 1951). These two collections are acknowledged as invaluable
sources for philological research, but all references are left in the original Greek. Fortunately, excellent translations of many such fragments
are available. Kathleen Freeman's *Ancilla to the Pre-Socratic Philosophers*
(1971) provides a fine, but laconic, summary of fragments that bear
directly on the earliest notions of rhetoric. A more literal and thorough
treatment of relevant fragments is presented in her other work, *The Pre-
Socratic Philosophers: A Companion to Diels*, Fragmente der Vorsokratiker
(1966). Rosamond Kent Sprague's *The Older Sophists* (1972) is a valuable
translation of fragments in *Die Fragmente der Vorsokratiker*. Readers of
Sprague's volume will find George Kennedy's "Gorgias" and Sprague's
own translation of "Dissoi Logoi or Dialexis" important sources for
early notions on rhetoric. Unfortunately, *The Older Sophists* is out of
print and, therefore, difficult to obtain. Lastly, a neglected but important collection of early fragments is G. S. Kirk and J. E. Raven's *The
Presocratic Philosophers* (1973). The advantage of the Kirk and Raven

collection is their integration of extended analysis and explication of fragments, which are presented both in the original Greek and in English. Other collections of such primary material exist, but readers of English will find those mentioned above the most beneficial, primarily because of the accessibility of translations and the thoroughness of the commentary.

Plato

One of the most important issues in classical rhetoric is the debate over the legitimacy of rhetoric as a discipline. Several primary sources reveal the controversy; in fact, the epistemological issues articulated by sophists such as Gorgias are evident in the fragments cited above. Essentially, the Platonic view on the acceptability of rhetoric as a system for acquiring knowledge is a counterstatement to the relativism that characterized sophistic thought. Students who are introduced to classical rhetoric will benefit from an exposure to both sides of this debate. While Plato's views on the credibility of rhetoric are evident in many dialogues, two are often seen as representative of his position, the *Gorgias* (ca. 387–385 B.C.) and the *Phaedrus* (ca. 370 B.C.). The *Gorgias* calls to question the sophistic claim that rhetoric has any systematic *techne*, or "art," and the *Phaedrus* examines the possibility of a rhetoric that could be acceptable as a *techne*.

Several translations of the *Gorgias* and the *Phaedrus* are available, and the choice of the most appropriate one depends on the needs of the reader. W. R. M. Lamb's translation of the *Gorgias* (1925) and H. N. Fowler's translation of the *Phaedrus* (1914), both of which appear in the Loeb Classical Library series, are excellent with the original Greek and the English appearing on facing pages. A minimum knowledge of the Greek alphabet makes these works uniquely valuable, since critical terms in Greek can be isolated easily and discussed in class. Two other editions of the *Gorgias* and the *Phaedrus* also warrant citation. The Greek edition of the *Gorgias* by E. R. Dodds (1959) provides excellent background information about the transmission of the text and the place of the *Gorgias* in Plato's dialogues. Similarly, the translation of the *Phaedrus* (1972) by R. Hackforth is an excellent edition for providing a brief, but synoptic, introduction with commentary throughout and headnotes paraphrasing each section. As indicated above, several other dialogues also capture the issues over rhetoric's province, but discussion of these would extend this essay beyond its limits. All of the extant dialogues of Plato are available through the Loeb Classical Library series, with several dialogues often appearing in each edition. Although outside the province of this essay, the writings of Isocrates

(436–338 B.C.) provide a valuable source of comparison with Plato on the practice of rhetoric in classical Athens. An excellent three-volume English translation of Isocrates' writing is provided by George Norlin and Larue Van Hook (1966, 1968) in the Loeb Classical Library series.

Aristotle

For many years the *Rhetorica ad Alexandrum* (ca. 340 B.C.) was believed to have been authored by Aristotle, and the work was even transmitted through the ages in the Aristotelian canon. Most scholars now agree that the work was probably authored by Anaximenes, but it is possible that this *techne*—considered the oldest extant manual of rhetoric—would have perished had it not been included among the writings of Aristotle. Two important works are available for readers of English. The Loeb Classical Library series offers a translation of the *Rhetorica ad Alexandrum* by H. Rackham (1937) that includes a helpful (and necessary) outline of this intricate, highly detailed treatise. E. M. Cope (1877) presents an analysis and commentary of the *Rhetorica ad Alexandrum* that makes an excellent companion volume to the Rackham edition cited above.

The primary work for Aristotle and, as some scholars believe, of classical rhetoric itself is his *Rhetoric* (ca. 335–330 B.C.), essentially (and arguably) because the *Rhetoric* established rhetoric as a discipline. Reading the *Rhetoric* in isolation from Aristotle's other treatises is a disservice to his objective of harmonizing knowledge, but only the English editions of the *Rhetoric* will be discussed here. Two of the most popular English editions of the *Rhetoric* are W. Rhys Roberts and Ingram Bywater's *Rhetoric and Poetics of Aristotle* (1954) and Lane Cooper's *The Rhetoric of Aristotle* (1960). Both of these works provide lucid translations, explanations, and—particularly in reference to the Cooper edition—a synoptic overview. Serious work on interpretation of philological issues within the *Rhetoric*, which is currently involving several researchers, is unavailable in these editions because of the exclusion of the Greek text. The translation by J. H. Freese, *The "Art" of Rhetoric* (1926), is an established version of the English edition and has the advantage of providing the Greek and English on facing pages along with a glossary of key terms.

Although analyses and commentaries are technically not considered "primary works," there are studies that so greatly facilitate our use of the English editions of the *Rhetoric* that they are included in this section. Edward M. Cope's *An Introduction to Aristotle's Rhetoric* (1867) is one of the distinguished contributions to scholarship in classical rhetoric and is essential for explicating Aristotle's views. Similarly, Edward

M. Cope and John Edwin Sandys's *The Rhetoric of Aristotle* (1877), while providing only the Greek text, offers three volumes of commentary that have served as the standard reference to the primary source for over one hundred years. Only recently have updated, and excellent, commentaries been published that bridge the one-hundred-year gap since the Cope and Sandys edition, William M. A. Grimaldi's commentaries on book I (1980) and book II (1988) of Aristotle's *Rhetoric*. Readers will find Grimaldi's discussion on *pistis* in the "Appendix" of the first volume a brilliant statement on the role of proof in Aristotle's methodology of rhetoric. In his commentary of book II, readers will find Grimaldi's treatment of *topoi* equally beneficial. In both commentaries, readers will find a more knowledgeable discussion of invention than offered in earlier commentaries. Plans are currently being made with Fordham University Press for a commentary of book III, which will complete the commentary of the *Rhetoric*. On an introductory level, Larry Arnhart's *Aristotle on Political Reasoning: A Commentary on the "Rhetoric"* (1981) provides a good general overview and explication of the text.

Cicero

For centuries the *Rhetorica ad Herennium* (ca. 86–82 B.C.) was believed to have been authored by Marcus Tullius Cicero and was included in the corpus of his *Rhetorica*. The work is now believed almost certainly not to have been written by Cicero but remains in his canon of treatises because exact authorship has yet to be determined. Similar to its Greek counterpart, the *Rhetorica ad Alexandrum*, the *Rhetorica ad Herennium* is the earliest complete Latin version of a technical manual. Reading of the text could be tedious, except that the storehouse of rhetorical figures and patterns of organization provide invaluable evidence for historians of rhetoric. Fortunately, readers of English will benefit from the excellent translation of the *Rhetorica ad Herennium* by Harry Caplan (1954). Titled *Ad C. Herennium de Ratione Dicendi (Rhetorica ad Herennium)*, Caplan's is one of the best editions of primary sources on rhetoric in the Loeb Classical Library series. The inclusion of the Latin text is an advantage to the reader, and Caplan's introduction and bibliography, while dated, are still regarded as a contribution in their own right.

Cicero's own works on rhetoric are extensive; in fact, much of the study of classical rhetoric in the Roman period is devoted to the analysis of his treatises. Earliest of these is the *De Inventione* (86 B.C.), a work that, although discounted by Cicero in his *De Oratore* as the product of a youthful mind, was one of the dominant rhetorical artifacts in the Latin-speaking West throughout the Middle Ages. Only one edition is readily available to readers of English, the H. M. Hubbell translation in the Loeb Classical Library series (1949). As is characteristic of the Loeb series, the original language of the text is also provided along with a bibliography. Many readers find that the *De Inventione* appears to be more on the arrangement of discourse than on invention and that important concepts of Cicero's developing views on the structure of rhetorical discourse are buried in wordy commentary. While such reactions to this important document are common, the Hubbell edition is helpful in providing a synoptic introduction and a bibliography.

Cicero's most famous treatise on rhetoric, and one of the primary texts for historians of rhetoric, is his *De Oratore* (55 B.C.). Written after his consulship, and after years of deliberative and forensic experience, the *De Oratore* is a comprehensive statement on rhetoric that is grounded in both theory and practice. While the dialogue form of *De Oratore* makes the interpretation of rhetorical principles difficult, the richness and utility of rhetoric for the welfare of the individual and of the state, revealed in the extended discussion, make it a valuable statement. Two major English translations are available. The J. S. Watson translation, *Cicero on Oratory and Orators*, served for years as the standard edition, and it is an index of the renewed interest in classical rhetoric that this edition was reissued in 1986 with a preface by Richard Leo Enos that updates the earlier introduction by Ralph A. Micken and foreword by David Potter. The Loeb Classical Library edition of *De Oratore* (1942, revised 1948) offers excellent translations by H. Rackham and E. W. Sutton. The difficulty of interpreting Cicero's own position on issues throughout the dialogue is alleviated by a thorough summary at the beginning of the two-volume edition, which includes section markings throughout and allows a quick and reliable reference to key passages. The Latin edition of Augustus S. Wilkins (1965), while not providing an English text, does give valuable commentary along with an insightful summary and analysis. Readers of *De Oratore* are strongly encouraged to examine Wilkins's Latin edition for serious study, as well as the summer 1988 issue of *Rhetorica*, which is devoted to presenting papers from the Rutgers University Conference on *De Oratore* in October 1987.

From 55 to 46 B.C., Cicero wrote a number of treatises on rhetoric, many of which are believed to be responses to comments he received about his *De Oratore*. The *Partitiones Oratoriae* (ca. 50 B.C.)—also referred to as *De Partitione Oratoria*—while not normally the subject of study by historians of rhetoric, does provide extended evidence on his later views of the compositional structure and arrangement of rhetorical discourse. Perhaps, with increased attention by historians to the heuristic procedures that guide the structuring of composition, this work will gain renewed attention, but it is now considered only a minor statement in the Ciceronian canon. To date, the only readily available English text of *Partitiones Oratoriae* is found in the Loeb Classical Library series (1942). H. Rackham is best known for his translation of *De Oratore*, which is included in the same volume, but readers will find his rendering of the *Partitiones Oratoriae* lucid if brief.

Similar to the *Partitiones Oratoriae*, Cicero's *De Optimo Genere Oratorum* (46 B.C.) is also a brief, and overlooked, statement on rhetoric. The major importance of this treatise is that it illustrates Cicero's relationship with, and indebtedness to, Hellenic rhetoric. The *De Optimo Genere Oratorum* was intended to serve as an introduction to Cicero's Latin edition of Demosthenes' *On the Crown*. His comments on the qualifications of the best sort of rhetor give insight to the values upon which his theory for the welfare of the state was based and complement his praise of Demosthenes in his *Orator*. A more detailed commentary on this relationship would enhance the merits of the translation by H. M. Hubbell in the Loeb Classical Library series (1949), but the standard of excellent translations that characterizes the series is maintained in this edition.

Cicero's *Brutus* (46 B.C.) is an invaluable work for historians of rhetoric. Through his accounting of scores of Roman orators, many of whom would be unknown without this treatise, Cicero indirectly reveals his admiration for the rhetors who preceded his generation. The major difficulty of the work is that the thorough chronicling of Roman orators makes mastery of the treatise, and synthesis of the precepts, difficult. The Loeb Classical Library translation by G. L. Hendrickson (1952) aids by providing a summary and introduction, but for a thorough accounting of this history of Roman rhetoric readers will need to consult G. V. Sumner's *The Orators in Cicero's* Brutus: *Prosopography and Chronology* (1973).

It could be argued that Cicero's *Topica* (44 B.C.) is a treatise that can strictly be considered outside the province of rhetoric, since the author's initial comments and reference to Aristotle's *Topica* imply that it ought to be taken only as a statement on dialectic. A reading of the treatise, however, reveals an extensive discussion of *loci communes* and their relationship to Greek *topoi*. The implications of Cicero's analysis reveal not only his indebtedness to Greek thought, and Aristotle in particular, but also his ability to integrate the methods and substance of other disciplines into his rhetorical theory. Similar to many other works in the Ciceronian *Rhetorica*, the English edition of his *Topica* is readily available only through the Loeb Classical Library series (1949). The translation by H. M. Hubbell is included in the volume with Cicero's *De Inventione* and *De Optimo Genere Oratorum*.

Stylistics, Criticism, and Argument

Research in classical rhetoric, and particularly in the interrelationships among the canons of rhetoric, has prompted an interest in the theoretical presuppositions grounding treatises on style and criticism. Fortunately, excellent English sources are available for such study. A clear example of this sort of work is the W. Rhys Roberts translation (1910) of the *De Compositione Verborum* of Dionysius of Halicarnassus (fl. 30 B.C.). The *De Compositione Verborum* (ca. 20–10 B.C.) is a detailed statement on literary composition that will be of interest not only to historians of rhetoric but to historical linguists and grammarians as well. The Roberts edition is an excellent source for the English reader because the Greek text is included with the translation, along with an introduction, notes, a glossary, and appendixes on such subjects as word order and pronunciation. Similarly, Stephen Usher's translation of critical essays by Dionysius of Halicarnassus in the Loeb Classical Library series (1974) provides valuable but indirect evidence of the theoretical standards implicit in such models of eloquence as Lysias and Demosthenes.

Inexpensive and lucid translations of Demetrius' *On Style* (first century A.D.) and Longinus' *On the Sublime* (ca. A.D. 40) are more readily available than the writings of Dionysius and are included with other, related classical texts. Demetrius' *On Style* includes examples from historians and poets as well as orators. The text also discusses letter-writing, which would become a popular subject for rhetoric in the Middle Ages and Renaissance. Two English editions are available. The Loeb Classical Library series provides a translation by W. Rhys Roberts (revised 1932), who devoted much of his scholarly career to translating and explicating treatises in classical rhetoric. This volume also includes Longinus' *On the Sublime* and Aristotle's *Poetics*. Another acceptable, and more easily available, English edition of Demetrius' *On Style* was published by Everyman's Library (1963). While this edition does not offer the Greek text, as does the Loeb Classical Library series, it includes editions of Aristotle's *Poetics* and Longinus' *On the Sublime*. Although the Everyman edition cannot be recommended for research, it does provide students with an inexpensive copy of important treatises on style and criticism.

Longinus' *On the Sublime* is commonly seen as one of the major texts in classical literary criticism. While *On the Sublime* is frequently discussed in rhetoric more as a point of departure from the pedantic rhetorical exercises that characterized much of the history of rhetoric in the first century A.D., the accessibility of English editions and the work's impact in the history of rhetoric warrant our attention. In addition to the editions mentioned in the preceding paragraph, the Penguin Classics series offers an inexpensive edition by T. S. Dorsch (1965); this edition is easy to read (the Roberts translation is used), and Dorsch's introduction provides a brief but broad overview of classical literary criticism.

The second century A.D. continued not only to make advances in stylistics and criticism but also to reapproach the classical notions of argument. Minucian's *On Epicheiremes* presents the systemic structuring of argument that complements the enthymeme. The translation by Prentice A. Meador, Jr. (1964), provides one of the few editions on the subject. Similarly, recent advances in neoclassical rhetoric have made apparent the importance of *stasis*. The writings of Hermogenes of Tarsus (fl. ca. A.D. 150) are among the most important contributions on the subject, ranking with Hermagoras of Temnos (second century B.C.). Ray Nadeau's translation of Hermogenes' *On Stasis* (1964) is highly recommended. Nadeau not only presents a careful translation of a highly technical subject but also provides an introduction and advances observations that are of value to serious historians of rhetoric. Complementing both Nadeau's translation and Hermogenes' discussion of *stasis* is Cecil W. Wooten's translation of Hermogenes' *On Types of Style* (1987). Wooten's translation, done over a six-year period, provides a clear understanding of Hermogenes' views; Wooten's two accompanying essays discuss Hermogenes' views on panegyric rhetoric, comparing his views with those of earlier critical theorists. Those readers interested in epideictic rhetoric will find this discussion particularly interesting.

Rhetoric and Roman Education: Seneca (The Elder) and Quintilian

Rhetoric thrived during the Roman Imperial period not so much for its political and forensic utility—which characterized the Ciceronian age—but because of its indisputable contributions to higher education in the ancient world. Until 1974, however, readers of English had to limit their study of Roman declamation to secondary sources. Michael Winterbottom's two-volume translation of the Elder Seneca's *Oratorum Sententiae Divisiones Colores* (ca. A.D. 37) in the Loeb Classical Library series (1974) provides a thesaurus of illustrations on the rhetorical exercises of *controversiae* and *suasoriae* that educated Romans. Unlike other treatises of rhetoric discussed in this section, Seneca's collection can be used as a reference for illustrating common topics in deliberative and forensic issues, since theoretical presuppositions driving the exercises are presented indirectly.

The most comprehensive and important statement of rhetoric in higher education is Quintilian's *Institutio oratoria* (ca. A.D. 94–95). The end product of a career of distinguished instruction, Quintilian's twelve-book treatise on the moral education of youth, and the concern for an ethical grounding to rhetoric, has established the *Institutio oratoria* as a landmark in the history of rhetoric. Researchers in the history of rhetoric stress the importance of this work not only for the moral plea for rhetoric—illustrated most pointedly in book 12—but also because Quintilian's compendious work provides important primary references on the history of rhetoric in Greece and Rome. Quintilian's enduring popularity has prompted English editions for several years. Unfortunately, many have become dated or have been so stringently edited that only the H. E. Butler translation in the Loeb Classical Library series (1920–1922) can be recommended. The value of this translation is enhanced by the synopsis of the books in the respective volumes, a summary of the life of Quintilian, and a letter from Trypho, his publisher.

Commentators and Historians of Rhetoric

Even in Antiquity, scholars were beginning to realize the value of preserving and recording the history of rhetoric. Plutarch's *Vitae Parallelae* (ca. A.D. 50–120) illustrates his attempts to record the deeds of prominent historical figures, many of whom helped to shape the history of rhetoric. Primary examples of such writings are his comparative accounts of the lives of Demosthenes and Cicero. B. Perrin's translation in the Loeb Classical Library series (1919) is a dated, but standard, reference for readers of English. It should also be noted that, although not strictly dealing with rhetorical theory, the popularization of the ten Attic orators in [Plutarch] *Vitae decem oratorum* helped to establish a standard for excellence throughout much of the history of rhetoric; this work was particularly popular in periods when rhetorical proficiency was taught not through the mastery of theory but through the study of models. The tenth volume of H. N. Fowler's translation of Plutarch's *Moralia* (1936) offers an introduction to the Attic orators that is too brief for the importance they had in the history of rhetoric, but it does offer a readable translation of the text.

Other historians of the period who earned their lasting recognition in other writings also commented on rhetoric. Tacitus, most famous for his *Annales,* presented an attack on the practices and objectives of rhetorical training during his own time and glorified Cicero and the orators of preceding generations in the *Dialogus* (ca. A.D. 84–85). Michael Winterbottom's revision of Wm. Peterson's translation of the

Dialogus (1970) is recommended; the Bobbs-Merrill edition (1967), which does provide an inexpensive text for students of the history of rhetoric, is not suggested for research.

Similar to Tacitus, Suetonius took time from his historical writing to chronicle the emergence of rhetoric as a formal discipline in Rome. Suetonius' *De Rhetoribus* (ca. A.D. 106–113) provides a wealth of information about the periods when the teaching of rhetoric was outlawed in Rome and about the use of stock declamations. Two English versions of this treatise are available. J. C. Rolfe's translation of Suetonius' writings in the Loeb Classical Library series (1914) provides a readable text but virtually no commentary. Readers who wish to understand the *De Rhetoribus* within its historical context are advised to consult the Richard Leo Enos translation (1972), which does include an extensive commentary.

Two additional documents are of interest to historians of rhetoric. Philostratus' *Vitae Sophistarum* (ca. A.D. 230–238) and Eunapius' *Vitae Sophistarum* (ca. A.D. 396) provide important information about the First and Second Sophistic. Illustrations of declamations along with invaluable references to sophists such as Gorgias help to provide a unique perspective to the history of rhetoric. Both of these important statements are available in English in the Loeb Classical Library series (1921), and, although dated, the translation by Wilmer C. Wright makes for clear reading.

Secondary Works

Reviews

It is only proper that any statement concerning a review of research acknowledge previous efforts. Although dated, two reviews of research in classical rhetoric continue to be beneficial. Charles S. Rayment's "A Current Survey of Ancient Rhetoric" (1958) provides a review of research. Similarly, for many years Maurice Platnauer's *Fifty Years (and Twelve) of Classical Scholarship* (1968) has been a standard reference for researchers in classical rhetoric. This volume contains specific sections on Greek and Roman rhetoric, but much of the research reviewed is from British and Continental sources with virtually no recognition of American contributions.

George A. Kennedy's 1975 review of research in *Classical Philology* will be very helpful to readers of English. Not only does Kennedy, himself a recognized authority on ancient rhetoric, synthesize European with American research, but he also directs the reader to needed areas of research. The utility of his review is demonstrated by the number of times it is cited in research as justification for an area of inquiry. Particularly useful is his commentary on George Kustas's study of Byzantine rhetoric (1973), which is available to American researchers only with extraordinary difficulty.

Those interested in a review of research that examines classical rhetoric within the larger framework of rhetorical theory are encouraged to consult Michael C. Leff's excellent "In Search of Ariadne's Thread: A Review of the Recent Literature on Rhetorical Theory" (1978). The value of this statement is Leff's ability to track a common theme, the epistemology of rhetoric, across a range of areas. Consequently, although classical research is not emphasized, the compatibility of topics with other domains makes relationships apparent that might otherwise be missed.

Reference Works and Bibliographies

Students and researchers of classical rhetoric require easily available sources for referring to the variety of concepts, individuals, and issues that are subsumed under the study of classical rhetoric. Three works are readily available to readers of English. The *Oxford Classical Dictionary* (2d ed., 1970), edited by N. G. L. Hammond and H. H. Scullard, is an invaluable source for quick and reliable information. The brief overviews of Greek and Latin rhetoric are synoptic, but accurate, and make for an excellent opening assignment to a new student of classical rhetoric. Several technical subjects are treated, and a list of sources often accompanies each entry; it is quite common to see this work by the desk of any researcher of classical rhetoric. On a much smaller scale, *Ancient Greek and Roman Rhetoricians: A Bibliographical Dictionary* (Bryant et al., 1968) offers an overview of prominent rhetoricians. While not recommended as a final source for researchers, it does provide a clear, readable accounting of prominent theorists; the discussion of Plato by Everett Lee Hunt is especially helpful. Lastly, the recent compilation of sources in the history of rhetoric under the editorship of Winifred Bryan Horner, *Historical Rhetoric: An Annotated Bibliography of Selected Sources in English* (1980), is intended for those who wish to have a thorough reference and introduction to the area. "The Classical Period," offered by Richard Leo Enos, was composed to respond to the revitalized interest in classical rhetoric, and particularly the emergence of neoclassical theorists of rhetoric and composition. While many of the works listed stress invention, the constraints of the publisher limited other entries and the length of discussion. Nonetheless, *Historical Rhetoric* is recommended as a source specifically directed to readers of English.

A detailed discussion of bibliographical studies for classical rhetoric must be limited here to general sources, but a specific collection of recommended works is provided in the Bibliography section at the end of this essay. Those who wish to keep abreast of philological research in rhetoric are encouraged to consult *L'Année Philologique*, which regularly publishes references to classical rhetoric. Similarly, references to studies in classical rhetoric growing out of communication studies in America are available in two Speech Communication Association sources: Ronald J. Matlon and Peter C. Facciola's *Index to Journals in Communication Studies through 1985* (1987); and Thomas W. Benson's *Speech Communication in the 20th Century* (1985), especially the chapter "The History of Rhetoric: The Reconstruction of Progress." In addition, the *Rhetoric Society Quarterly* regularly publishes bibliographies in classical rhetoric, and the *Rhetoric Newsletter* of the International Society for the History of Rhetoric updates its members on current research among colleagues in the organization.

Historical Studies: General, Specific, and Pedagogical

Many readers of English were introduced to the history of rhetoric through the pioneer efforts of Charles Sears Baldwin's *Ancient Rhetoric and Poetic* (1959). However, Baldwin's work is less a history than a summary and digest of ancient authors and was replaced as the essential secondary source by George A. Kennedy's *The Art of Persuasion in Greece* (1963). It is through Kennedy's efforts that many readers of English were widely exposed to the rich history of classical rhetoric. In fact, it is not too much to say that Kennedy's *The Art of Persuasion in Greece* and Edward P. J. Corbett's *Classical Rhetoric for the Modern Student* (1965, 1971, 1990) did more to encourage the neoclassical movement in rhetoric for readers of English than any two other works. In testimony to his efforts, Kennedy's work, which is still widely used, is being expanded and modified by subsequent research—much of which his work helped to promote. Similarly, Corbett's text has gone through three editions and is complemented by Winifred Bryan Horner's *Rhetoric in the Classical Tradition* (1988). While other works, such as Werner Jaeger's *Paideia: The Ideals of Greek Culture* (1945), J. W. H. Atkins's *Literary Criticism in Antiquity* (1934), Albin Lesky's *A History of Greek Literature* (1966), and Rudolf Pfeiffer's *History of Classical Scholarship from the Beginnings to the End of the Hellenistic Age* (1968), provide a larger framework to examine rhetoric, Kennedy's *The Art of Persuasion in Greece* has yet to be replaced for its central emphasis on rhetoric.

It should also be noted, however, that interest in specialized studies focusing on periods and cultures is developing. Robert W. Smith's excellent study, *The Art of Rhetoric in Alexandria: Its Theory and Practice in the Ancient World* (1974), provides insight to the impact of classical rhetoric in Greco-Roman Egypt from 300 B.C. to A.D. 400. Similar attention is being paid to Byzantine studies. While Kennedy ("Later Greek Philosophy and Rhetoric," 1980; *Greek Rhetoric under Christian Emperors*, 1983) and Conley ("Byzantine Teaching on Figures and Tropes," 1986) should be cited for their scholarship on Byzantine rhetoric, the only comprehensive work is George Kustas's *Studies in Byzantine Rhetoric* (1973). As indicated earlier, Kustas's volume, although written in English, was published in Greece and is extremely difficult to obtain in the United States. Two of the most recent contributions to specialized studies of ancient rhetoric focus on New Testament literature through rhetoric. George Kennedy's *New Testament Interpretation through Rhetorical Criticism* (1984) applies principles of rhetoric to the analysis of sacred literature. Kennedy's work has been so well received because he brings to his investigation a thorough knowledge of rhetorical criticism and an approach which provides new insights to the exegesis of the New Testament. From a somewhat different perspective, James L. Kinneavy's *Greek Rhetorical Origins of Christian Faith: An Inquiry* (1987) also examines New Testament literature through rhetoric. Kinneavy's approach, however, more thoroughly grounds his analysis in the social and theological issues of the time, particularly the interaction of Greek schools in Palestine with rabbinical education. Kinneavy also offers a detailed analysis of the concept of "faith" (*pistis*), showing not only its different meaning(s) from the Old Testament but also its expansiveness within the New Testament. Kinneavy attributes much of this difference to the influence of Greek thought and, specifically, the infusing of classical rhetoric in Palestine. There is little doubt that one of the most noteworthy of all recent contributions is the effort by scholars of classical rhetoric to provide analyses with more depth than the generalized histories of a period, and Kinneavy's work is a fine example of the results of that effort.

George A. Kennedy's scholarly dominance in the history of Greek rhetoric is paralleled, to a somewhat lesser extent, in Roman rhetoric. For many years only works such as Martin L. Clarke's *Rhetoric at Rome* (1953), J. F. D'Alton's *Roman Literary Theory and Criticism* (1962), and J. Wright Duff's two-volume work on the literary history of Rome (1964, 1967) served as the basic histories for English readers. Kennedy's *The Art of Rhetoric in the Roman World: 300 B.C.–A.D. 300* (1972) provides the comprehensive statement on rhetoric welcomed by historians of the discipline. While *The Art of Rhetoric in the Roman World* has not gained the popularity of his *The Art of Persuasion in Greece*, the volume is regarded as a standard source by researchers, and the section on Cicero (discussed later in this essay) is well worth reading. Those interested in Roman rhetoric, however, are strongly encouraged to read the excellent treatise by A. D. Leeman, *Orationis Ratio: The Stylistic Theories and Practice of the Roman Orators, Historians and Philosophers* (1963). Leeman's two-volume work is a carefully prepared and thoroughly documented source that will frequently aid researchers.

Several histories of rhetoric have emphasized education and the preservation of rhetorical traditions that grew out of antiquity. H. I. Marrou's *A History of Education in Antiquity* (1964), Donald Lemen Clark's *Rhetoric in Greco-Roman Education* (1957), and Aubrey Gwynn's *Roman Education from Cicero to Quintilian* (1926) are the best known of these works. There are also studies that do not stress new scholarly research but attempt to acquaint students with the field through a review of the history of classical rhetoric. James J. Murphy's *A Synoptic History of Classical Rhetoric* (1972) was reissued in 1983 with errors corrected and appendixes attached. James L. Golden, Goodwin F. Berquist, and William E. Coleman's *The Rhetoric of Western Thought* (3d ed., 1983) and their accompanying anthology, *Essays of the Rhetoric of the Western World* (1990), continue to expand both in audience and in coverage; of all the texts in the history of rhetoric this one is the most responsive to integrating new information and topics. Both of these textbooks on the history of rhetoric advance no claims beyond acquainting new students with an overview of rhetoric's sources of social and intellectual power. The dominant, and possibly the most provocative, of these historical statements is George Kennedy's *Classical Rhetoric and Its Christian and Secular Tradition from Ancient to Modern Times* (1980). While the scope of this work—as evidenced by the title—and the consistency of its quality across periods are debated by reviewers (see Michael C. Leff's "The Classical Tradition in Rhetoric: Three Views of George A. Kennedy's Synthesis," 1981), there should be little surprise that the early chapters on the Greek and Roman periods have been well received. Kennedy's discussion of *letteraturizzazione*, or the transformation of rhetoric from its primary function of oral persuasion to its secondary function of written literary expression, is important for understanding the relationship between oral and written expression. Brian Vickers's *In Defence of Rhetoric* (1988) also offers a history of rhetoric, but from a fixed point of view. While the scholarship is excellent, particularly those chapters dealing with classical rhetoric, Vickers's own conservative opinions and preferences often color his interpretations and direct the readers in an unnecessarily judgmental manner. Readers who can adjudicate the merits of Vickers's views on their own terms will be able to appreciate the careful scholarly attention he obviously directed to the creation of this work. The recent publication of Thomas M. Conley's *Rhetoric in the European Tradition* (1990), however, will provide upper-division and graduate students with an alternative to the Kennedy volume. Conley's reputation for detail is apparent in his chapter-by-chapter summaries, suggestions for further reading, and even outlines of classical texts. *Rhetoric in the European Tradition* is so new that critics have not yet had time to assess its merits, but there is every indication that Conley's textbook provides a combination of scholarship and pedagogy that will attract serious students of classical rhetoric. An equally attractive prospect for enhancing our knowledge of rhetoric in the classical period is the volume edited by James J. Murphy titled *A Short History of Writing Instruction from Ancient Greece to Twentieth-Century America* (1990). The chapters on ancient Greece (Kathleen Ethel Welch) and Rome (James J. Murphy) should provide a more specific discussion of composition practices and pedagogy than previous, general histories of rhetoric have offered.

Rhetoricians

Perhaps the most difficult and constraining task of this review is to select studies from the scores of excellent research on the most prominent figures in the history of rhetorical theory. Such a task immediately omits research on the Attic orators and such distinguished efforts as Richard C. Jebb's *The Attic Orators from Antiphon to Isaeos* (1962). Moreover, the limitations of this inquiry call not only for passing over contemporary research but also for omitting rhetorical theorists who, while making noteworthy contributions to the history of rhetoric, are not directly relevant to the objectives of this study. With these caveats and apologies in mind, it is appropriate to make a chronological examination of the most important figures.

Many scholars are interested in the proto-history of rhetoric; that is, in evidence of the development of notions about the structuring of discourse long before rhetoric emerged as an established discipline. Much of this interest has been fueled by studies examining the relationship of orality and literacy, particularly in ancient Greece. Although not strictly considered statements on rhetoric, the philological researches of Milman Parry (1932, 1971), G. S. Kirk (1976), and Berkley Peabody (1975) have made an excellent case for continued examination of rhetorical techniques in the earliest Greek literature and indirectly refute the claim of D. A. G. Hinks (1940) that studies of rhetoric prior to Corax and Tisias are "irrelevant" to the discipline. Despite the quality of these works, however, it was not until the publication of Eric A.

Havelock's *Preface to Plato* (1963) that attention was drawn to reexamining the relationship between oral and written composition and the epistemological issues attendant with the technology of writing. The interest generated from *Preface to Plato* resulted not only in its redistribution (1982) but also in the publication of Havelock's essays in his *The Literate Revolution in Greece and Its Cultural Consequences* (1982). The generalization made in Havelock's works was in part popularized by Walter J. Ong's *Orality and Literacy: The Technologizing of the Word* (1982) and Havelock's own retrospective statement, *The Muse Learns to Write: Reflections on Orality and Literacy from Antiquity to the Present* (1986). Much of the debate over Havelock's observations centers on the claims he advances about what conceptual processes are facilitated by literacy and what processes cannot exist without literacy. By far the most balanced examination of the issues in this debate is found in *Language and Thought in Early Greek Philosophy* (1983). This volume, edited by Kevin Robb, includes an excellent introduction by Havelock himself and essays that directly challenge many of the claims of Havelock. Particularly important is Arthur W. H. Adkins's "Orality and Philosophy," which not only critiques Havelock's claims but summarizes them at the beginning of the essay. Robert J. Connors's "Greek Rhetoric and the Transition from Orality" (1986) also offers a view on Havelock's notion of orality and the implications it holds for Hellenic rhetoric. Finally, those who wish to see an extended discussion of orality and literacy written directly for an audience of rhetoricians are encouraged to read Tony M. Lentz's *Orality and Literacy in Hellenic Greece* (1989). Lentz's excellent treatment of reading in ancient Greece alone is sufficient to merit praise. Other examples of studies that have emphasized the proto-history of rhetoric are Richard Leo Enos's "The Hellenic Rhapsode" (1978) and "Emerging Notions of Heuristic, Eristic, and Protreptic Rhetoric in Homeric Discourse: Proto-Literate Conniving, Wrangling and Reasoning" (1981) and K. E. Wilkerson's "From Hero to Citizen: Persuasion in Early Greece" (1982).

A considerable amount of research has resulted from the debate over the legitimacy and province of rhetoric as a discipline. Studies emphasizing Plato's views most helpful to readers of English are Everett Lee Hunt's "Plato and Aristotle on Rhetoric and Rhetoricians" (1920), which endures as required reading for students of classical rhetoric. W. K. C. Guthrie's *Socrates* (1971) also provides a perspective on Plato's dialogue character. For provocative interpretations of Plato's views on rhetoric, however, readers are encouraged to consult Edwin Black's (1958) and David S. Kaufer's (1978) interpretations of Plato's philosophical and epistemological position toward rhetoric. An excellent, but expensive, collection about Plato's position on rhetoric is Keith V. Erickson's *Plato: True and Sophistic Rhetoric* (1979). One of the best ways to examine both Plato's and Aristotle's views on rhetoric is to compare them with their respective opinions on poetics. For this perspective, there are few works better than Gerald F. Else's *Plato and Aristotle on Poetry* (1986). Edited and completed by Peter Burian after Else's death, this volume provides an excellent perspective on these two great thinkers, one that clarifies, for example, the *Republic* and book III of the *Rhetoric* on issues relevant to rhetoric.

In addition to the well-regarded commentaries on Aristotle's *Rhetorica* by Edward M. Cope (1867), Cope and John Edwin Sandys (1877), and William M. A. Grimaldi (1980, 1988) discussed earlier, several other noteworthy contributions to explicating Aristotle's views on rhetoric are available to readers of English. One of the best collections of scholarship on Aristotelian rhetoric is the volume edited by Keith V. Erickson, *Aristotle: The Classical Heritage of Rhetoric* (1974). The advantage of the Erickson collection is that it draws together some of the foremost essays on the subject from scholars in various disciplines. All of the essays in the collection merit attention, but readers will find the essay by Friedrich Solmsen, "The Aristotelian Tradition in Ancient Rhetoric," to be a fine historical statement and a good overview of the main points of the *Rhetorica*. Also included in this collection are important studies on the enthymeme (Lloyd Bitzer), the example (Gerard A. Hauser), and *topoi* (William M. A. Grimaldi and Donovan J. Ochs).

An extensive collection of studies on Aristotelian rhetoric is also available in Winifred Bryan Horner's *Historical Rhetoric: An Annotated Bibliography of Selected Sources in English* (1980), but two studies are particularly worthy of note. William M. A. Grimaldi's "Studies in the Philosophy of Aristotle's *Rhetoric*" (1972) is a comprehensive monograph that provides a detailed analysis of Aristotle's notion of the enthymeme in particular and rhetorical argument in general. Wilbur Samuel Howell's "Aristotle and Horace on Rhetoric and Poetics" (1968) is one of the clearest statements on the differences between rhetoric and poetics and explicates the distinctions between nonmimetic and mimetic discourse that established them as separate disciplines.

There is little doubt that two of the most dynamic issues in the study of Aristotle's *Rhetoric* are the relationship of rhetoric to philosophy and the "epistemology" of Aristotle's *Rhetoric*. Robert N. Gaines's 1986 discussion of the dialectical nature of rhetoric and Eugene Garver's claim that the *Rhetoric* can be read as a work of philosophy (1986) without ignoring essential differences in science (1988) stress relationships between opinion and knowledge. Topics such as ethos provide the arena to discuss the relationship of ethics and rhetoric in which issues of philosophy and politics are critical. Robert C. Rowland and Deanna F. Womack's "Aristotle's View on Ethical Rhetoric" (1985) provides the sort of synthesis that makes apparent how rhetoric interacts with philosophically oriented ethical issues that bear on society. One of the most recent and insightful discussions of ethos is Roger D. Cherry's "*Ethos Versus Persona: Self-representation in Written Discourse*" (1988), in which he reviews and reevaluates conventional notions of ethos and the range of meaning (and confusion) that can be generated from an imprecise understanding of self-representation.

Cicero is commonly acknowledged by historians of rhetoric as the most dominant figure in the Latin-speaking West, and the amount of research devoted to his works testifies to his contributions. Unlike Plato and Aristotle, however, no anthology of research is readily available for Ciceronian rhetoric. A series of essays edited by T. A. Dorey on Cicero (1965) comes closest to a set of readings, but the work is dated and not all the essays deal directly with rhetoric. A short list of suggested readings for Cicero's *Rhetorica* is provided in the summer 1988 issue of *Rhetorica*. As indicated earlier, however, the best overview of Cicero's contributions is found in George A. Kennedy's *The Art of Rhetoric in the Roman World* (pp. 103–300). Kennedy provides a readable account of Cicero as a theoretician and practitioner of rhetoric while presenting his discussion in the context of the forces and figures shaping the period. Although much has been written about Cicero as an advocate, far fewer studies have been devoted to his theoretical work. James M. May's *Trials of Character: The Eloquence of Ciceronian Ethos* (1988), for example, provides an excellent analysis of ethos as exhibited by Cicero's career as an orator but has little to say about his theoretical views on the concept. Paul Prill's discussion of Cicero's theory and practice in securing good will (1986) is a more balanced but smaller study than May's work. Cecil W. Wooten's *Cicero's* Philippics *and Their Demosthenic Model: The Rhetoric of Crisis* (1983) is a thorough study of Ciceronian oratory but, excluding chapter 7, provides little perspective that is grounded in rhetorical theory. The summer 1978 issue of the *Central States Speech Journal*, however, is primarily devoted to discussing aspects of Cicero's theoretical views on rhetoric and explicating his view of the relationship between theory and practice. The introduction to the Latin edition of Cicero's *De Oratore* by Augustus S. Wilkins (1965) does present a fine, if dated, overview of Cicero's theoretical works. Richard Leo Enos's *The Literate Mode of Cicero's Legal Rhetoric* (1988) is an effort to compare Cicero's theory with his practice as an advocate and offers the first in-depth study in classical rhetoric of a historical individual's ability in oral and written rhetoric.

George A. Kennedy presents a needed biographical profile of Quintilian in his *Quintilian* (1969) and integrates this information within his *The Art of Rhetoric in the Roman World* (1972). A brief but informative sketch of Quintilian also appears in the *Oxford Classical Dictionary* (2d ed., 1970). Much of the research on Quintilian is devoted more to his impact throughout the history of rhetoric than to the particular contributions inherent in his *Institutio oratoria*, but Keith V. Erickson's excellent bibliography on Quintilian in the *Rhetoric Society Quarterly* (1981) provides a valuable collection of difficult-to-locate studies. Two available works do provide treatment of Quintilian's theoretical position. Marsh H. McCall, Jr., discusses Quintilian's views on style in *Ancient Rhetorical Theories of Simile and Comparison* (1969), and A. D. Leeman analyzes Quintilian's views in *Orationis Ratio: The Stylistic Theories and Practice of the Roman Orators, Historians and Philosophers* (1963). James J. Murphy's previously mentioned essay on writing instruction in Rome (1990) is written from Quintilian's perspective, but it is clear that readers of English are in need of additional studies of a theorist whose impact extends throughout the history of rhetoric.

A discussion of research on the sophists and the sophistic movement is extremely difficult to isolate, and it is impossible to fix the sophists to a specific point in the history of rhetoric because of the pervasiveness and endurance of their impact. Excellent research on the First Sophistic is available to readers of English. Mario Untersteiner's *The Sophists* (1954) is commonly, and correctly, regarded as the most authoritative statement on the early sophists. Untersteiner's meticulous attention to detail and thoroughness of citation make this a superior study. W. K. C. Guthrie's *The Sophists* (1971) is also worthy of praise, and both works deserve to be read carefully. Susan C. Jarratt's 1987 discussions of sophistic practices have much to say about how historians have viewed sophists and how a sophistic perspective itself would do much to revise our approach to historical research.

Everett Lee Hunt's synoptic essay "On the Sophists" (1965) directed attention to the important role sophists played in the history of rhetoric. Recently, however, in-depth treatment of individual sophists has become increasingly popular, with particular emphasis on Gorgias of Leontini. Studies by C. P. Segal (1962), Bruce E. Gronbeck (1972), Richard A. Engnell (1973), and Richard Leo Enos (1976) have all stressed the contributions of Gorgias as a serious thinker of rhetoric. An interesting comparison of Gorgias with Plato and Aristotle is offered in Jacqueline de Romilly's *Magic and Rhetoric in Ancient Greece* (1975). While works such as G. B. Kerferd's *The Sophistic Movement* (1981) and Enos's "Aristotle, Empedocles and the Notion of Rhetoric" (1987) have tried to view the First Sophistic from an intellectual context, it is also clear that much more work is needed on the individual sophists who are now seen as little more than straw men for Socrates in Plato's dialogues. Out of such work a more sensitive understanding of the sophists should emerge and John Poulakos's (1983, 1984) insights on the nature of sophistic rhetoric and its distinction from Aristotelian rhetoric should be continued.

The 105th annual meeting of the American Philological Association in 1973 witnessed a strong interest in research of the Second Sophistic, sometimes called the "Greek Renaissance." The coordinator of this effort was G. W. Bowersock, whose excellent *Greek Sophists in the Roman Empire* (1969) is a fine statement about the place of the Second Sophistic within the Roman world. Out of the American Philological Association meeting came a monograph entitled *Approaches to the Second Sophistic* (1974). Unfortunately, this valuable collection of papers by such scholars as George Kennedy is virtually unavailable today. It is, nonetheless, strongly recommended as an excellent introduction to the period; excluding the works mentioned above, the only other such introduction available is Charles Sears Baldwin's dated account in *Medieval Rhetoric and Poetic (to 1400): Interpreted from Representative Works* (1959). More specialized studies on the sophists within their historical context are in I. Avotins's "The Holders of the Chairs of Rhetoric at Athens" (1975) and Richard Leo Enos's "The Effects of Imperial Patronage on the Rhetorical Tradition of the Athenian Second Sophistic" (1977). Lastly, although these works do not deal directly with the Second Sophistic, readers interested in comparing the Greek techniques for declamation with their Roman counterparts are encouraged to consult S. F. Bonner's excellent *Roman Declamation in the Late Republic and Early Empire* (1949), Harry Caplan's "The Decay of Eloquence at Rome in the First Century" (1944), and A. F. Sochatoff's "Basic Rhetorical Theories of the Elder Seneca" (1939). D. A. Russell's *Greek Declamation* (1983) is a work of superior scholarship, providing the first detailed illustration of the marked differences between Greek and Roman declamation. Particularly striking in Russell's study is the important role that *stasis* played in Greek declamation. One of the best, and most recent, contributions to understanding the social and political forces that shaped not only sophists but literary enterprises at large is Barbara K. Gold's *Literary Patronage in Greece and Rome* (1987). Gold's examination of the notion of patronage makes evident the constraints of "benefits" that writers had to be concerned with in their compositions. Gold's lack of discussion of rhetoric's history is the only shortcoming of an otherwise fine contribution.

Specialized Concepts

Although many of the concepts and heuristic processes central to rhetoric are subsumed, and have been discussed, in earlier sections, there are several works worthy of attention and even repetition. The concept of *stasis*, for example, has occupied the attention of rhetoricians for much of the classical period. Fortunately, the excellent article by Otto A. L. Dieter, "*Stasis*" (1950), although difficult to read because of the density of the material and thoroughness of treatment, persists as one of the most important essays in classical rhetoric. Studies following Dieter's essay have helped to explain the notion of *stasis*, the most beneficial of which are presented by Ray Nadeau in his two *Speech Monographs* essays (1958, 1959) and his excellent survey of classical systems of *stases* in *Greek, Roman and Byzantine Studies* (1959). After Dieter and Nadeau, research on *stasis* becomes much more specialized, as is apparent in the writings of James C. Backes (1960), Wayne N. Thompson (1972), and the thoroughly documented study by Ray D. Dearin (1976); in fact, the Dearin essay itself provides a fine review of research on *stasis*. Michael Carter's "*Stasis* and *Kairos*: Principles of Social Construction in Classical Rhetoric" (1988) is a recent effort to explain two critical concepts in rhetoric by showing their relationship historically and in respect to contemporary theory. David Goodwin's "*Controversiae, Meta-Asystatae* and the New Rhetoric" (1989) offers a thorough discussion of *stasis* that makes specific ties with contemporary notions of *loci* as discussed by Chaim Perelman and L. Olbrechts-Tyteca in their *The New Rhetoric: A Treatise on Argumentation* (Notre Dame: University of Notre Dame Press, 1969) and by Kenneth Burke in his dramatistic pentad. The Carter and Goodwin essays both provide illustrations of how *stasis* theory merits further inquiry for its historical importance and contemporary value to rhetorical theory.

The argumentative structures of enthymeme, epicheireme, and example have been discussed in earlier sections. Particular reference is again paid to William M. A. Grimaldi's (1972) and James A. McBurney's (1936) studies on the enthymeme. Similarly, studies by David A. Church and Robert S. Cathcart (1965) and Gary Cronkhite (1966) on the epicheireme provide important, and needed, information. Studies on the example by Gerard A. Hauser (1968, 1985, 1987) and William Lyon Benoit (1980, 1987) are helpful interpretations of Aristotle's views, but the most valuable statement on paradigmatic reasoning in classical rhetoric is made by William M. A. Grimaldi in the appendix to his commentary on Aristotle's *Rhetorica* (1980). As discussed earlier, Grimaldi's studies on the example, enthymeme, *pistis*, and *topoi* should be required reading for all serious students of classical rhetoric. Lastly, the concept of *topoi* is embedded in many of the works discussed earlier, but readers will find the statements of William M. A. Grimaldi (1974, 1980, 1988) and Donovan J. Ochs (1969, 1982, 1989) the most helpful of all those discussed. It is clear, however, that a considerable amount of research on heuristic processes is still required if the merits of classical rhetoric are to be fully realized.

Needed Areas for Future Research

There are several areas of research that merit attention. First, very little has been done on the proto-history of rhetoric; that is, studies that examine the emergence of rhetorical techniques in oral and written literature prior to rhetoric's canonization as a formal discipline. Second, much more work needs to be done in the epistemology generating classical rhetorical theories, particularly with understanding sophistic rhetoric and the interaction of heuristic processes. Although such topics have recently been discussed in several articles, continued study is required before the presuppositions grounding ancient views on the relationship between thought and discourse can be realized. Third, much of the evidence of classical rhetoric is still in need of collection, analysis, and synthesis. Such work will require not only proficiency in textual analysis and philological research but also "fieldwork" at libraries and archaeological sites. This need is particularly serious both in the study of literary fragments of sophists and in the collection and analysis of such nontraditional, but invaluable, evidence as epigraphical sources. Fourth, as Kennedy correctly indicates in his 1975 review article, the impact of classical rhetoric across cultures and through time is still in need of study. It is known, for example, that classical rhetoric was influential, and in some cases even preserved by the Byzantine Empire and Arab world, yet relatively little is known about these phenomena. Lastly, the theories of classical rhetoric have survived throughout our history in part because of their utility. The resurgence of classical rhetoric in departments of English is an illustration of the power of these theories. One of the most important tasks for historians and theoreticians of classical rhetoric is to introduce, refine, and possibly modify the heuristic and stylistic processes of classical rhetorical theory for the resolution of contemporary communication problems so that the benefits of rhetoric, which have been evident for centuries, can continue to be made apparent through scholarly research.

There is little doubt that this final item has been the most dynamic concern of not only classical rhetoricians but historians of rhetoric in general. *Festschriften* such as the 1984 *Essays on Classical Rhetoric and Modern Discourse* edited by Robert J. Connors, Lisa S. Ede, and Andrea A. Lunsford in honor of Edward P. J. Corbett, as well the recent publication of Corbett's own collected articles (1989), explicitly discuss the merits of applying classical rhetoric to contemporary rhetoric and composition studies. Other essays, particularly those by S. Michael Halloran (1982), John T. Gage (1983), John Hagaman (1986), and Kathleen Ethel Welch (1987, 1988), have all sought to clarify the nature and application of classical rhetoric for modern readers. James J. Murphy's "Implications of the 'Renaissance of Rhetoric' in English Departments" (1989) and the recent publication of the 1988 CCCC panel discussion, "Octolog: The Politics of Historiography" (*Rhetoric Review*, 1988), capture the currency and importance of pedagogical issues. Out of much of this discussion has emerged an understanding that traditional scholarship is not incompatible with applied research or literary and communication studies and, indeed, that much can be learned from realizing their compatibility (see Richard Leo Enos's "The Classical Tradition(s) of Rhetoric: A Demur to the Country Club Set," 1987). Two of the best illustrations of this synthesis are Jean Dietz Moss's *Rhetoric and Praxis: The Contribution of Classical Rhetoric to Practical Reasoning* (1986) and Jasper Neel's *Plato, Derrida, and Writing: Deconstruction, Composition and Influence* (1988). What has become apparent since the first writing of this essay is that while much work still needs to be done, there is an ever-growing awareness of classical rhetoric's importance both for its historical significance and for its contributions to current concerns of literacy.

Bibliography

This bibliography is intended to provide full citations for works referred to in the essay. For the sake of coherence, the references listed will be divided into three categories: primary works, secondary works, and selected bibliographies. The "Primary Works" section will adhere as closely as possible to the chronology and order of presentation of primary sources mentioned in the essay. The "Secondary Works" section will list works in alphabetical order. The "Selected Bibliographies" section will provide a sampling of collections for further study. In a few cases, additional studies have been listed that, while not the focus of specific commentary in the essay, are recommended to the reader. Hopefully, this bibliography will be both a sampling and a foundation upon which further reading and research can be based.

Primary Works

Pre-Socratic Philosophers and Sophists:
Homeric to ca. the Peloponnesian War

Ancilla to the Pre-Socratic Philosophers. Edited by Kathleen Freeman. Oxford: Basil Blackwell, 1971.

Artium scriptores: Reste der voraristotelischen Rhetorik. Edited by Ludwig Radermacher. Vienna: Rudolf M. Rohrer, 1951.

Die Fragmente der Vorsokratiker. Edited by Hermann Diels and Walther Kranz. 2 vols. Dublin: Weidmann, 1972.

The Older Sophists. Edited by Rosamond Kent Sprague. Columbia: University of South Carolina Press, 1972.

The Pre-Socratic Philosophers: A Companion to Diels, Fragmente der Vorsokratiker. Edited by Kathleen Freeman. 2d ed. Oxford: Basil Blackwell, 1966.

The Presocratic Philosophers: A Critical History with a Selection of Texts. Edited by G. S. Kirk and J. E. Raven. Cambridge: Cambridge University Press, 1973.

Plato

Plato: Euthyphro—Apology—Crito—Phaedo—Phaedrus. Translated by H. N. Fowler. The Loeb Classical Library. Cambridge: Harvard University Press, 1914.

Plato: Gorgias—A Revised Text with Introduction and Commentary. Edited by E. R. Dodds. Oxford: Clarendon Press, 1959.

Plato: Lysis—Symposium—Gorgias. Translated by W. R. M. Lamb. The Loeb Classical Library. Cambridge: Harvard University Press, 1925.

Plato's Phaedrus: *Translated with an Introduction and Commentary.* Translated by R. Hackforth. Cambridge: Cambridge University Press, 1972.

Aristotle

[Anaximenes.] *Rhetorica ad Alexandrum.* Translated by H. Rackham (Preceded by *Problems, Books XXII-XXXVIII.* Translated by W. S. Hett.) The Loeb Classical Library. Cambridge: Harvard University Press, 1937.

The "Art" of Rhetoric. Translated by J. H. Freese. The Loeb Classical Library. Cambridge: Harvard University Press, 1926.

Rhetoric and Poetics of Aristotle. Translated by W. Rhys Roberts and Ingram Bywater. Introduction and notes by Friedrich Solmsen. New York: Modern Library, 1954.

The Rhetoric of Aristotle. Edited by Edward M. Cope and John Edwin Sandys. 3 vols. Cambridge: Cambridge University Press, 1877.

The Rhetoric of Aristotle. Translated by Lane Cooper. New York: Appleton-Century-Crofts, 1960.

Cicero

[Cicero.] *Ad C. Herennium de Ratione Dicendi (Rhetorica ad Herennium).* Translated by Harry Caplan. The Loeb Classical Library. Cambridge: Harvard University Press, 1954.

Brutus. Translated by G. L. Hendrickson. *Orator.* Translated by H. M. Hubbell. The Loeb Classical Library. Cambridge: Harvard University Press, 1952.

Cicero on Oratory and Orators. Translated by J. S. Watson. Introduction by Ralph A. Micken. Foreword by David Potter. Preface by Richard Leo Enos. Carbondale: Southern Illinois University Press, 1986.

De Inventione—De Optimo Genere Oratorum—Topica. Translated by H. M. Hubbell. The Loeb Classical Library. Cambridge: Harvard University Press, 1949.

De Oratore. Books I-II. Translated by E. W. Sutton and H. Rackham. The Loeb Classical Library. Cambridge: Harvard University Press, 1942. Revised, 1948.

De Oratore. Book III. De Fato—Paradoxoa Stoicorum—De Partitione Oratoria. Translated by H. Rackham. The Loeb Classical Library. Cambridge: Harvard University Press, 1942.

M. Tulli Ciceronis De Oratore Libri Tres. Edited by Augustus S. Wilkins. Hildesheim: Georg Olms Verlag, 1965.

Stylistics, Criticism, and Argument

Dionysius of Halicarnassus: The Critical Essays. Translated by Stephen Usher. Vol. 1. The Loeb Classical Library. Cambridge: Harvard University Press, 1974.

Dionysius of Halicarnassus: On Literary Composition. Edited with an introduction, translation, notes, glossary, and appendixes by W. Rhys Roberts. London: Macmillan and Co., 1910.

(Aristotle), The Poetics and Longinus, On the Sublime. Translated by W. Hamilton Fyfe. *Demetrius, On Style.* Translated by W. Rhys Roberts. The Loeb Classical Library. Rev. ed. Cambridge: Harvard University Press, 1932.

Aristotle's Poetics, Demetrius on Style, Longinus on the Sublime. Introduction by John Warrington. Translated by John Warrington, T. A. Moxon, and H. L. Havell. London and New York: Everyman's Library, 1963.

Aristotle, Horace, Longinus: Classical Literary Criticism. Translated by T. S. Dorsch. London: Penguin, 1965.

(Minucian.) Meador, Prentice A., Jr. "Minucian, On Epicheiremes: An Introduction and Translation." *SM* 31 (March 1964): 54–63.

(Hermogenes.) Nadeau, Ray. "Hermogenes's *On Stasis*: A Translation with an Introduction and Notes." *SM* 31 (November 1964): 361–424.

(————.) Wooten, Cecil W. *Hermogenes' On Types of Style.* Chapel Hill and London: University of North Carolina Press, 1987.

Rhetoric and Roman Education: Seneca (The Elder) and Quintilian

Seneca: Controversiae, I-VI. Translated by Michael Winterbottom. Vol. 1. The Loeb Classical Library. Cambridge: Harvard University Press, 1974.

Seneca: Controversiae, VII-X. Suasoriae. Translated by Michael Winterbottom. Vol. 2. The Loeb Classical Library. Cambridge: Harvard University Press, 1974.

The Institutio oratoria *of Quintilian.* Translated by H. E. Butler. 4 vols. The Loeb Classical Library. Cambridge: Harvard University Press, 1920–1922.

Commentators and Historians of Rhetoric

Plutarch: Moralia (Lives of the Ten Orators). Translated by H. N. Fowler. Vol. 10. The Loeb Classical Library. Cambridge: Harvard University Press, 1936.

Plutarch: Parallel Lives; Demosthenes and Cicero—Alexander and Caesar. Translated by B. Perrin. The Loeb Classical Library. Cambridge: Harvard University Press, 1919.

Tacitus: Agricola. Translated by M. Hutton, revised by R. M. Ogilvie. *Germania*. Translated by M. Hutton, revised by E. H. Warmington. *Dialogus*. Translated by Wm. Peterson, revised by Michael Winterbottom. The Loeb Classical Library. Cambridge: Harvard University Press, 1970.

Tacitus: Agricola, Germany, Dialogue on Orators. Translated with an introduction and notes by Herbert W. Benario. Indianapolis: Bobbs-Merrill Co., 1967.

Suetonius: The Lives of the Caesars (continued), The Lives of Illustrious Men. Translated by J. C. Rolfe. Vol. 2. The Loeb Classical Library. Cambridge: Harvard University Press, 1914.

(Suetonius.) Enos, Richard Leo. "When Rhetoric Was Outlawed in Rome: A Translation and Commentary of Suetonius's Treatise on Early Roman Rhetoricians." *SM* 39 (March 1972): 37–45.

Philostratus: Lives of the Sophists. Eunapius: Lives of the Philosophers and Sophists. Translated by Wilmer C. Wright. The Loeb Classical Library. Cambridge: Harvard University Press, 1921.

Secondary Works

Arnhart, Larry. *Aristotle on Political Reasoning: A Commentary on the "Rhetoric."* DeKalb: Northern Illinois University Press, 1981.

Atkins, J. W. H. *Literary Criticism in Antiquity: A Sketch of Its Development*. 2 vols. Cambridge: Cambridge University Press, 1934.

Avotins, I. "The Holders of the Chairs of Rhetoric at Athens." *HSCP* 79 (1975): 313–24.

Backes, James C. "Aristotle's Theory of *Stasis* in Forensic and Deliberative Speech in the Rhetoric." *CSSJ* 12 (Autumn 1960): 6–8.

Baldwin, Charles Sears. *Ancient Rhetoric and Poetic*. Gloucester, Mass.: Peter Smith, 1959.

———. *Medieval Rhetoric and Poetic (to 1400): Interpreted from Representative Works*. Gloucester, Mass.: Peter Smith, 1959.

Benoit, William Lyon. "Aristotle's Example: The Rhetorical Induction." *QJS* 66 (April 1980): 182–92.

———. "On Aristotle's Example." *PR* 20 (Fall 1987): 261–67.

Benson, Thomas W., ed. *Speech Communication in the 20th Century*. Carbondale: Southern Illinois University Press, 1985.

Bitzer, Lloyd. "Aristotle's Enthymeme Revisited." *QJS* 45 (December 1959): 399–408.

Black, Edwin. "Plato's View of Rhetoric." *QJS* 44 (December 1958): 361–74.

Bonner, S. F. *Roman Declamation in the Late Republic and Early Empire*. Liverpool: Liverpool University Press, 1949.

Bowersock, G. W. *Greek Sophists in the Roman Empire*. Oxford: Clarendon Press, 1969.

Bowersock, G. W., ed. *Approaches to the Second Sophistic*. Ephrata, Pa.: Science Press, 1974.

Brandes, Paul D. "Evidence in Aristotle's Rhetoric." *SM* 28 (March 1961): 21–28.

Bryant, Donald C., Robert W. Smith, Peter D. Arnott, Erling B. Holtsmark, and Galen O. Rowe, eds. *Ancient Greek and Roman Rhetoricians: A Bibliographical Dictionary*. Columbia, Mo.: Artcraft Press, 1968.

Caplan, Harry. "The Decay of Eloquence at Rome in the First Century." In *Studies in Speech and Drama in Honor of Alexander M. Drummond*, edited by Herbert A. Wichlens, 295–325. Ithaca: Cornell University Press, 1944.

Carter, Michael. "*Stasis* and *Kairos*: Principles of Social Construction in Classical Rhetoric." *RR* 7 (Fall 1988): 97–112.

Cherry, Roger D. "*Ethos* Versus Persona: Self-Representation in Written Discourse." *WC* 5 (July 1988): 251–76.

Church, David A., and Robert S. Cathcart. "Some Concepts of the Epicheireme in Greek and Roman Rhetoric." *WS* 29 (Summer 1965): 140–47.

Clark, Donald Lemen. *Rhetoric in Greco-Roman Education*. New York: Columbia University Press, 1957.

Clarke, Martin L. *Rhetoric at Rome*. London: Cohen & West, 1953.

Conley, Thomas M. "Byzantine Teaching on Figures and Tropes." *Rhetorica* 4 (Autumn 1986): 335–74.

———. *Rhetoric in the European Tradition*. New York and London: Longman, 1990.

Connors, Robert J. "Greek Rhetoric and the Transition from Orality." *PR* 19 (Winter 1986): 38–65.

Connors, Robert J., Lisa S. Ede, and Andrea A. Lunsford, eds. *Essays on Classical Rhetoric and Modern Discourse*. Carbondale: Southern Illinois University Press, 1984.

Cope, Edward M. *An Introduction to Aristotle's Rhetoric: With Analysis, Notes and Appendices*. London: Macmillan Co., 1867.

Corbett, Edward P. J. *Classical Rhetoric for the Modern Student*. 3d ed. New York: Oxford University Press, 1990.

———. *Selected Essays of Edward P. J. Corbett*. Edited by Robert J. Connors. SMU Studies in Composition and Rhetoric. Dallas: Southern Methodist University Press, 1989.

Cronkhite, Gary. "The Enthymeme as Deductive Rhetorical Argument." *WS* 30 (Spring 1966): 129–34.

D'Alton, J. F. *Roman Literary Theory and Criticism.* New York: Russell and Russell, 1962.

Dearin, Ray D. "The Fourth *Stasis* in Greek Rhetoric." In *Rhetoric and Communication*, edited by Jane Blankenship and Hermann G. Stelzner, 3–16. Urbana: University of Illinois Press, 1976.

de Romilly, Jacqueline. *Magic and Rhetoric in Ancient Greece.* Cambridge: Harvard University Press, 1975.

Dieter, Otto A. L. "*Stasis.*" *SM* 17 (August 1950): 345–69.

Dobson, John F. *The Greek Orators.* Freeport, N.Y.: Books for Libraries Press, 1971.

Dorey, T. A., ed. *Cicero.* New York: Basic Books, 1965.

Duff, J. Wright. *A Literary History of Rome: From the Origins to the Close of the Golden Age.* Edited by A. M. Duff. London: Ernest Benn, 1967.

———. *A Literary History of Rome in the Silver Age: From Tiberius to Hadrian.* Edited by A. M. Duff. 3d ed. London: Ernest Benn, 1964.

Ehninger, Douglas W. "The Classical Doctrine of Invention." *Gavel* 39 (March 1957): 59–62, 70.

———. "On Systems of Rhetoric." *PR* 1 (Summer 1968): 131–44.

Else, Gerald F. *Plato and Aristotle on Poetry.* Edited by Peter Burian. Chapel Hill and London: University of North Carolina Press, 1986.

Engnell, Richard A. "Implications for Communication of the Rhetorical Epistemology of Gorgias of Leontini." *WS* 37 (Summer 1973): 175–84.

Enos, Richard Leo. "Aristotle, Empedocles and the Notion of Rhetoric." In *In Search of Justice: The Indiana Tradition in Speech Communication*, edited by Richard J. Jensen and John C. Hammerback, 5–21. Amsterdam: Rodopi, 1987.

———. "The Classical Tradition(s) of Rhetoric: A Demur to the Country Club Set." *CCC* 38 (October 1987): 283–90.

———. "The Effects of Imperial Patronage on the Rhetorical Tradition of the Athenian Second Sophistic." *CQ* 25 (Spring 1977): 3–10.

———. "Emerging Notions of Heuristic, Eristic, and Protreptic Rhetoric in Homeric Discourse: Proto-Literate Conniving, Wrangling and Reasoning." In *Selected Papers from the 1981 Texas Writing Research Conference*, edited by Maxine C. Hairston and Cynthia L. Selfe, 44–64. Austin: University of Texas at Austin, 1981.

———. "The Epistemological Foundation for Cicero's Litigation Strategies." *CSSJ* 26 (Summer 1975): 207–14.

———. "The Epistemology of Gorgias's Rhetoric: A Re-examination." *SSJ* 42 (Fall 1976): 35–51.

———. "The Hellenic Rhapsode." *WS* 42 (Spring 1978): 134–43.

———. *The Literate Mode of Cicero's Legal Rhetoric*. Carbondale: Southern Illinois University Press, 1988.

Erickson, Keith V. "The Lost Rhetorics of Aristotle." *SM* 43 (August 1976): 229–37.

Erickson, Keith V., ed. *Aristotle: The Classical Heritage of Rhetoric*. Metuchen, N.J.: Scarecrow Press, 1974.

———. *Plato: True and Sophistic Rhetoric*. Amsterdam: Editions Rodopi, 1979.

Gage, John T. "Teaching the Enthymeme: Invention and Arrangement." *RR* 2 (September 1983): 38–50.

Gaines, Robert N. "Aristotle's Rhetorical Rhetoric?" *PR* 19 (Summer 1986): 194–200.

Garver, Eugene. "Aristotle's *Rhetoric* as a Work of Philosophy." *PR* 19 (Winter 1986): 1–22.

———. "Aristotle's *Rhetoric* on Unintentionally Hitting the Principles of the Sciences." *Rhetorica* 6 (Autumn 1988): 381–93.

Gold, Barbara K. *Literary Patronage in Greece and Rome*. Chapel Hill and London: University of North Carolina Press, 1987.

Golden, James L., Goodwin F. Berquist, and William E. Coleman. *The Rhetoric of Western Thought*. 3d ed. Dubuque, Iowa: Kendall/Hunt Publishing Co., 1983.

Golden, James L., Goodwin F. Berquist, and William E. Coleman, eds. *Essays on the Rhetoric of the Western World*. Dubuque, Iowa: Kendall/Hunt Publishing Co., 1990.

Goodwin, David. "*Controversiae, Meta-Asystatae* and the New Rhetoric." *RSQ* 19 (Summer 1989): 205–16.

Grimaldi, William M. A., S.J. "The Aristotelian Topics." In *Aristotle: The Classical Heritage of Rhetoric*, edited by Keith V. Erickson, 176–93. Metuchen, N.J.: Scarecrow Press, 1974.

———. *Aristotle, Rhetoric I: A Commentary*. Bronx, N.Y.: Fordham University Press, 1980.

———. *Aristotle, Rhetoric II: A Commentary*. Bronx, N.Y.: Fordham University Press, 1988.

———. "Rhetoric and Truth: A Note on Aristotle, Rhetoric 1355a." *PR* 11 (Summer 1978): 173–77.

———. "Studies in the Philosophy of Aristotle's *Rhetoric*." *Hermes: Zeitschrift für klassische Philologie* 25 (1972): 1–151.

Gronbeck, Bruce E. "Gorgias on Rhetoric and Poetic: A Rehabilitation." *SSJ* 38 (Fall 1972): 27–38.

Guthrie, W. K. C. *Socrates*. Cambridge: Cambridge University Press, 1971.

———. *The Sophists*. Cambridge: Cambridge University Press, 1971.

Gwynn, Aubrey. *Roman Education from Cicero to Quintilian*. Oxford: Oxford University Press, 1926.

Hagaman, John. "Modern Use of *Progymnasmata* in Teaching Rhetorical Invention." *RR* 5 (Fall 1986): 22–29.

Halloran, S. Michael. "Aristotle's Concept of *Ethos*, or if not His Somebody Else's." *RR* 1 (September 1982): 58–63.

Hammond, N. G. L., and H. H. Scullard, eds. *The Oxford Classical Dictionary*. 2d ed. Oxford: Clarendon Press, 1970.

Hauser, Gerard A. "Aristotle's Example Revisited." *PR* 18 (Summer 1985): 171–80.

———. "The Example in Aristotle's *Rhetoric*: Bifurcation or Contradiction?" *PR* 1 (Spring 1968): 78–90.

———. "Reply to Benoit." *PR* 20 (Fall 1987): 268–73.

Havelock, Eric A. *The Literate Revolution in Greece and Its Cultural Consequences*. Princeton: Princeton University Press, 1982.

———. *The Muse Learns to Write: Reflections on Orality and Literacy from Antiquity to the Present*. New Haven and London: Yale University Press, 1986.

———. *Preface to Plato*. Cambridge: Harvard University Press, 1963, 1983.

Hendrickson, G. L. "The Origin and Meaning of the Ancient Characters of Style." *AJP* 26 (1905): 249–90.

Hinks, D. A. G. "Tisias and Corax and the Invention of Rhetoric." *Classical Quarterly* 34 (April 1940): 61–69.

Horner, Winifred Bryan. *Rhetoric in the Classical Tradition*. New York: St. Martin's Press, 1988.

Horner, Winifred Bryan, ed. *Historical Rhetoric: An Annotated Bibliography of Selected Sources in English*. Boston: G. K. Hall, 1980.

Howell, Wilbur Samuel. "Aristotle and Horace on Rhetoric and Poetics." *QJS* 54 (December 1968): 325–39.

Hunt, Everett Lee. "On the Sophists." In *The Province of Rhetoric*, edited by Joseph Schwartz and John A. Rycenga, 69–84. New York: Ronald Press Co., 1965.

———. "Plato and Aristotle on Rhetoric and Rhetoricians." *QJS* 6 (June 1920): 35–56.

Jaeger, Werner. *Paideia: The Ideals of Greek Culture*. Translated by Gilbert Highet. 3 vols. New York: Oxford University Press, 1945.

———. "The Rhetoric of Isocrates and Its Cultural Ideal." In *The Province of Rhetoric*, edited by Joseph Schwartz and John A. Rycenga, 84–111. New York: Ronald Press Co., 1965.

Jarratt, Susan C. "The First Sophists and the Uses of History." *RR* 6 (Fall 1987): 67–78.

———. "Toward a Sophistic Historiography." *Pre/Text* 8 (Spring/Summer 1987): 9–26.

Jebb, Richard C. *The Attic Orators from Antiphon to Isaeos*. 2 vols. New York: Russell and Russell, 1962.

Kaufer, David S. "The Influence of Plato's Developing Psychology on His Views of Rhetoric." *QJS* 64 (February 1978): 63–78.

Kennedy, George A. *The Art of Persuasion in Greece*. Princeton: Princeton University Press, 1963.

———. *The Art of Rhetoric in the Roman World: 300 B.C.–A.D. 300*. Princeton: Princeton University Press, 1972.

———. *Classical Rhetoric and Its Christian and Secular Tradition from Ancient to Modern Times*. Chapel Hill: University of North Carolina Press, 1980.

———. *Greek Rhetoric under Christian Emperors*. Princeton: Princeton University Press, 1983.

———. "Later Greek Philosophy and Rhetoric." *PR* 13 (Summer 1980): 181–97.

———. *New Testament Interpretation through Rhetorical Criticism*. Chapel Hill and London: University of North Carolina Press, 1984.

———. *Quintilian*. New York: Twayne Publishers, 1969.

———. "Review Article: The Present State of the Study of Ancient Rhetoric." *Classical Philology* 70 (December 1975): 278–82.

Kerferd, G. B. *The Sophistic Movement*. London: Cambridge University Press, 1981.

Kinneavy, James L. *Greek Rhetorical Origins of Christian Faith: An Inquiry*. New York and Oxford: Oxford University Press, 1987.

Kirk, G. S. *Homer and the Oral Tradition*. Cambridge: Cambridge University Press, 1976.

Kustas, George. *Studies in Byzantine Rhetoric*. Salonika, Greece: Patriarchal Institute for Patristic Studies, 1973.

Leeman, A. D. *Orationis Ratio: The Stylistic Theories and Practice of the Roman Orators, Historians and Philosophers*. 2 vols. Amsterdam: Adolf M. Hakkert, 1963.

Leff, Michael C. "In Search of Ariadne's Thread: A Review of the Recent Literature on Rhetorical Theory." *CSSJ* 29 (Summer 1978): 73–91.

Leff, Michael C., ed. "The Classical Tradition in Rhetoric: Three Views of George A. Kennedy's Synthesis." *QJS* 67 (May 1981): 206–37.

Lentz, Tony M. *Orality and Literacy in Hellenic Greece*. Carbondale: Southern Illinois University Press, 1989.

Lesky, Albin. *A History of Greek Literature*. Translated by James Willis and Cornelis de Heer. London: Methuen, 1966.

Lundy, Susan Ruth, and Wayne N. Thompson. "Pliny, a Neglected Roman Rhetorician." *QJS* 66 (December 1980): 407–17.

McBurney, James A. "The Place of the Enthymeme in Rhetorical Theory." *SM* 3 (1936): 49–74.

McCall, Marsh H., Jr. *Ancient Rhetorical Theories of Simile and Comparison*. Cambridge: Harvard University Press, 1969.

Marrou, H. I. *A History of Education in Antiquity*. Translated by George Lamb. New York: New American Library, 1964.

May, James M. *Trials of Character: The Eloquence of Ciceronian Ethos*. Chapel Hill and London: University of North Carolina Press, 1988.

Meador, Prentice A., Jr. "The Classical Epicheireme: A Re-Examination." *WS* 30 (Summer 1966): 151–55.

Moss, Jean Dietz, ed. *Rhetoric and Praxis: The Contribution of Classical Rhetoric to Practical Reasoning*. Washington, D.C.: Catholic University of America Press, 1986.

Mudd, Charles. "The Enthymeme and Logical Validity." *QJS* 45 (December 1959): 409–14.

Murphy, James J. "Implications of the 'Renaissance of Rhetoric' in English Departments." *QJS* 75 (August 1989): 335–43.

Murphy, James J., ed. *A Short History of Writing Instruction from Ancient Greece to Twentieth-Century America*. Davis, Calif.: Hermagoras Press, 1990.

———. *A Synoptic History of Classical Rhetoric*. Berkeley: University of California Press, 1972. Rev. ed., Davis, Calif.: Hermagoras Press, 1983.

Nadeau, Ray. "Classical Systems of *Stases* in Greek: Hermagoras to Hermogenes." *Greek, Roman and Byzantine Studies* 2 (January 1959): 51–71.

———. "Hermogenes on 'Stock Issues' in Deliberative Speaking." *SM* 25 (March 1958): 59–66.

———. "Some Aristotelian and Stoic Influences on the Theory of *Stasis*." *SM* 26 (November 1959): 248–54.

Neel, Jasper. *Plato, Derrida, and Writing: Deconstruction, Composition and Influence*. Carbondale: Southern Illinois University Press, 1988.

Ochs, Donovan J. "Aristotle's Concept of Formal Topics." *SM* 36 (November 1969): 419–25.

———. "Cicero and Philosophic *Inventio*." *RSQ* 19 (Summer 1989): 217–27.

———. "Cicero's *Topica*: A Process View of Invention." In *Explorations in Rhetoric: Studies in Honor of Douglas Ehninger*, edited by Ray E. McKerrow, 107–18. Glenview, Ill.: Scott, Foresman and Co., 1982.

"Octolog: The Politics of Historiography." *RR* 7 (Fall 1988): 5–49.

Ong, Walter J. *Orality and Literacy: The Technologizing of the Word*. London and New York: Methuen Press, 1982.

Parry, Adam, ed. *The Making of Homeric Verse: The Collected Papers of Milman Parry*. Oxford: Clarendon Press, 1971.

Parry, Milman. "Studies in the Epic Technique of Oral Verse-Making, II. The Homeric Language as the Language of Oral Poetry." *HSCP* 43 (1932): 1–50.

Peabody, Berkley. *The Winged Word: A Study in the Technique of Ancient Greek Oral Composition as Seen Principally through Hesiod's* Works and Days. Albany: State University of New York Press, 1975.

Pfeiffer, Rudolf. *History of Classical Scholarship from the Beginnings to the End of the Hellenistic Age*. Oxford: Clarendon Press, 1968.

Platnauer, Maurice, ed. *Fifty Years (and Twelve) of Classical Scholarship*. 2d ed. Oxford: Basil Blackwell, 1968.

Poulakos, John. "Rhetoric, the Sophists, and the Possible." *CM* 51 (September 1984): 215–26.

———. "Toward a Sophistic Definition of Rhetoric." *PR* 16 (Winter 1983): 35–48.

Prill, Paul. "Cicero in Theory and Practice: The Securing of Good Will in the *Exordia* of Five Forensic Speeches." *Rhetorica* 4 (Spring 1986): 93–109.

Rayment, Charles S. "A Current Survey of Ancient Rhetoric." *Classical World* 52 (December 1958): 75–91.

Robb, Kevin, ed. *Language and Thought in Early Greek Philosophy*. LaSalle, Ill.: Hegeler Institute (Monist Library of Philosophy), 1983.

Roberts, W. Rhys. *Greek Rhetoric and Literary Criticism*. New York: Longmans, Green & Co., 1928.

Rowland, Robert C., and Deanna F. Womack. "Aristotle's View on Ethical Rhetoric." *RSQ* 15 (Winter–Spring 1985): 13–31.

Russell, D. A. *Greek Declamation*. Cambridge: Cambridge University Press, 1983.

Sattler, William M. "Conceptions of Ethos in Ancient Rhetoric." *SM* 14 (1947): 55–65.

———. "Some Platonic Influences in the Rhetorical Works of Cicero." *QJS* 35 (April 1949): 164–69.

Segal, C. P. "Gorgias and the Psychology of the Logos." *HSCP* 66 (1962): 99–155.

Smith, Robert W. *The Art of Rhetoric in Alexandria: Its Theory and Practice in the Ancient World*. The Hague: Martinus Nijhoff, 1974.

Sochatoff, A. F. "Basic Rhetorical Theories of the Elder Seneca." *Classical Journal* 34 (March 1939): 345–54.

Solmsen, Friedrich. "The Aristotelian Tradition in Ancient Rhetoric."

AJP 62 (1941): 35–50, 169–90. Reprinted in *Aristotle: The Classical Heritage of Rhetoric*, edited by Keith V. Erickson, 278–309. Metuchen, N.J.: Scarecrow Press, 1974.

Sumner, G. V. *The Orators in Cicero's* Brutus: *Prosopography and Chronology*. Toronto: University of Toronto Press, 1973.

Thompson, Wayne N. "*Stasis* in Aristotle's *Rhetoric*." *QJS* 58 (April 1972): 134–41.

Thonssen, Lester, and A. Craig Baird. "Cicero and Quintilian on Rhetoric." In *The Province of Rhetoric*, edited by Joseph Schwartz and John A. Rycenga, 137–57. New York: Ronald Press Co., 1965.

Untersteiner, Mario. *The Sophists*. Translated by Kathleen Freeman. New York: Philosophical Library, 1954.

Vickers, Brian. *In Defence of Rhetoric*. Oxford: Clarendon Press, 1988.

Wagner, Russell H. "The Rhetorical Theory of Isocrates." In *Readings in Rhetoric*, edited by Lionel Crocker and Paul A. Carmack, 169–83. Springfield, Ill.: Charles C. Thomas, 1965.

Welch, Kathleen Ethel. "A Critique of Classical Rhetoric: The Contemporary Appropriation of Ancient Discourse." *RR* 6 (Fall 1987): 79–86.

———. "The Platonic Paradox: Plato's Rhetoric in Contemporary Rhetoric and Composition Studies." *WC* 5 (January 1988): 3–21.

Wilkerson, K. E. "From Hero to Citizen: Persuasion in Early Greece." *PR* 15 (Spring 1982): 104–25.

Wilkinson, L. P. *Golden Latin Artistry*. Cambridge: Cambridge University Press, 1963.

Wooten, Cecil W. *Cicero's* Philippics *and Their Demosthenic Model: The Rhetoric of Crisis*. Chapel Hill and London: University of North Carolina Press, 1983.

Yates, Frances Amelia. *The Art of Memory*. London and Chicago: Routledge and University of Chicago Press, 1966.

Selected Bibliographies

Allen, Walter. "A Survey of Selected Ciceronian Bibliography, 1939–1953." *Classical World* 47 (1953–1954): 129–39.

Benoit, William L. "A Brief Bibliography of Sources on Isocrates in English." *RSQ* 11 (Fall 1981): 263–64.

Caplan, Harry. "Bibliography." In [*Cicero*] *Ad C. Herennium de Ratione Dicendi (Rhetorica ad Herennium)*, translated by Harry Caplan, xli–xliv. The Loeb Classical Library. Cambridge: Harvard University Press, 1954.

Enos, Richard Leo. "The Classical Period." In *Historical Rhetoric: An*

Annotated Bibliography of Selected Sources in English, edited by Winifred Bryan Horner, 1–41. Boston: G. K. Hall, 1980.

————. "Early Concepts of Greek Rhetoric and Discourse: A Selected Bibliography." *RSQ* 10 (Winter 1980): 49–50.

————. "Epigraphical Sources for the History of Hellenic Rhetoric." *RSQ* 9 (Summer 1979): 169–76.

Enos, Richard Leo, and Dean N. Constant. "A Bibliography of Ciceronian Rhetoric." *RSQ* 6 (Spring 1976): 21–28.

Enos, Richard Leo, and Honora Mary Rockar. "General Works on the Development of Writing and Scripts." *RSQ* 10 (Fall 1980): 263–65.

Enos, Richard Leo, and Howard E. Sypher. "A Bibliography for the Study of Classical Invention." *RSQ* 7 (Spring 1977): 53–57.

Erickson, Keith V. "Plato's Philosophy of Rhetoric: A Research Guide." *RSQ* 7 (Summer 1977): 78–90.

————. "Quintilian's *Institutio oratoria* and *Pseudo-Declamationes*." *RSQ* 11 (Winter 1981): 45–62.

Lentz, Tony M. "The Oral Tradition in Transition: A Bibliography Relevant to the Study of Reading in Hellenic Greece." *RSQ* 8 (Spring 1978): 82–98.

Matlon, Ronald J., and Peter C. Facciola. *Index to Journals in Communication Studies through 1985*. Falls Church, Va.: Speech Communication Association, 1987.

THE MIDDLE AGES

James J. Murphy
and Martin Camargo

Scholarship to 1942

Although the serious study of medieval rhetoric has increased considerably over the past two decades, the first movements in that direction came in the middle of the last century and were accelerated by several works published in the 1930s and 1940s. The medieval period itself was long neglected or misunderstood. In the sixteenth century, for example, the poet Edmund Spenser referred to Chaucer as a literary diamond in a dunghill of an age. Nineteenth-century figures like William Morris and Alfred Lord Tennyson, who romanticized the middle ages, perpetuated a sense of unreality about the period. The rhetoric of such a period was not likely to be worthy of study.

The first major change in attitude toward rhetoric of that period came in Germany in the 1850s and 1860s, when scholars began to realize that certain "historical" documents—letters, contracts, formulas—were in fact not records of real events but models or even teaching exercises for medieval students of the *ars dictaminis*, or art of letter-writing. This discovery led to the publication in 1863 of a landmark collection of Latin texts: Ludwig Rockinger, *Briefsteller und Formelbücher des eilften bis vierzehnten Jahrhunderts*. Rockinger's introduction is not very pertinent today, but his set of eighteen texts, which includes both letter-writing manuals and model letter collections, is still quite useful, and the book was in fact reprinted in 1961.

Because much rhetorical material was taught by grammarians during the middle ages, another important nineteenth-century collection deserves mention. In 1868, M. C. Thurot, "Notices et extraits de divers manuscrits latins pour servir à l'histoire des doctrines grammaticales au moyen age," was published in a special issue of *Notices et Extraits*. Thurot's set of studies, lists, and text excerpts is still extremely valuable, and the book was reprinted in 1964.

The next major advance came in a different rhetorical field, and some

45

six decades later, with the publication in 1924 of Edmond Faral's *Les arts poétiques du XIIe et du XIIIe siècles*. Faral furnishes the Latin texts or summaries of six major *artes poetriae*, with brief biographies of their authors, together with a useful analysis of their basic doctrines and a brief chapter on the medieval use of the tropes and figures of the pseudo-Ciceronian *Rhetorica ad Herennium*. Faral's book triggered a wave of interest in the literary influences of the *artes*, especially the *Poetria nova* of Geoffrey of Vinsauf; a key article by John M. Manly ("Chaucer and the Rhetoricians," 1926) was among the first of more than fifty such studies. *Les arts poétiques* was reprinted in 1958.

The first major modern study of medieval preaching theory appeared at almost the same time as Faral's book, in 1926. By the Cambridge don Gerald R. Owst, this work was *Preaching in Medieval England: An Introduction to Sermon Manuscripts of the Period, c. 1350–1450*. This marvelously detailed study of both theory and practice remains a standard. Then, in a remarkable scholarly coincidence, three extremely important guides to the study of medieval preaching theory appeared within three years of each other. Harry Caplan's *Mediaeval Artes Praedicandi: A Hand-List* came out in 1934. Then in 1936 Father Th.-M. Charland's *Artes praedicandi: contribution à l'histoire de la rhétorique au moyen âge* was published, the same year as Caplan's *Supplement* to his basic 1934 handlist. Caplan and Charland between them listed some three hundred treatises of the *ars praedicandi*, or art of preaching, many anonymous, and almost all still in manuscript. Today, more than five decades later, only about twenty-five are available in any printed form. Charland's book includes an excellent summary of theory, the biographies of known authors, lists of manuscripts, and the Latin texts of two preaching manuals by Thomas Waleys and Robert of Basevorn. Like Faral and Rockinger, Charland remains indispensable for any serious study of rhetoric in the middle ages.

Meanwhile, in 1928 Charles S. Baldwin had produced *Medieval Rhetoric and Poetic*, with useful summaries of some medieval treatises; he paid little attention to developments in rhetoric after the thirteenth century, however, and stresses unduly the role of dialectic. The "Poetic" in his title is largely Chaucerian. (Four years earlier he had completed another volume on the same plan, *Ancient Rhetoric and Poetic*.) Moreover, since the work of Charland and Caplan had not yet been done, Baldwin paid comparatively little detailed attention to preaching theories.

By the time of World War II it was clear that, in addition to the long-documented survival of ancient rhetorical texts (especially those of Cicero), there was considerable interest during the middle ages in rhetorical theories developed by medieval writers in the three fields of letter-writing, verse-writing, and sermon-making. Taking together the three basic collections of Latin treatises—those by Rockinger, Faral, and Charland—there was ample text material in hand for further study.

Richard McKeon's landmark "Rhetoric in the Middle Ages" (1942) was an effort at a synthesis of what had been learned to that point. McKeon used the relations between the three arts of the medieval *trivium*—grammar, rhetoric, and dialectic—to place the rhetorical forms of the middle ages in an understandable context. Although the article is still referred to frequently and does contain some valuable citations and other information, it is densely, even obscurely written and over-emphasizes the influence of dialectic on medieval rhetorical theory. Nevertheless, many readers may find it worth the careful reading that its sometimes murky prose will require.

The Present State of Scholarship

Basic Resources

In some respects the medieval period is now one of the best covered, since we now have in print a general bibliography and a partial one, two collections of translations in addition to a number of individual translations, a volume of essays dealing with medieval rhetoric, a number of key studies, and finally a one-volume history of rhetoric for the period from Saint Augustine to the Renaissance. All of these have appeared within the past two decades.

Besides these publications specifically relating to medieval rhetoric, there are also several important encyclopedic projects under way that will include many items relating to the subject. The first fascicles of *Lexikon des Mittelalters* began to appear in 1978; the German-language *Lexikon* is published by Artemis & Winkler of Munich, West Germany, and is planned for five volumes and an index volume. Articles are generally short, with emphasis on summary rather than detail, and have brief bibliographies at the end. Excellent articles appear in the first volume on *Ars dictaminis* (Hans Martin Schaller) and *Ars praedicandi* (Franz Quadlbauer), though the article on *Ars poetica, ars versificatoria* (R. Düchting) is less satisfactory in its omission of most scholarship of the last twenty years.

A second, more narrowly focused German-language work is the planned *Historisches Wörterbuch der Rhetorik*, directed by Walter Jens and Gert Ueding and to be published by Niemeyer of Tübingen, West Germany. Most articles will be similar in length to those in the *Lexikon*, though major areas of research will be allotted more space. The first volume is scheduled for publication in 1991.

In contrast to the brevity of the *Lexikon*, the twelve-volume *Dictionary of the Middle Ages* (New York: Charles Scribner's Sons, 1982–1989) includes articles ranging up to ten thousand words on major subjects. Western European rhetoric, for instance, has eight thousand words in an article by James J. Murphy (10:351–64), while separate essays are devoted to Arabic, Persian, and Hebrew rhetoric (Andras Hamori and Jerome Clinton, 10:345–49) and to Byzantine rhetoric (Robert Browning, 10:349–51). The *Dictionary* also includes articles on dialectic, grammar, the major genres of medieval rhetoric, and a number of important rhetorical authors like Boethius and Geoffrey of Vinsauf. A short bibliography accompanies each essay.

Finally, the Typologie des sources du moyen âge occidental currently has in press a series of monographs (in English), several of them quite lengthy, on the four major "genres" of medieval rhetoric: Marianne Briscoe, *Artes praedicandi*; Martin Camargo, *Ars dictaminis, Artes dictandi*; Douglas Kelly, *The Arts of Poetry and Prose*; and John Ward, *Ciceronian Rhetoric in Treatise, Scholion and Commentary*. Several other fascicles in this series, for example that of Giles Constable (*Letters and Letter-Collections*), contain material useful to students of medieval rhetoric.

A major advantage of an encyclopedic entry, of course, is that it usually represents a distillation of the major elements in a subject by an expert in the field. (Paradoxically, this is less true of the treatment of medieval rhetoric in the latest edition of *The Encyclopaedia Britannica*, where the article on "Rhetoric" by Thomas O. Sloane takes a broad and conceptual view of the subject that may be of less value to one interested specifically in rhetoric of the middle ages.)

Bibliographies

The standard bibliography for medieval rhetoric is James J. Murphy, *Medieval Rhetoric: A Select Bibliography* (2d ed., 1989), containing 971 citations arranged under nine headings: Background Studies, Early Middle Ages, High Middle Ages, Letter-Writing: *Ars dictaminis*, Poetics and Grammar: *Ars poetriae*, Sermon Theory: *Ars praedicandi*, University Disputation and Scholastic Method, Various Sources, and Renaissance. Many items are annotated. A listing of forty key books and articles concludes the volume.

A bibliography of more limited scope that may be useful for beginning the study of medieval rhetoric is that of Luke Reinsma, "The Middle Ages," in Winifred Bryan Horner, ed., *Historical Rhetoric: An Annotated Bibliography of Selected Sources in English* (1980). All 235 primary and secondary sources are annotated; Reinsma points out that he has concentrated on the more recent of the secondary works (30 percent of them since 1970), with special attention to "liberally documented" sources whose notes can facilitate further study. He also notes that nearly half of his citations are not in the first edition of the Murphy bibliography (1971). The Reinsma bibliography lists primary sources chronologically and secondary sources alphabetically by author rather than by field or chronological period; while some readers may find this a disadvantage, the extensive annotation may be of assistance. (Additional remarks on bibliography may be found below in the section on Journals and Series.) Also useful is a general medieval bibliography that includes many items relating to rhetoric: *Medioevo Latino: Bolletino bibliografico della cultura europea dal secolo VI al XIII*, edited by Claudio Leonardi as a bibliographic appendix to the journal *Studi Medievale*; the first volume appeared in 1980.

Translations

Two collections of translations are now available. The first to appear was *Three Medieval Rhetorical Arts* (1971), edited by Murphy. This set of original translations includes the editor's rendering of Anonymous of Bologna, *The Principles of Letter-Writing* (1135)—still the only *ars dictaminis* so far rendered into English—Geoffrey of Vinsauf, *The New Poetics* (ca. 1210), translated by Jane Baltzell Kopp; and Robert of Basevorn, *The Form of Preaching* (1322), translated by Father Leopold Krul, O.S.B. The three works are essentially complete. An appendix includes excerpts from the two works of Aristotle used in medieval universities for training in *disputatio*, his *Topics* and *On Sophistical Refutations*. An introduction (vii-xxiii) outlines the place of the three translated texts in the "preceptive tradition" of the middle ages.

The second collection, while more extensive in some respects (thirty-six authors are named), is more difficult to assess because it includes items at three levels: complete translations, translations of excerpts, and nine "commentaries" of a page or two that cite translations available elsewhere. This collection is Joseph M. Miller, Michael H. Prosser, and Thomas W. Benson, eds., *Readings in Medieval Rhetoric* (1973). Some of the translations included were first published elsewhere; Father Joseph Miller is the sole translator of the original renderings in the volume. A few of the works translated may strike some readers as trivial—for instance, Hildebert of Lavardin's Second Sermon for Pentecost—but the volume also presents for the first time in English some extremely valuable texts for the history of medieval rhetoric; especially noteworthy are texts of the excerpts from Priscian, Martianus Capella,

Isidore of Seville, Rabanus Maurus, Walafrid Strabo, Alberic of Monte Cassino, Alain de Lille, Giles of Rome, and Thomas of Todi. Nevertheless, the reader might well have a mixed reaction to the items gathered in this collection.

Other translations of individual works will be of interest. A number of key texts of the *ars poetriae* are now available in English. One of the most important is Traugott Lawler's *The* Parisiana Poetria *of John of Garland* (1974). John of Garland was a prominent early thirteenth-century grammar master who undertook to prepare a single book that could give the reader everything he needed to know about composing prose, quantitative verse, or rhymed syllabic verse. As John says in his prologue, "the art of composition is here channeled in a short stream." Lawler's work contains the Latin text facing the English. With its careful and extensive notes giving frequent cross-references to other works of the time (especially those of Geoffrey of Vinsauf), this volume can be an invaluable introduction to the whole relationship of grammar and rhetoric in the late twelfth and early to mid-thirteenth centuries.

The *Poetria nova* and *Documentum* of Geoffrey of Vinsauf have both been translated—the *Poetria nova* three times—and further editions and commentaries are in preparation. One translation of the *Poetria nova* has already been noted above (Murphy, *Three Arts*, 1971). Another with some unique features is that of Ernest A. Gallo, *The* Poetria nova *and Its Sources in Early Rhetorical Doctrine* (1971); Gallo provides a Latin text (basically Faral's) and a facing prose translation and then devotes a hundred pages (133–236) to a discussion of the poem's ancient rhetorical sources. The doctrine of *amplificatio* gets special attention. Gallo uses the method of parallel passages to argue derivation from Horace's *Ars poetica*, Cicero's *De inventione*, and the pseudo-Ciceronian *Rhetorica ad Herennium*, though his parallels to the *Institutio oratoria* of Quintilian are less convincing.

The most highly regarded translation of Vinsauf's work, however, has been that of Margaret F. Nims, *The Poetria Nova of Geoffrey of Vinsauf* (1967). A crisp translation close to the flavor of the difficult Latin text, coupled with economical yet revealing notes, has made this by far the preferred version of the poem's text, though some readers may prefer a translation with a more extensive introduction.

Vinsauf's prose *Documentum de modo et arte dictandi et versificandi*, which presents substantially the same doctrine as his hexameter *Poetria nova*, has been translated by Roger P. Parr as *Instruction in the Method and Art of Speaking and Versifying* (1968).

The *Ars versificatoria* of the twelfth-century author Matthew of Vendôme has been translated three times. The earliest, partial version is by

Gallo, "Matthew of Vendome: Introductory Treatise on the Art of Poetry" (1974); Gallo summarizes some sections instead of offering a direct translation. Complete renderings are found in *Matthew of Vendôme: The Art of Versification*, translated by Aubrey E. Galyon (1980), and *Ars versificatoria (The Art of the Versemaker)*, translated by Roger P. Parr (1981). The new edition of Matthew's Latin text by Franco Munari (1988) may well inspire a fourth translation.

Eberhard the German's *Laborintus* was translated as a Cornell Master's thesis by Evelyn Carlson in 1930. One other major Latin work in this tradition, Gervase of Melkley's *De arte versificatoria et modo*, was only summarized by Faral, but it was later edited in Germany by Hans-Jürgen Gräbener under the title *"Ars poetica"* in *Forschungen zur romanischen Philologie* 17 (1965). Catherine Yodice Giles's Ph.D. dissertation (Rutgers, 1973) includes a translation of Gräbener's text.

A new approach to medieval concepts of language use is found in a recent set of translations of scholastic documents dealing with literary theory: *Medieval Literary Theory and Criticism, c. 1100–c. 1375: The Commentary Tradition* (1988), edited by Alastair Minnis and A. B. Scott with David Wallace. This book now makes available a wide range of treatises dealing with language, grammar, rhetoric, and poetics.

Translations are more plentiful when one turns to the *ars praedicandi*, or preaching manual, but here it must be noted that fewer than a dozen of the three-hundred-odd known treatises are available in English, while editions of the Latin texts still number only about twenty-five. Details of the Latin texts may be secured in the Murphy bibliography for such authors as Francis Eiximenis, Hugh of St. Victor, or Martin of Cordova. The *Ars componendi sermones* of Ranulph Higden, edited by Margaret Jennings, was published in Leiden in 1990. The Miller-Prosser-Benson collection discussed above includes translated excerpts from the manuals of Alain de Lille, Rabanus Maurus, Guibert of Nogent, Humbert of Romans, and Thomas of Todi. In addition, both Murphy and Reinsma in their bibliographies list translations of Simon Alcock, Thomas Waleys, Henry of Hesse, and Pseudo-Aquinas. One of the longest (and in the eyes of one historian of the subject, most "typical") treatises is the *Form of Preaching* (1322) of Robert of Basevorn, translated by Leopold Krul in Murphy's *Three Arts* (1971). One rendering not listed in either the Reinsma or Murphy bibliography is Harry C. Hazel, Jr., "Translation, with Commentary, of the Bonaventuran *Ars concionandi*" (1972); this work was at one time erroneously attributed to Saint Bonaventure. Harry Caplan's *Of Eloquence* (1970) reprints his earlier journal translations of "Henry of Hesse" and "Pseudo-Aquinas."

Gillian R. Evans has translated the *Ars praedicandi* of Alain de Lille as

The Art of Preaching (1981), from the Patrologia latina text of Migne, describing it as a "working text" necessary until a critical edition of the Latin text is prepared to supplant the "far from satisfactory" Migne text.

As was noted earlier, only one *ars dictaminis* or letter-writing manual has so far appeared in English; this is the so-called Anonymous of Bologna, *Principles of Letter-Writing*, in the Murphy collection *Three Arts*. However, some interesting aspects of the tradition may be seen in Charles H. Haskins, "The Life of Medieval Students as Illustrated by Their Letters" (1929).

Most of the foundational works of the late classical period and the early middle ages are now available in some kind of English version and will generally repay the reading—Saint Augustine, Martianus Capella, Priscian, Isidore of Seville, Cassiodorus, Boethius, Bede, Rabanus Maurus, and Alcuin. For details see the bibliography at the end of this essay.

Surveys and General Studies

Since World War II a number of surveys or extensive studies have attempted to place in perspective the larger number of medieval rhetorical treatises that have come to light. Some older works were still in use, such as Paul Abelson's *The Seven Liberal Arts* (1906) and Louis J. Paetow's *The Arts Course at Medieval Universities with Special Reference to Grammar and Rhetoric* (1910). Then in 1943 John W. H. Atkins wrote *English Literary Criticism: The Medieval Phase*, whose lengthy analysis of Geoffrey of Vinsauf and other authors of the *artes poetriae* sparked another wave of journal articles dealing with rhetoric in literature.

The most useful book of the immediate postwar period, however, proved to be Ernst R. Curtius, *European Literature and the Latin Middle Ages* (1953), translated from the original 1948 German version. The basic thesis of the book is that *topoi* or rhetorical topics can be used to analyze the impact of rhetoric on medieval habits of literary development; with examples from several national literatures as well as from Latin, Curtius popularized for a time the search for "themes" as well as rhetorical figures in medieval literary works. The book is so richly documented that it is well worth studying today. It was reprinted in 1967.

Another provocative general study worth perusal is Erich Auerbach, *Literary Language and Its Public in Late Latin Antiquity and in the Middle Ages* (1965). As its title indicates, this book raises some useful generic questions about communication in the middle ages.

As the titles of Atkins's, Curtius's, and Auerbach's works indicate, a literary approach to the study of medieval rhetoric seemed for a time to be dominant among scholars. Meanwhile, however, a number of parallel studies were going on relating to such diverse subjects as preaching, Italian humanism, the *ars dictaminis*, medieval grammar, the *disputatio* in universities, the *trivium*, and medieval commentaries on the rhetoric of Cicero. See the bibliography at the end of this essay for a selection from the English-language scholarship in these areas published during the past thirty years. Space does not permit a detailed listing here, but the important point is that these studies represent a widespread and continuing set of investigations into what is increasingly regarded as a very complex subject.

The "standard history of medieval rhetoric" (to use Reinsma's term) appeared in 1974 with the publication of Murphy's *Rhetoric in the Middle Ages: A History of Rhetorical Theory from Saint Augustine to the Renaissance*. Its preface declares that it traces the medieval history of the "preceptive rhetorical tradition"—the fundamental concept of order and plan in discourse—first laid down in ancient Greece and then transmitted to the middle ages through Roman writers. The book is divided into six chapters and an epilogue. The first three chapters deal with ancient rhetorical theory and its continuations: the ancient traditions, Saint Augustine and the age of transition (to A.D. 1050), and the medieval survival of classical traditions. The second set of three chapters discusses three medieval "genres" of verse-writing, letter-writing, and preaching. An epilogue describes the fifteenth-century rediscovery of the complete texts of Quintilian's *Institutio* and Cicero's *De oratore*.

Rhetoric in the Middle Ages argues that Greek and Roman rhetoric was committed to the discovery of precepts that could be used to plan and present future discourse. These discoveries were amalgamated into books like Aristotle's *Rhetoric* or Cicero's *De inventione*. Roman education, built around rhetorical preparation for civic life, systematically applied the Isocratean trilogy of Talent, Education, and Practice to devise a complex training program of great efficiency. Both grammatical and rhetorical precepts were employed. This educational program outlasted the culture that gave it birth, transmitting Roman rhetorical educational practices directly into the middle ages. Early medieval writers like Saint Augustine defended the values of Roman rhetorical training in the face of Christian distrust of pagan ideas, and the so-called encyclopedists (Martianus Capella, Isidore of Seville, and Cassiodorus) digested basic rhetorical doctrines as part of their surveys of ancient learning. Thus men of the high middle ages—A.D. 1050–1400— inherited both a respect for Roman rhetoric and a set of texts (mainly Ciceronian) presenting its theory. Commentary writers of the twelfth and thirteenth centuries further popularized these ideas. Medieval rhetoric to a great extent then became a series of adaptations of Ciceronian rhetoric to particular needs of the times, with applications to problems of letter-writing, verse-writing, and preaching. In the universities, however, the basic communicative methodology remained the *disputatio* derived from principles of Aristotelian dialectic. *Rhetoric in the Middle Ages* was reissued as a paperback in 1981.

The ground covered in Murphy's landmark book was surveyed more briefly by Martin Camargo in the chapter "Rhetoric" in *The Seven Liberal Arts in the Middle Ages* (1983). Also useful is Peter Dronke's "Medieval Rhetoric," in *Literature and Western Civilization* (1973).

There are two recent general surveys of rhetorical history with a segment on the middle ages. One is George A. Kennedy, *Classical Rhetoric and Its Christian and Secular Tradition from Ancient to Modern Times* (1980). Kennedy, already well known for *The Art of Persuasion in Greece* (1963) and *The Art of Rhetoric in the Roman World* (1972), sets out in this book "to define classical rhetoric and its tradition by examining the various strands of thought which are woven together in different ways at different times" (3). He includes an interesting chapter on Judeo-Christian rhetoric, and another on Greek rhetoric in the middle ages; he devotes twenty pages to Latin rhetoric in the period, covering fourteen topics very briefly. The reader should remember, though, that Kennedy's purpose is to seek traces of the later history of classical rhetoric, not to write a history of every period.

The second survey is Thomas M. Conley's *Rhetoric in the European Tradition* (1990). Each of the ten chapters is followed by brief outlines of the major works discussed; for the medieval Latin chapter the authors are Augustine, Alcuin, Notker Labeo, William of Auvergne, and Robert de Basevorn. Conley also includes a chapter on late antique and Byzantine Greek rhetoric. Treatments are necessarily brief, but most readers will probably find his coverage objective as well as synoptic.

An equally brief but more significant treatment of medieval rhetoric may be found in Paul O. Kristeller, "Philosophy and Rhetoric from Antiquity to the Renaissance" (1979). Kristeller's notes alone would be worth the reading. His reflections on the developmental role of *dictamen* are particularly valuable. (For parallel views about the importance of the medieval *ars dictaminis* in terms of later Renaissance humanism, see Jerrold Seigel, *Rhetoric and Philosophy in Renaissance Humanism* [1968], especially chapter 7, "From the *dictatores* to the Humanists," and Ronald Witt, "Medieval 'Ars dictaminis' and the Beginnings of Humanism" [1982].)

Readers interested in a more inductive approach to the various facets of medieval rhetoric may be interested in a collection of fourteen essays edited by Murphy under the title *Medieval Eloquence: Studies in the Theory and Practice of Medieval Rhetoric* (1978). Part 1 includes six essays on rhetorical theory: Michael Leff on Boethius, John O. Ward on Ciceronian commentaries, Ernest Gallo on Geoffrey of Vinsauf, Charles B. Faulhaber on Guido Faba's *dictamen*, Margaret Jennings on Ranulph Higden's preaching manual, and M. B. Parkes on the rhetorical uses of punctuation. Part 2 contains eight examinations of rhetoric as applied to various literatures: Calvin Kendall on Bede's Latin, Jackson J. Campbell on Old English literature, Murphy on an early Middle English poem, Douglas Kelly on Old French literature, Aldo Scaglione on Dante, Robert O. Payne on Chaucer, Samuel Jaffe on Gottfried von Strassburg, and Josef Purkart on Boncompagno of Signa. Taken together, these essays with their notes and other references can provide an illuminating introduction to the subject.

Journals and Series

Most humanistic journals will consider articles dealing with the history of rhetoric. Even a rapid scan of the bibliography at the end of this essay will show that significant items dealing with medieval rhetoric have appeared in such journals as *Speculum, Medium Ævum, Studi Medievali, Medieval Studies, Medievalia et Humanistica*, and *Review of English Studies*. Articles from these and similar journals are indexed in the annual *MLA Bibliography*.

For journals in the speech/communication field there is now a useful index covering publications through 1985: Ronald J. Matlon, *Index to Journals in Communication Studies through 1985* (Falls Church, Va.: Speech Communication Association, 1987). Among the journals indexed are several that have carried numerous relevant articles: *Quarterly Journal of Speech, Communication Monographs* (formerly *Speech Monographs*), *Western Speech Communication Journal* (formerly *Western Speech*), *Southern Speech Journal*, and *Central States Speech Journal*. Cross-references in the Matlon volume permit searches for subjects and periods as well as for authors and titles.

Perhaps the most important new resource is the quarterly *Rhetorica: A Journal of the History of Rhetoric*, published by the University of California Press for the International Society for the History of Rhetoric. The first issue appeared in Spring 1983.

An important but so far little known series is the *Cahiers de l'Institut du Moyen-Âge Grec et Latin* (*CIMAGL*, 1969–), begun at the University of Copenhagen under the general editorship of the late Jan Pinborg. The *CIMAGL* include texts and studies relating to the middle ages.

This brief overview cannot of course offer complete coverage of the many studies that European and American scholars have devoted to medieval rhetoric over the past several decades. The bibliography at the end of this essay—itself necessarily highly selective—can point to additional resources. What is heartening, however, is that after centuries of comparative neglect there is now a strong interest in exploring medieval ideas of communication. The next section will examine the frontiers of our present knowledge and suggest some possible new lines of inquiry.

Six Issues for Future Scholarship

I. *Texts.* Some textual problems occur in any field, but in a field as comparatively uncharted as medieval rhetoric there is a need for the publication of the medieval texts that can provide evidence for our assessment of the subject. There are at least three hundred unedited *artes praedicandi* or preaching manuals; there are perhaps four hundred unedited *artes dictaminis*—Emil Polak of Queensborough Community College has been touring Europe uncovering hitherto unknown treatises by the score. It is not only a deep interest in medieval literature, certainly, that has produced so many studies relating to the *ars poetriae*; it must be remembered that Faral's basic Latin texts have been in print for almost seventy years. So far we lack that kind of textual control for preaching manuals, or letter-writing treatises and commentaries, or school texts. Without numerous texts to compare, the average scholarly reader is at the mercy of the summarizer and survey-writer.

Somewhat the same thing can be said in this decreasingly Latinic age about the value of translations. The Latin-less reader is also at the mercy of the summarizer, unless he or she has a readable version of the texts to compare with what the surveyor alleges. Directors of theses and dissertations might well bear this need in mind when counseling their students about making a "contribution to knowledge."

Jacques Maritain once remarked that the history of philosophy was not the same as the history of its books. The same is no doubt true of medieval rhetoric, but at the same time the written record of ideas and their applications over the centuries of the middle ages can surely be of immense assistance to us in trying to understand that period.

II. *The educational background.* This may be treated under two headings:

A. *The history of education.* Insofar as rhetoric deals with a basic and essential social ability—the power to speak or to write—it has been closely related to education since the days of Plato, Isocrates, and Aristotle. It was embedded in the whole Roman approach to education. All evidence points to this continued relation of rhetoric to education even into our own times.

Yet we have barely begun to approach this question for the middle ages. The rough outlines of medieval educational history have long been in place, in the works of such writers as Henri Marrou, Hastings Rashdall, Foster Watson, Louis Paetow, Theodore Haarhoff, Lynn Thorndike, Arthur F. Leach, Pearl Kibre, and Lowrie Daly. (For details see the Murphy bibliography.) More recently there have been studies of medieval elementary education: by Cora E. Lutz (1977), Nicholas I. Orme (1973, 1976), by Murphy (1967, 1980), and by Marjorie Curry Woods (1985, 1989). Rashdall's *The Universities of Europe in the Middle Ages* (1936) has been supplemented and in some cases surpassed by Gordon Leff, *Paris and Oxford Universities in the Thirteenth and Fourteenth Centuries* (1968), and especially by what is probably the most perceptive treatment, A. B. Cobban, *The Medieval Universities: Their Development and Organization* (1970). Cobban's publisher (Methuen) has declined to reprint the book, now out of print. Cobban's masterful correlation of the diverse forces in medieval university life, from student power to theological controversy, makes this book indispensable for anyone wishing to study the relation of rhetoric to other arts in that particular educational environment. Cobban's more recent book concentrates on Oxford and Cambridge: *The Medieval English Universities: Oxford and Cambridge to c. 1500* (1988).

Nevertheless, what would be gratefully received today would be a definitive study of the place of rhetoric in both university and non-university education of the middle ages. The question of whether the "Seven Liberal Arts" ever actually functioned as a unit in medieval education might then find an answer. The changing roles of *dialectica* and *grammatica* would then be easier to assess. The relative worth of the rhetoric of Cicero, of Aristotle, and of Quintilian at different times could be analyzed. Arabic and Greek influences could be studied. Above all, the precise contributions of commentaries—so typically an adjunct of a teaching situation—might be more carefully understood.

Once the educational history of the middle ages is well charted, with or without direct studies of the place of rhetoric, it will be easier to grasp the pervasive influence that the educational backgrounds of medieval writers must surely have had on their ways of thinking, their modes of composition, and even their choices of word patterns.

B. *Educational biographies.* A good start in the direction of a history of medieval education might well be made by systematically investigating the educational biographies of major writers. As John W. Baldwin has shown so well in his *Masters, Princes, and Merchants* (1970), the influence of even one teacher like Peter the Chanter can spread like the ripples from a rock thrown in a pond. Helene Wieruszowski's study of

Arezzo (1953) shows the influence of the schools of one town. Studies of the dictaminal writer Guido Faba by Ernst H. Kantorowicz (1941–1943), Virgilio Pini (1956), and Charles Faulhaber (1978) demonstrate how much of the *ars* or theory of a master can be gleaned from careful study of his antecedents. Edith Rickert's landmark essay on "Chaucer at School" (1931) offers a model for such studies in relation to a literary figure.

Much could be learned from intensive study of, for instance, the Thomas Chabham (or Chobham) who seems to have been the first or at least a very early writer of an *ars praedicandi* outlining the so-called thematic sermon. The Latin text of his *Summa de arte praedicandi* has now been edited by Franco Morenzoni (1988). Writing about A.D. 1200, he was clearly conversant with Horace, Sedulius, Aristotle, Cicero, Peter Lombard, Abelard, Peter the Chanter, and half a dozen other authors, and capable of comparing Cicero's *orationes* to the sermons of the Church Fathers. Who taught him? Where? In what way? And what impelled him to chart what proved to be a new course for sermon-making? In this case we do know the rudiments of his biography, and perhaps with more study the connections can be made. But we need many such.

There now prove to have been many more schools in medieval France, England, Italy, and Germany than once was thought. Who attended them, and what effect, if any, did they have on the theory and practice of rhetoric in the middle ages? These are fruitful avenues of inquiry.

III. *Definition and scope of medieval rhetoric.* There seem to be two quite different understandings of the nature of "rhetoric" regardless of the historical period under study. One says that rhetoric is a certain definable body of principles, usually embodied in texts, and applied in various ways as times and circumstances change; the other says that rhetoric is always culture-bound and is substantially different in each time and place. (These are of course the extremes, and most scholarship partakes of both.) While this difference may seem merely an abstraction of little importance to the historian, it does have practical consequences in terms of the evidence that scholars are willing to accept in respect to medieval rhetoric. A case in point is the early history of the study of the *ars dictaminis*: some scholars (for example, Paetow and C. S. Baldwin) saw it as a theory and often simply equated it with the whole of medieval rhetoric, while others (for example, Atkins) dismissed it as merely a medieval habit or practice with no theoretical aspect. The first view saw it as an application in the middle ages of ancient Roman ideas, while the other view saw it as a mere practice, limited to a time and place.

This general problem will need resolution as research uncovers more and more examples of rhetorical practice—poems, letters, sermons, histories—to assess against the *scientia* or *ars* of the theoretical treatises of the middle ages. There may be no immediate solution to the problem, short of improving our whole concept of the historiography of medieval rhetoric, but in this writer's view it remains an important bar to a consensus as to the nature and scope of the subject.

In this connection the student of medieval rhetoric would do well to examine carefully some of the excellent general studies of medieval culture that have lately appeared: see in the bibliography, for instance, items by Judson B. Allen, Marcia L. Colish, Peter Dronke, Robert O. Payne, and Winthrop Wetherbee.

IV. *The role of dictamen*. There are two scholarly debates in progress in this area, one about the origins of the *ars dictaminis* and another about its outcomes. There seems to be general agreement about the midlife of *dictamen*, as Kristeller points out: "The body of literature that belongs to *dictamen* and its related enterprises is very large indeed, and exceeds by far in bulk anything comparable that has been preserved from classical antiquity, and anything else remotely rhetorical, such as the rhetorical commentaries on Cicero, produced in the Middle Ages" ("Philosophy and Rhetoric from Antiquity to the Renaissance," 241).

While there is less agreement about its beginnings, the matter is in part one of definition (as noted above). Typical of one point of view is the 1971 article by Murphy titled "Alberic of Monte Cassino: Father of the Medieval *Ars dictaminis*," discussing the first known theoretical treatises in the genre. On the other hand, William Patt ("The Early 'Ars dictaminis' as Response to a Changing Society," 1978), among others, has pointed to the practice of tenth-century writers composing letters according to the five parts of the standard *ars dictaminis*. Was Alberic's work, then, merely the confirmation of an existing practice, or did it instead analyze a current tendency and elevate it to a theoretical level? Implicit in this issue is the question of "art" versus "practice" mentioned earlier. It could well be that both sides of the issue are correct. In any case further investigation can only benefit our general understanding.

There is still a great deal of work to be done to assess the influence of the *ars dictaminis* during the high middle ages—not only on chancery affairs but also on letters in general including the vernacular—but of great interest also is the history of the *ars dictaminis* toward the end of the middle ages. Renaissance humanists often looked to classical models for letter composition, and the controversy over "Ciceronianism" enhanced such movements; certainly by the sixteenth century there was available a new epistolography that turned away from medieval patterns. Yet Lidia Winniczuk has shown that some of the medieval manuals continued to be printed into the sixteenth century. Meanwhile, it seems clear that the *ars dictaminis* as a genre allowed Italian writers (as well as some French and English) a form in which to include new ideas of literary theory; for that matter Kristeller and Seigel among others have shown how individual *dictatores* used their dictaminal talents to introduce "humanist" ideas. Guido Faba and Justus Lipsius were both interested in letters: how do they differ? A history of ideas about letter-writing for, say, the period 1450–1650 might provide a highly illuminating perspective on that period.

V. *The relation of rhetoric and grammar to the* ars poetriae. When Edmond Faral completed *Les arts poétiques* in 1924 he not only pointed to Ciceronian influences but actually organized his summaries of works like Geoffrey of Vinsauf's *Poetria nova* under the five Roman rhetorical canons of Invention, Arrangement, Style, Memory, and Delivery. Those elements are certainly visible in the Faral texts; in fact many of the subsequent studies simply refer to those writers as "rhetoricians." Beginning in 1964, however, Murphy ("A New Look at Chaucer and the Rhetoricians") argued that this line of reasoning was leading scholars to overlook the contributions to the *ars poetriae* by principles of the medieval *ars grammatica*. This argument did not win universal acceptance, especially in the absence of a definitive history of medieval grammar; perhaps the strongest single rebuttal appeared in a 1968 article by Richard F. Schoeck titled "On Rhetoric in Fourteenth-Century Oxford." (The title reflects the fact that it is intended as a reply to a 1965 article by Murphy titled "Rhetoric in Fourteenth-Century Oxford.") Schoeck objects to placing the *ars poetriae* within a grammatical tradition, saying that to do so would be a distortion of the meaning of grammar. In Murphy's *Rhetoric in the Middle Ages* (1974) a chapter is devoted to a brief history of medieval grammar and analysis of the six *artes poetriae*, with the added argument that all the authors of these *artes* were in fact teachers of grammar who regarded grammar as their main subject and used Ciceronian rhetoric only to supplement it in forming "preceptive grammar."

The issue is one both of definition and of principle, with implications for our understanding of medieval attitudes toward language use. Did it make any difference to Geoffrey of Vinsauf what his precepts were called? We know that the fourteenth-century preaching theorist Robert of Basevorn did consciously call on the preacher to use interchangeably the lores of rhetoric, of grammar, and of dialectic, pointing as well to models like Saint Bernard who might be imitated regardless of precepts. Was that attitude also prevalent a century earlier? Was it prevalent among grammar teachers? In the first Christian century, Quintilian had warned that grammarians would try to take over the province of rhetoricians: was this still a problem in the age of Geoffrey of Vinsauf? The difficulty, in other words, is that we need to distinguish between what we wish to call things today and what medieval writers may or may not have called things. Perhaps Geoffrey would not have cared one way or another, given the pragmatic tendencies of medieval usage that employed anything from any period or from any art if it seemed useful. On the other hand, given the jurisdictional problems of medieval education, the title of a master or of a book might have made a good deal of difference.

The definitive history of medieval grammar (and of rhetoric, and of dialectic) that might illuminate these questions is still in the future. Meanwhile the issue itself is worth keeping in mind when we soberly give modern names to medieval phenomena.

VI. *Sermons and sermon theory.* We do not yet know enough to make a sure judgment about whether the theory of the "thematic sermon" preceded or followed the widespread making of such sermons. The genesis of the treatises offering this sermon theory itself is now fairly clear, datable almost precisely to A.D. 1200 in the works of Alexander Ashby and Thomas Chobham. (For details see Murphy, *Rhetoric in the Middle Ages,* chapter 6.) The proliferation of the *artes praedicandi* shortly afterward is well documented by Caplan, Charland, Woodburn O. Ross, Charles H. E. Smyth, and Dorothea Roth, with several hundred now identified. Yet a question remains, not unlike one posed in relation to the *ars dictaminis*: do Ashby and Chobham in effect offer a rationale for existing practice, or does the proposed thematic plan represent a breakthrough? Some careful examination of surviving twelfth-century sermons might provide the beginnings of an answer to that question.

There is also a broader problem in connection with the study of this whole area: Who is best equipped to study medieval sermons? Literary historians seeking influences on medieval writers often pick over the texts of sermons looking for passages; cultural historians look for social implications; theologians look for doctrinal matters; biographers sometimes count sermons of their subjects the way they would list book titles. By and large, rhetoricians have not taken up the challenge of looking at sermons holistically, the way they look at orations or speeches of other ages—that is, as whole oral compositions delivered in a certain time and place for a given reason. Audience analysis, as a result, is almost entirely neglected.

The whole matter of deciding *how* to study medieval sermons remains to be settled. Some attention to this problem would surely pay immense dividends, especially now that more and more sermon texts are becoming available. (In this respect it is heartening to see the establishment of the *Medieval Sermon Studies Newsletter*, edited by Gloria Cigman, Department of English, Warwick University, Coventry, England.)

A final note. What runs through all the works cited here, and resides in the six issues raised here, is the conviction on the part of hundreds of twentieth-century scholars that medieval theories of communication are worth the study. The more we learn, the more we see what needs to be learned. What is involved is a thousand years of human interest in one of the most complex activities of mankind—the ability to translate thought into speech or writing. Our study of that past might well illuminate our own future.

Bibliography

Since there are specialized bibliographies available for medieval rhetoric, no attempt is made here to list every item that might be of interest. Nevertheless, this bibliography is self-sufficient—that is, it does include the major citations necessary to undertake a study of the subject. All books and articles cited in the text are listed here more fully. For convenience, basic modern studies, bibliographies, collections of texts and translations, and recent studies are grouped together in separate sections.

Basic Modern Studies

Since modern studies of medieval rhetoric have proliferated to a bewildering degree, the following list is provided as a basic selection of works useful for understanding the subject. Most are books, but the reader is cautioned that much of the recent work on the medieval arts of discourse continues to appear in journal articles rather than in books.

Abelson, Paul. *The Seven Liberal Arts: A Study in Mediaeval Culture.* Columbia University Teachers' College Contributions to Education, no. 11. New York: Teachers' College, Columbia University, 1906. Reprinted: New York: AMS Press, 1972.

Arbusow, Leonid H. N. *Colores rhetorici: Eine Auswahl rhetorischer Figuren und Gemeinplätze als Hilfsmittel für akademische Übungen an mittelalterlichen Textin.* Göttingen: Vandenhoeck & Ruprecht, 1948. 2d ed., edited by Helmut Peters, 1963. Reprinted: Geneva: Slatkine Reprints, 1974.

Atkins, John W. H. *English Literary Criticism: The Medieval Phase.* New York: Macmillan Co.; Cambridge: Cambridge University Press, 1943. Reprinted: London: Methuen; New York: Peter Smith, 1952.

Auerbach, Erich. *Literary Language and Its Public in Late Latin Antiquity and in the Middle Ages.* Translated by Ralph Manheim. Bollingen Series, no. 74. New York: Pantheon Books; Princeton: Princeton University Press, 1965.

Baldwin, Charles S. *Medieval Rhetoric and Poetic (to 1400) Interpreted from Representative Works.* New York: Macmillan Co., 1928. Reprinted: Gloucester, Mass.: Peter Smith, 1959; St. Clair Shores, Mich.: Scholarly Press, 1976.

Camargo, Martin. "Rhetoric." In *The Seven Liberal Arts in the Middle Ages*, edited by David L. Wagner, 96–124. Bloomington: Indiana University Press, 1983.

Caplan, Harry. *Of Eloquence: Studies in Ancient and Mediaeval Rhetoric.* Edited by Anne King and Helen North. Ithaca: Cornell University Press, 1970.

Charland, Th.-M. *Artes praedicandi: contribution à l'histoire de la rhétorique au moyen âge.* Publications de l'Institut d'Études Médiévales d'Ottowa, 7. Paris: J. Vrin; Ottawa: Institut d'Études Médiévales, 1936.

Conley, Thomas M. *Rhetoric in the European Tradition.* New York: Longman, 1990.

Curtius, Ernst R. *European Literature and the Latin Middle Ages.* Translated by Willard R. Trask. Bollingen Series, no. 36. New York: Pantheon Books, 1953. Reprinted: Princeton: Princeton University Press, 1967.

Dargan, Edwin C. *A History of Preaching.* 2 vols. New York: A. C. Armstrong & Son, 1905–1912. Reprinted: Burt Franklin Research and Source Works Series, no. 177. New York: Burt Franklin, 1968.

Denholm-Young, Noël. "The Cursus in England." In *Oxford Essays in Medieval History Presented to Herbert Edward Salter,* 68–103. Oxford: Clarendon Press, 1934. Reprinted: Freeport, N.Y.: Books for Libraries Press, 1968. Reprinted in Denholm-Young, *Collected Papers on Mediaeval Subjects,* 26–55. Oxford: B. Blackwell, 1946. Reprinted with revisions in Denholm-Young, *Collected Papers of N. Denholm-Young,* 42–73. Cardiff: University of Wales Press, 1969.

Dronke, Peter. "Mediaeval Rhetoric." In *Literature and Western Civilization,* edited by David Daiches and A. Thorlby, 2:315–45. London: Aldus, 1973.

Faral, Edmond. *Les arts poétiques du XIIᵉ et du XIIIᵉ siècles: Recherches et documents sur la technique littéraire du moyen âge.* Bibliothèque de l'Ecole des Hautes Etudes. Paris: Champion, 1924, 1962.

Kennedy, George A. *Classical Rhetoric and Its Christian and Secular Tradition from Ancient to Modern Times.* Chapel Hill: University of North Carolina Press, 1980.

Kristeller, Paul O. "Rhetoric in Medieval and Renaissance Culture." In *Renaissance Eloquence: Studies in the Theory and Practice of Renaissance Rhetoric,* edited by James J. Murphy, 1–19. Berkeley: University of California Press, 1983.

Lausberg, Heinrich. *Handbuch der literarischen Rhetorik.* 2 vols. Munich: M. Hueber, 1960.

McKeon, Richard. "Rhetoric in the Middle Ages." *Speculum* 17 (1942): 1–32. Reprinted with revisions in *Critics and Criticism: Ancient and Modern,* edited by R. S. Crane, 260–96. Chicago: University of Chicago Press, 1952, 1975. Reprinted from Crane in *The Province of Rhetoric,* edited by Joseph Schwartz and John A. Rycenga, 172–212. New York: Ronald Press Co., 1965.

Murphy, James J. *Rhetoric in the Middle Ages: A History of Rhetorical Theory from Saint Augustine to the Renaissance.* Berkeley, Los Angeles, and London: University of California Press, 1974, 1981.

Murphy, James J., ed. *Medieval Eloquence: Studies in the Theory and Practice of Medieval Rhetoric.* Berkeley, Los Angeles, and London: University of California Press, 1978.

Owst, Gerald R. *Preaching in Medieval England: An Introduction to Sermon Manuscripts of the Period, c. 1350–1450.* Cambridge Studies in Medieval Life and Thought. Cambridge: Cambridge University Press, 1926. Reprinted: New York: Russell & Russell, 1965.

Robins, R. H. *Ancient & Mediaeval Grammatical Theory in Europe with Particular Reference to Modern Linguistic Doctrine.* London: G. Bell & Sons, 1951. Reprinted: Port Washington, N.Y., and London: Kennikat Press, 1971.

Smyth, Charles H. E. *The Art of Preaching: A Practical Survey of Preaching in the Church of England, 747–1939.* London: S.P.C.K.; New York: Macmillan Co., 1940. Reprinted: London: S.P.C.K., 1953.

Thurot, M. C. "Notices et extraits de divers manuscrits latins pour servir à l'histoire des doctrines grammaticales au moyen age." *Notices et Extraits des Manuscrits de la Bibliothèque Impériale,* no. 22, 2. Paris: Imprimerie Impériale, 1868. Reprinted: Frankfurt-am-Main: Minerva, 1964.

Ward, John O. *"Artificiosa Eloquentia* in the Middle Ages: The Study of Cicero's *De inventione,* the *Ad Herennium* and Quintilian's *De institutione oratoria* from the early Middle Ages to the Thirteenth Century, with special reference to the schools of northern France." 2 vols. Ph.D. dissertation, University of Toronto, 1972.

Bibliographies

Caplan, Harry. *Medieval Artes Praedicandi: A Hand-List.* Cornell Studies in Classical Philology, 24. Ithaca: Cornell University Press, 1934. *Supplement,* 1936.

Faulhaber, Charles. "Rétoricas clásicas y medievales en bibliotecas castellanas." *Abaco* 4 (1973): 151–300.

Medioevo Latino: Bolletino bibliografico della cultura europea dal secolo VI al XIII. Edited by Claudio Leonardi. Appendix to *Studi Medievale,* 1980–.

Murphy, James J. *Medieval Rhetoric: A Select Bibliography.* Toronto Medieval Bibliographies, 3. Toronto: University of Toronto Press, 1971. 2d ed., 1989.

Reinsma, Luke. "The Middle Ages." In *Historical Rhetoric: An Annotated*

Bibliography of Selected Sources in English, edited by Winifred Bryan Horner, 45–108. Boston: G. K. Hall, 1980.

Scaglione, Aldo D. "The Historical Study of *Ars Grammatica*: A Bibliographic Survey." In his *Ars Grammatica: A Bibliographic Survey, Two Essays on the Grammar of the Latin and Italian Subjunctive, and a Note on the Ablative Absolute,* 11–43. Janua Linguarum, Series Minor, no. 77. The Hague and Paris: Mouton, 1970.

Schneyer, Johann Baptist. *Repertorium der lateinischen Sermones des Mittelalters für die Zeit von 1150–1350.* Beiträge zur Geschichte der Philosophie des Mittelalters, 43. 7 vols. Münster: Aschendorff, 1969–1976.

The Educational Background

Rhetoric has been deeply involved with schools since the earliest times, and the changing relationships in the middle ages among grammar, rhetoric, and dialectic in the set of arts called the *trivium* make it even more important for modern readers to understand the place of rhetoric in medieval education. These relationships changed greatly from time to time and place to place. The history of both elementary and university education is involved. No single standard history of medieval education has yet appeared, though the following works can provide a good deal of information about the subject.

Baldwin, John W. *Masters, Princes, and Merchants: The Social Views of Peter The Chanter and His Circle.* Princeton: Princeton University Press, 1970.

Bernstein, Alan E. *Pierre d'Ailly and the Blanchard Affair: University and Chancellor of Paris at the Beginning of the Great Schism.* Leiden: E. J. Brill, 1978.

Bliese, John. "The Study of Rhetoric in the Twelfth Century." *QJS* 63 (1977): 364–83.

Cobban, A. B. *The Medieval English Universities: Oxford and Cambridge to c. 1500.* Berkeley: University of California Press; Aldershot: Scolar, 1988.

———. *The Medieval Universities: Their Development and Organization.* London: Methuen, 1970.

Contreni, John. *The Cathedral School of Laon from 850 to 930: Its Manuscripts and Masters.* Münchener Beiträge zur Mediävistik und Renaissance-Forschung, 29. Munich: Arbeo-Gesellschaft, 1978.

History of Universities. Edited by Charles B. Schmitt. Amersham, Eng.: Avebury Publishing Co., 1981–.

Leff, Gordon. *Paris and Oxford Universities in the Thirteenth and Four-*

teenth Centuries: An Institutional and Intellectual History. New Dimensions in History: Essays in Comparative History. New York, London, and Sydney: John Wiley & Sons, 1968. Reprinted: Huntington, N.Y.: R. E. Krieger Publishing Co., 1975.

Lutz, Cora E. "Remigius' Ideas on the Classification of the Seven Liberal Arts." *Traditio* 12 (1956): 65–86.

———. *Schoolmasters of the Tenth Century*. Hamden, Conn.: Archon Books, 1977.

Murphy, James J. "Literary Implications of Instruction in the Verbal Arts in Fourteenth Century England." *LSE*, n.s. 1 (1967): 119–35.

———. "The Teaching of Latin as a Foreign Language in the Twelfth Century." *Historiographia Linguistica* 7, nos. 1/2 (1980): 159–75.

Orme, Nicholas I. *Education in the West of England 1066–1548*. Exeter: University of Exeter Press, 1976.

———. *English Schools in the Middle Ages*. London: Methuen, 1973.

Paetow, Louis J. *The Arts Course at Medieval Universities with Special Reference to Grammar and Rhetoric*. University Studies of the University of Illinois, nos. 3, 7. Champaign: University of Illinois Press, 1910. Reprinted: Dubuque, Iowa: Wm. C. Brown Reprint Library, n.d.

Rashdall, Hastings. *The Universities of Europe in the Middle Ages*. 3 vols. 2d ed., rev. by F. M. Powicke and A. B. Emden. Oxford: Clarendon Press, 1936.

Riché, Pierre. *Les Ecoles et l'enseignement dans l'Occident chrétien de la fin du Vᵉ siècle*. Paris: Aubier Montaigne, 1979.

———. *Education and Culture in the Barbarian West from the Sixth through the Eighth Century*. 3d ed. Translated by John J. Contreni. Columbia: University of South Carolina Press, 1978.

Scaglione, Aldo. "Aspetti delle arti del trivio fra medioevo e rinascimento." *Medioevo Romanza* 3 (1976): 265–91.

Sirisai, Nancy G. *Arts and Sciences at Padua: The Studium of Padua before 1350*. Pontifical Institute of Mediaeval Studies, Studies and Texts, no. 25. Toronto: Pontifical Institute of Mediaeval Studies, 1973.

Stump, Eleonore. "Dialectic in the Eleventh and Twelfth Centuries: Garlandus compotista." *History and Philosophy of Logic* 1 (1980): 1–18.

Thorndike, Lynn. *University Records and Life in the Middle Ages*. New York: Columbia University Press, 1944. Reprinted: New York: Norton, 1975.

Weisheipl, James A. "Curriculum of the Faculty of Arts at Oxford in the Early Fourteenth Century." *MS* 26 (1964): 143–85.

———. "Developments in the Arts Curriculum at Oxford in the Early Fourteenth Century." *MS* 28 (1966): 151–75.

————. "The Parisian Faculty of Arts in Mid-Thirteenth Century: 1240–1270." *ABR* 25 (1974): 200–217.

Wieruszowski, Helene. "Arezzo as a Center of Learning and Letters in the Thirteenth Century." *Traditio* 9 (1953): 321–91. Reprinted in *Politics and Culture in Medieval Spain and Italy*, 387–474. Storia e Letteratura, Raccolta di Studi e Testi, no. 121. Rome: Edizioni de Storia e Letteratura, 1971.

————. *The Medieval University: Masters, Students, Learning.* Princeton: Van Nostrand Reinhold, 1966.

Translations and Recent Editions of Primary Sources

This too is a selective list, designed to be representative rather than exhaustive.

It should be noted that an edition of a text may be very valuable even for readers unfamiliar with Latin or other medieval languages, since such works may often have extensive introductions that explain the relevance of the text and thus place it within the context of medieval culture. Two good examples may be seen below in Polak's book on Jacques de Dinant, with its English commentary as well as Latin text, and in the Thomson/Murphy edition of Ventura da Bergamo, which relates the edited text to the genre of the *ars dictaminis*.

Details of other medieval texts published prior to 1970 may be found in Murphy, *Medieval Rhetoric*, and usually also in Reinsma, "The Middle Ages" (with some supplementary data on certain works), listed above under Bibliographies.

A. Collections of Two or More Works

Miller, Joseph M., Michael H. Prosser, and Thomas W. Benson, eds. *Readings in Medieval Rhetoric.* Bloomington: Indiana University Press, 1973.
  Martianus Capella, "The Book of Rhetoric" (*De nuptiis Philologiae et Mercurii*, V)
  Pseudo-Augustine, *On Rhetoric*
  Emporius the Orator, *Concerning Ethopeia*
  Rufinus of Antioch, *Verses . . . On the Word Arrangement and Metres in Oratory*
  Priscian the Grammarian, *Fundamentals Adapted from Hermogenes*
  Anicius M. S. Boethius, *An Overview of the Structure of Rhetoric*
  Cassiodorus Senator, "On Rhetoric" (*Institutiones divinarum et saecularium litterarum* II.2)
  Isidore of Seville, "Concerning Rhetoric" (*Etymologies* II. 1–15)

Venerable Bede, *Concerning Figures and Tropes*
Rabanus Maurus, *On the Training of the Clergy*, III. 19
Walafrid Strabo, *Verse on the Five Parts of Rhetoric*
Alberic of Monte Cassino, *Flowers of Rhetoric*
Guibert of Nogent, *A Book about the Way a Sermon Ought To Be Given*
Philip of Harveng, *On the Training of the Clergy*
Alain de Lille, *A Compendium on the Art of Preaching*
Brunetto Latini, *Li Livres dou Tresor*, III. 60–65
Giles of Rome, *On the Difference between Rhetoric, Ethics and Politics*, Part I.
Thomas of Todi, *The Art of Giving Sermons and of Preparing Conferences* (excerpts).
(The book also includes brief excerpts from other texts.)
Murphy, James J., ed. *Three Medieval Rhetorical Arts.* Berkeley: University of California Press, 1971.
Anonymous of Bologna, *The Principles of Letter-Writing*
Geoffrey of Vinsauf, *The New Poetics*
Robert of Basevorn, *The Form of Preaching*
Rockinger, Ludwig, ed. *Briefsteller und Formelbücher des eilften bis vierzehnten Jahrhunderts.* 2 vols. Quellen und Eröterungen zur bayerischen und deutschen Geschichte, 9. Munich, 1863–1864. Reprinted (in one volume): New York: Burt Franklin, 1961.
Nine Latin texts of the *ars dictaminis* and *ars notariae*, with some texts of formularies

Faral, *Les arts poétiques*, Charland, *Artes praedicandi*, and Caplan, *Of Eloquence* (listed above under Basic Modern Studies) also include Latin texts of *artes poetriae* and *artes praedicandi* respectively.

B. Individual Translations or Recent Editions

This list concentrates on translations, regardless of their age, but cites only recent Latin or other editions not found in the Murphy or Reinsma bibliographies, listed above.

Alain of Lille. *Art of Preaching.* Translated by Gillian R. Evans. Kalamazoo, Mich.: Medieval Institute, 1981.
Alcock, Simon. "Simon Alcock on Expanding the Sermon." Translated by Mary F. Boynton. *Harvard Theological Review* 34 (1941): 201–16.
Alcuin. *The Rhetoric of Alcuin & Charlemagne; a Translation, with an Introduction, the Latin Text, and Notes.* Edited and translated by Wilbur S. Howell. Princeton: Princeton University Press, 1941. Reprinted: New York: Russell & Russell, 1965.

Al-Farabi. *Deux ouvrages inédits sur la rhétorique.* Edited by J. Langlade and P. Grinaschi. Beirut, 1971.

Alfonso d'Alpraox. "El 'Ars praedicandi' de Fr. Alfonso d'Alprao O.F.M.: Aportacion al estudio de la teoría de la predicacion en la Península Ibérica." Edited by Albert G. Hauf. *Archivum Franciscanum Historicum* 72 (1979): 233–329.

d'Andeli, Henri. *The Battle of the Seven Arts: A French Poem by Henri d'Andeli, Trouvère of the Thirteenth Century.* Edited and translated by Louis J. Paetow. Memoirs of the University of California, no. 4, 1. Berkeley: University of California Press, 1914. Reprinted as pt. 1 of Paetow's *Two Medieval Satires on the University of Paris.* Berkeley: University of California Press, 1927.

Anonymous. *An Early Commentary on the* Poetria nova *of Geoffrey of Vinsauf.* Edited and translated by Marjorie Curry Woods. New York and London: Garland, 1985.

Augustine. *On Christian Doctrine.* Translated by D. W. Robertson. Library of Liberal Arts, 80. New York: Bobbs-Merrill, 1958.

Averroes' Three Short Commentaries on Aristotle's "Topics," "Rhetoric," and "Poetics." Edited and translated by Charles E. Butterworth. Albany: State University of New York Press, 1977.

Bene of Florence. *Bene Florentini Candelabrum.* Edited by Giancarlo Alessio. Thesaurus Mundi, 23. Padua: Antenore, 1983.

Boethius. *Boethius's De topicis differentiis: Translated, with Notes and Essays on the Text.* Edited by Eleonore A. Stump. Ithaca and London: Cornell University Press, 1978.

Buridan, John. "Buridan's *Quaestiones super Rhetoricam Aristotelis.*" Edited by Karin M. Fredborg. In *The Logic of John Buridan: Acts of the 3rd European Symposium on Medieval Logic and Semantics, Copenhagen 16. –21. November 1975,* edited by Jan Pinborg, 47–59. Copenhagen: Museum Tusculanum, 1976.

Capella, Martianus. *Martianus Capella and the Seven Liberal Arts,* vol. 2: *The Marriage of Philology and Mercury.* Translated by William H. Stahl, Richard Johnson, and E. L. Burge. Columbia University Records of Civilization, Sources and Studies, no. 84. New York: Columbia University Press, 1977.

Cassiodorus Senator. *An Introduction to Divine and Human Readings by Cassiodorus Senator; Translated with an Introduction and Notes.* Translated by Leslie W. Jones. Columbia University Records of Civilization, Sources and Studies, no. 40. New York: Columbia University Press, 1946. Reprinted: New York: W. W. Norton & Co., 1969.

Dybinus, Nicholas. *Nicolaus Dybinus' "Declaratio Oracionis de Beata Dor-*

othea": Studies and Documents in the History of Late Medieval Rhetoric. Edited by Samuel P. Jaffe. Wiesbaden: Steiner, 1974.

Eberhard the German. "The *Laborintus* of Eberhard rendered into English with Introduction and Notes." Translated by Evelyn Carlson. Master's thesis, Cornell University, 1930.

Geoffrey of Vinsauf. *Documentum de modo et arte dictandi et versificandi (Instruction in the Method and Art of Speaking and Versifying).* Translated by Roger P. Parr. Mediaeval Philosophical Texts in Translation, no. 17. Milwaukee: Marquette University Press, 1968.

———. "The New Poetics." Translated by Jane Baltzell Kopp. In *Three Medieval Rhetorical Arts*, edited by James J. Murphy, 29–108. Berkeley: University of California Press, 1971.

———. *The* Poetria nova *and Its Sources in Early Rhetorical Doctrine.* Edited by Ernest A. Gallo. De Proprietatibus Litterarum, Series Maior, no. 10. The Hague and Paris: Mouton, 1971.

———. *The Poetria Nova of Geoffrey of Vinsauf.* Translated by Margaret F. Nims. Toronto: Pontifical Institute of Mediaeval Studies, 1967.

Higden, Ranulph. Ars Componendi Sermones *of Ranulph Higden, O.S.B.: A Critical Edition.* Edited by Margaret Jennings. Davis Medieval Texts and Studies, 6. Leiden: E. J. Brill, 1990.

Hugh of St. Victor. *The Didascalicon of Hugh of St. Victor: A Medieval Guide to the Arts; Translated from the Latin with an Introduction and Notes.* Translated by Jerome Taylor. Columbia University Records of Civilization, Sources and Studies, no. 64. New York and London: Columbia University Press, 1961.

Humbert of Romans. *Treatise on Preaching by Humbert of Romans.* Translated by Dominican Students, Province of St. Joseph. Edited by Walter M. Conlon. Westminster, Md.: Newman Press, 1951. Reprinted: London: Blackfriars Publications, 1955.

Isidore of Seville. "The Rhetoric and Dialectic of Isidorus of Seville: A Translation and Commentary." Translated by Dorothy V. Cerino. Master's thesis, Brooklyn College, 1938.

Jacques de Dinant. *A Textual Study of Jacques de Dinant's "Summa dictaminis."* Edited by Emil J. Polak. Études de philologie et d'histoire, 28. Geneva: Droz, 1975.

John of Garland. *The* Parisiana Poetria *of John of Garland; Edited with Introduction, Translation, and Notes.* Edited and Translated by Traugott Lawler. Yale Studies in English, no. 182. New Haven and London: Yale University Press, 1974.

John of Salisbury. *The Metalogicon of John of Salisbury: A Twelfth-Century Defense of the Verbal and Logical Arts of the Trivium; Translated with an*

Introduction & Notes. Translated by Daniel D. McGarry. Berkeley and Los Angeles: University of California Press, 1955, 1971.

Juan Gil de Zamora. *Dictaminis Epithalamium*. Edited by Charles Faulhaber. Biblioteca degli Studi Mediolatini e Volgari, n.s. 2. Pisa: Pacini, 1978.

Latini, Brunetto. "Book Three of Brunetto Latini's *Tresor*: An English Translation and Assessment of its Contribution to Rhetorical Theory." Translated by James R. East. Ph.D. dissertation, Stanford University, 1960.

Matthew of Vendôme. *Mathei Vindocinensis Opera*, vol. 3: *Ars versificatoria*. Edited by Franco Munari. Rome: Storia e Letteratura, 1988.

————. *Matthew of Vendôme*: Ars Versification (*The Art of the Versemaker*). Translated by Roger P. Parr. Milwaukee: Marquette University Press, 1981.

————. *Matthew of Vendôme: The Art of Versification*. Translated by Aubrey E. Galyon. Ames: Iowa State University Press, 1980.

————. "Matthew of Vendôme: Introductory Treatise on the Art of Poetry." Translated by Ernest Gallo. *Proceedings of the American Philosophical Society* 118 (1974): 51–92.

Pseudo-Bonaventure. "Translation, with Commentary, of the Bonaventuran *Ars concionandi*." Translated by Harry C. Hazel, Jr. Ph.D. dissertation, Washington State University, 1972.

Siguinus, Magister, *Ars lectoria: Un Art de lecture à haute voix du onzième siècle*. Edited by C. H. Kneepkeus and H. F. Reijnders. Leiden: E. J. Brill, 1979.

Thierry of Chartres. *The Latin Rhetorical Commentaries*. Edited by Karin M. Fredborg. Toronto: Pontifical Institute of Mediaeval Studies, 1988.

Ventura da Bergamo. "Dictamen as a Developed Genre: The *Brevis doctrina* of Ventura da Bergamo." Edited by David Thomson and James J. Murphy. *SMed*, 3d ser. 23 (1982): 361–86.

Waleys, Thomas. "Thomas Waleys' *De modo componendi sermones* Rendered into English." Translated by Dorothy E. Grosser. Master's thesis, Cornell University, 1949.

Some Recent Studies

Included here are all works mentioned in the essay for which a full bibliographical description has not yet been given and some of the most useful studies in English published since 1960. For studies in languages other than English and for earlier studies in English, the reader should consult Murphy, *Medieval Rhetoric: A Select Bibliography* (1971, 1989).

Letter-writing

Banker, James R. "The *Ars dictaminis* and Rhetorical Textbooks at the Bolognese University in the Fourteenth Century." *M&H*, n.s. 5 (1974): 153–68.

———. "Giovanni di Bonandrea and Civic Values in the Context of the Italian Rhetorical Tradition." *Manuscripts* 18 (1974): 3–20.

Benson, Robert. "Proto-humanism and Narrative Technique in Early Thirteenth-Century Italian 'Ars dictaminis.'" In *Boccaccio: Secoli di vita. Atti del Congresso Internationale: Boccaccio 1975*, 31–50. Acura di Marga Cottino-Jones e Edward F. Tuttle. Los Angeles: Center for Medieval and Renaissance Studies; Ravenna: Longo, 1979.

Bloch, H. "Monte Cassino's Teachers and Library in the High Middle Ages." Vol. 19 of *La scuola nell'occidente latino dell'alto medioevo*. Spoleto: Settimane di studio del Centro Italiano di studi sull'alto medioevo, 1972.

Camargo, Martin. "The English Manuscripts of Bernard of Meung's *Flores dictaminum*." *Viator* 12 (1981): 197–219.

———. "*Libellus de arte dictandi rhetorice* Attributed to Peter of Blois." *Speculum* 59 (1984): 16–41.

———. "Toward a Comprehensive Art of Written Discourse: Geoffrey of Vinsauf and the *Ars dictaminis*." *Rhetorica* 6 (1988): 167–94.

Constable, Giles. *Letters and Letter-Collections*. Turnhout: Brepols, 1976.

———. "The Structure of Medieval Society According to the *Dictatores* of the Twelfth Century." In *Law, Church, and Society: Essays in Honor of Stephan Kuttner*, edited by Kenneth Pennington and Robert Sommerville, 253–67. Philadelphia: University of Pennsylvania Press, 1977.

Dalzell, Ann. "The *forma dictandi*: Attributed to Albert of Morra and Related Texts." *MS* 39 (1977): 440–65.

Davis, Hugh H. "'De rithmis' of Alberic of Monte Cassino: A Critical Edition." *MS* 28 (1966): 198–227.

East, James R. "Brunetto Latini's Rhetoric of Letter Writing." *QJS* 54 (1968): 241–46.

Faulhaber, Charles B. *Latin Rhetorical Theory in Thirteenth and Fourteenth Century Castile*. University of California Publications in Modern Philology, no. 103. Berkeley, Los Angeles, and London: University of California Press, 1972.

Gehl, Paul F. "From Monastic Rhetoric to *Ars dictaminis*: Traditionalism and Innovation in the Schools of Twelfth-Century Italy." *ABR* 34 (1983): 33–47.

Haskins, Charles H. "The Early *Artes dictandi* in Italy." In his *Studies in*

Mediaeval Culture, 170–92. New York: Frederick Ungar; Oxford: Clarendon Press, 1929. Reprinted: New York: Frederick Ungar, 1965.

———. "The Life of Medieval Students as Illustrated by Their Letters." *American Historical Review* 3 (1897–1898): 203–29. Revised and expanded in his *Studies in Mediaeval Culture*, 1–35. New York: Frederick Ungar; Oxford: Clarendon Press, 1929. Reprinted: New York: Frederick Ungar, 1965.

Hill, Sidney R., Jr. "*Dictamen*: That Bastard of Literature and Law." *CSSJ* 24 (1973): 17–24.

Janson, Tore. *Prose Rhythm in Medieval Latin from the 9th to the 13th Century*. Acta Universitatis Stockholmiensis, Studia Latina Stockholmiensia, no. 20. Stockholm: Almqvist & Wiskell International, 1975.

Kane, Peter E. "*Dictamen*: The Medieval Rhetoric of Letter-Writing." *CSSJ* 21 (1970): 224–30.

Kantorowicz, Ernst H. "An 'Autobiography' of Guido Faba." *MARS* 1 (1941–1943): 253–80. Reprinted in his *Selected Studies*, 194–212. Locust Valley, N.Y.: J. J. Augustin, 1965.

Kristeller, Paul O. "Matteo de'Libri, Bolognese Notary of the Thirteenth Century and His *Artes dictaminis*." In *Miscellanea Giovanni Galbiati*, 2:283–320. Fontes Ambrosiani, 26. Milan, 1951.

———. "Philosophy and Rhetoric from Antiquity to the Renaissance." Part 5 in *Renaissance Thought and Its Sources*, edited by Michael Mooney, 211–60 (notes 312–27). New York: Columbia University Press, 1979.

Kuhn, Sherman M. "Cursus in Old English: Rhetorical Ornament or Linguistic Phenomenon?" *Speculum* 47 (1972): 188–206. See also Smedick, "*Cursus* in Middle English," below.

Lanham, Carol D. Salutatio. *Formulas in Latin Letters to 1200: Syntax, Style, and Theory*. Münchener Beiträge zur Mediävistik und Renaissance—Forschung, no. 22. Munich: Arbeo-Gesellschaft, 1975.

Lawton, David A. "Gaytryge's Sermon, *Dictamen*, and Middle English Alliterative Verse." *MP* 76 (1979): 329–43.

Murphy, James J. "Alberic of Monte Cassino: Father of the Medieval *Ars dictaminis*." *ABR* 22 (1971): 129–46. See also Patt, "The Early 'Ars dictaminis' as Response to a Changing Society," below.

Patt, William D. "The Early 'Ars dictaminis' as Response to a Changing Society." *Viator* 9 (1978): 133–35.

Pini, Virgilio, ed. "La *Summa de vitiis et virtutibus* di Guido Faba." *Quadrivium* 1 (1956): 41–152.

Polak, Emil J. "Latin Epistolography of the Middle Ages and Renaissance: Manuscript Evidence in Poland." *Eos* 73 (1985): 349–62.

Richardson, Malcolm. "The *Dictamen* and Its Influence on Fifteenth-Century English Prose." *Rhetorica* 2 (1984): 207–26.

Robinson, I. S. "The 'colores rhetorici' in the Investiture Contest." *Traditio* 32 (1976): 209–38.

Seigel, Jerrold. *Rhetoric and Philosophy in Renaissance Humanism: The Union of Eloquence and Wisdom, Petrarch to Valla*. Princeton: Princeton University Press, 1968.

Sitzmann, Marion. "Lawrence of Aquilega and the Origins of the Business Letter." *ABR* 28 (1977): 180–87.

Smedick, Lois K. "*Cursus* in Middle English: *A Talking of De Love of God* Reconsidered." *MS* 37 (1975): 387–406. See also Kuhn, "Cursus in Old English," above.

Taylor, John. "Letters and Letter-collections in England, 1300–1420." *Nottingham Medieval Studies* 28 (1980): 57–70.

Triska, Josef. "Prague Rhetoric and the *Epistolare dictamen* (1278) of Henricus de Isernia." *Rhetorica* 3 (1985): 183–200.

Tunberg, Terence O. "What Is Boncompagno's 'Newest Rhetoric'?" *Traditio* 42 (1986): 299–334.

Voigts, Linda E. "Letter from a Middle English Dictaminal Formulary in Harvard Law Library MS 43." *Speculum* 56 (1981): 575–81.

Wieruszowski, Helene. "Rhetoric and the Classics in Italian Education of the Thirteenth Century." *Studia Gratiana* 11 (1967): 169–208.

———. "Twelfth-century 'Ars dictaminis' in the Barberini Collection of the Vatican Library." *Traditio* 18 (1962): 382–93.

Winniczuk, Lidia. *Epistolografia*. Biblioteka Meandra, 19. Warsaw, 1952.

Witt, Ronald. "Boncompagno and the Defense of Rhetoric." *MARS* 16 (1986): 1–31.

———. "Medieval 'Ars dictaminis' and the Beginnings of Humanism: A New Construction of the Problem." *RQ* 35 (1982): 1–35.

———. "On Bene of Florence's Conception of the French and Roman *Cursus*." *Rhetorica* 3 (1985): 77–98.

Poetics and Grammar

Alford, John A. "Grammatical Metaphor: A Survey of Its Use in the Middle Ages." *Speculum* 57 (1982): 728–60.

Allen, Judson B. *The Ethical Poetic of the Later Middle Ages*. Toronto: University of Toronto Press, 1981.

———. "Hermann the German's Averroistic Aristotle and Medieval Poetic Theory." *Mosaic* 9 (1976): 67–81.

Baltzell, Jane. "Rhetorical 'Amplification' and 'Abbreviation' and the Structure of Medieval Narrative." *Pacific Coast Philology* 2 (1967): 32–39.

Beale, Walter H. "Rhetoric in the Old English Verse-paragraph." *Neu-philologische Mitteilungen* 80 (1979): 133–42.

Boggess, William F. "Artistotle's *Poetics* in the Fourteenth Century." *SP* 67 (1970): 278–94.

Clogan, Paul. "Literary Genres in a Medieval Textbook." *M&H*, n.s. 11 (1982): 199–209.

Colker, Marvin L. "New Evidence that John of Garland Revised the *Doctrinale* of Alexander de Villa Dei." *Scriptorium* 28 (1974): 68–71.

Conley, Thomas. "Byzantine Teaching on Figures and Tropes: An Introduction." *Rhetorica* 4 (1986): 335–74.

Frey, Leonhard H. "Rhetoric of Latin Christian Epic Poetry." *Annuale medievale* 2 (1961): 15–30.

Gibson, Margaret. "Early Scholastic 'Glosule' to Priscian, 'Institutiones Grammaticae': The Text and Its Influence." *SMed*, n.s. 3:20 (1979): 235–54.

Gibson, Margaret T., and J. E. Tolson. "Summa of Petrus Helias on Priscianus minor." *CIMAGL* 27 (1978): 2–158.

Giles, Catherine Yodice. "Gervais of Melkley's Treatise on the Art of Versifying and the Method of Composing in Prose." Ph.D. dissertation, Rutgers University, 1973.

Gronbeck-Tedesco, John L. "An Application of Medieval Rhetorical Invention to Dramatic Composition: Matthew of Vendome's *Ars versificatoria* and *Milo*." *Theatre Journal* 32 (1980): 235–47.

Guisberti, F., ed. "Twelfth Century Theological Grammar." In *Materials for a Study on Twelfth Century Scholasticism*, edited by A. Maierù and G. Polara, 87–109. History of Logic, 2. Naples: Bibliopolis, 1982.

Haidu, P. "Repetition: Modern Reflections on Medieval Aesthetics." *Modern Language Notes* 92 (1977): 875–87.

Harbert, Bruce, ed. *Thirteenth-Century Anthology of Rhetorical Poems. Glasgow MS. Hunterian V.8.14.* Toronto Medieval Latin Texts, 4. Toronto: Centre for Medieval Studies, 1975.

Hunt, Richard W. *History of Grammar in the Middle Ages: Collected Papers.* Edited by Geoffrey L. Bursill-Hall. Amsterdam Studies in the Theory and History of Linguistic Science; Series III: Studies in the History of Linguistics, vol. 5. Amsterdam: Mouton, 1980.

Hunt, Tony. "Aristotle, Dialectic, and Courtly Literature." *Viator* 10 (1979): 95–129.

Huntsman, Jeffrey F. "Grammar." In *The Seven Liberal Arts in the Middle Ages*, edited by David L. Wagner, 58–95. Bloomington: Indiana University Press, 1983.

Irvine, Martin. "Medieval Grammatical Theory and Chaucer's *House of Fame*." *Speculum* 60 (1985): 850–76.

Kelly, Douglas. *Medieval Imagination: Rhetoric and the Poetry of Courtly Love.* Madison: University of Wisconsin Press, 1978.

———. "The Scope of the Treatment of Composition in the Twelfth- and Thirteenth-Century Arts of Poetry." *Speculum* 41 (1966): 261–78.

———. "Theory of Composition in Medieval Narrative: Poetry and Geoffrey of Vinsauf's *Poetria nova.*" *MS* 31 (1969): 117–48.

Kelly, Henry Ansgar. "*Occupatio* as Negative Narration: A Mistake for *Occultatio/Praeteritio.*" *MP* 74 (1977): 311–15.

Kliman, Bernice W. "John Barbour and Rhetorical Tradition." *Annuale Medievale* 18 (1977): 106–35.

Lawler, Traugott F. "John of Garland and Horace: A Medieval School-man faces the *Ars poetica.*" *Classical Folia* 22 (1968): 3–13.

Lubienski-Bedenhami, H. "The Origins of the Fifteenth-Century View of Poetry as 'seconde rhétorique.'" *MLR* 7 (1979): 26–38.

McKeon, Richard. "Poetry and Philosophy in the Twelfth Century: The Renaissance of Rhetoric." *MP* 43 (1946): 217–34. Reprinted in *Critics and Criticism: Ancient and Modern,* edited by R. S. Crane, 297–318. Chicago: University of Chicago Press, 1952, 1975.

McPherson, Clair Wade. "The Influence of Latin Rhetoric on Old English Poetry." Ph.D. dissertation, University of Washington, 1980.

Manly, John M. "Chaucer and the Rhetoricians." Warton Lecture on English Poetry. *Proceedings of the British Academy* 12 (1926): 95–113. Reprinted in *Chaucer Criticism, the Canterbury Tales: An Anthology,* edited by Richard J. Schoeck and Jerome Taylor, 268–90. Notre Dame: University of Notre Dame Press, 1960. See also Murphy, "A New Look at Chaucer and the Rhetoricians," below.

Marshall, J. H. "Observations on the Sources of the Treatment of Rhetoric in the *Leys d'Amors.*" *MLR* 64 (1969): 39–52.

Matonis, Ann. "Rhetorical Patterns in *Marwnad Llywelyn ap Gruffudd* by Gruffudd ab yr Ynad Coch." *Studia Celtica* 14–15 (1979–1980): 188–92.

Minnis, Alastair J. "Literary Theory in Discussions of *Formae tractandi* by Medieval Theologians." *NLH* 11 (1979–1980): 133–45.

Minnis, Alastair, and A. B. Scott, eds., with David Wallace. *Medieval Literary Theory and Criticism, c. 1100–c. 1375: The Commentary Tradition.* Oxford: Clarendon Press, 1988.

Murphy, James J. "A New Look at Chaucer and the Rhetoricians." *Review of English Studies,* n.s. 15 (1964): 1–20.

———. "Rhetoric in Fourteenth-Century Oxford." *MAE* 34 (1965): 1–20.

Nims, Margaret F. "*Translatio*: 'Difficult Statement' in Medieval Poetic Theory." *University of Toronto Quarterly* 43 (1974): 215–30.

O'Donnell, J. Reginald. "Sources and Meaning of Bernard Silvester's Commentary on the *Aeneid*." *MS* 24 (1962): 233–49.

Olsson, Kurt O. "Rhetoric, John Gower, and the Late Medieval *Exemplum*." *M&H*, n.s. 8 (1977): 185–200.

Patterson, Linda M. *Troubadours and Eloquence*. Oxford: Clarendon Press, 1975.

Payne, Robert O. "Chaucer and the Art of Rhetoric." In *Companion to Chaucer Studies*, edited by Beryl Rowland, 42–64. Rev. ed. Toronto, New York, and London: Oxford University Press, 1979.

———. *The Key of Remembrance: A Study of Chaucer's Poetics*. New Haven and London: Yale University Press, 1963. Reprinted: Westport, Conn.: Greenwood Press, 1973.

Scaglione, Aldo. "Rhetoric in Italian Literature: Dante and the Rhetorical Theory of Sentence Structure." In *Medieval Eloquence: Studies in the Theory and Practice of Medieval Rhetoric*, edited by James J. Murphy, 252–69. Berkeley, Los Angeles, and London: University of California Press, 1978.

Schoeck, Richard J. "On Rhetoric in Fourteenth-Century Oxford." *MS* 30 (1968): 214–25. See also Murphy, "Rhetoric in Fourteenth-Century Oxford," above.

Schultz, James A. "Classical Rhetoric, Medieval Poetics, and the Medieval Vernacular Prologue." *Speculum* 59 (1984): 1–15.

Shapiro, Marianne. "Figurality in the *Vita Nuova*: Dante's New Rhetoric." *Dante Studies* 97 (1979): 107–27.

Thomson, David. "Oxford Grammar Masters Revisited." *MS* 45 (1983): 298–310.

Trimpi, Wesley. "Quality of Fiction: The Rhetorical Transmission of Literary Theory." *Traditio* 30 (1974): 1–118.

Woods, Marjorie Curry. "An Unfashionable Rhetoric in the Fifteenth Century." *QJS* 9 (1989): 312–20.

Ziolkowski, Jan. "Avatars of Ugliness in Medieval Literature." *MLR* 79 (1984): 1–20.

Zumthor, Paul. "From Hi(story) to Poem, or the Paths of Pun: The Grands Rhétoriqueurs of Fifteenth-Century France." *NLH* 10 (1979): 231–63.

———. "Great Game of Rhetoric." *NLH* 12 (1980–1981): 493–508.

Sermon Theory

Bataillon, Louis-Jacques. "Approaches to the Study of Medieval Sermons." *LSE*, n.s. 11 (1980): 19–35.

Brilioth, Ingve. *Brief History of Preaching*. Translated by Karl E. Mattson. Philadelphia: Fortress Press, [1965].

Cespedes, Frank V. "Chaucer's Pardoner and Preaching." *Journal of English Literary History* 44 (1977): 1–18.

Chobham, Thomas. *Summa de arte praedicandi*. Edited by Franco Morenzoni. Corpus Christianovum. Continuatio Medievalis, 82. Turnhout: Brepols, 1988.

D'Avray, David L. *Preaching of the Friars: Sermons Diffused from Paris before 1300*. Oxford: Clarendon Press; New York: Oxford University Press, 1985.

———. "Wordlists in the 'Ars faciendi sermones' of Geraldus de Piscario." *Franciscan Studies* 38 (1978): 184–193.

Dieter, Otto A. L. "*Arbor picta*: The Medieval Tree of Preaching." *QJS* 51 (1965): 123–44.

Evans, Gillian R. *Alan of Lille: The Frontiers of Theology in the Later Twelfth Century*. Cambridge: Cambridge University Press, 1983.

———. "Book of Experience: Alain of Lille's Use of the Classical Rhetorical Topos in His Pastoral Writing." *Analecta Cisterciensia* 32 (1977 for 1976): 113–21.

Evans, Gillian R., and David L. d'Avray. "Unusual 'Ars Praedicandi.'" *MAE* 49 (1980): 26–31.

Gallick, Susan. "*Artes Praedicandi*: Early Printed Editions." *MS* 39 (1977): 477–89.

Gatch, Milton McC. *Preaching and Theology in Anglo-Saxon England: Aelfric and Wulfstan*. Toronto: University of Toronto Press, 1977.

Gillespie, Vincent. "*Doctrina* and *Predicacio*: The Design and Function of Some Pastoral Manuals." *LSE*, n.s. 11 (1980): 36–50.

Hazel, Harry C., Jr. "Bonaventuran 'Ars concionandi.'" In *S. Bonaventura, 1274–1974: II, Studia de vita, mente, fontibus et operibus sancti Bonaventurae*, 435–46. Rome: Quarrachi, 1973.

———. "The Bonaventuran 'Ars concionandi.'" *WS* 36 (1972): 241–50.

———. "Translation, with Commentary of the Bonaventuran *Ars concionandi*." Ph.D. dissertation, Stanford University, 1972.

Jennings, Margaret. *The Ars Componendi Sermones of Ranulph Higden*. Leiden: E. J. Brill, 1990.

———. "Monks and the *Artes Praedicandi* in the Time of Ranulph Higden: An Acknowledgement." *Revue bénédictine* 87 (1977): 389–90.

———. "Preacher's Rhetoric: The *Ars componendi sermones* of Ranulph Higden." In *Medieval Eloquence: Studies in the Theory and Practice of Medieval Rhetoric*, edited by James J. Murphy, 112–26. Berkeley, Los Angeles, and London: University of California Press, 1978.

———. Letson, D. R. "Form of the Old English Homily." *ABR* 30 (1979): 399–431.

McGuire, B. P. "Cistercians and the Rise of the 'Exemplum' in Early

Thirteenth Century France: A Reevaluation of Paris B.N. Ms. lat 15912." *Classica et Medievalia* 34 (1983): 211–67.

McGuire, Michael, and John H. Patton. "Preaching in the Mystic Mode: The Rhetorical Art of Meister Eckhart." *CM* 44 (1977): 263–72.

Roberts, Phyllis B. *Stephanus de Lingua-Tonante: Studies in the Sermons of Stephen Langton.* Studies and Texts, 16. Toronto: Pontifical Institute for Mediaeval Studies, 1968.

Ross, Woodburn O., ed. *Middle English Sermons.* Early English Text Society, 209. London: Early English Text Society, 1940.

Roth, Dorothea. *Die mittelalterliche Predigttheorie und das Manuale curatorum des Johann Ulrich Surgant.* Basler Beiträge zur Geschichtswissenschaft, 58. Basel, 1956.

Rouse, Richard H., and Mary A. Rouse. *Preachers, Florilegia and Sermons: Studies on the* Manipulus Florum *of Thomas of Ireland.* Toronto: University of Toronto Press, 1979.

Tedesco, John L. "Theology in Two Medieval Tractates on Preaching: A Comparative Study." *SSJ* 41 (1976): 177–88.

Trout, John M. "Alain of Lille and the Art of Preaching in the Twelfth Century." *Bulletin de théologie ancienne et médiévale* 12 (1980): 642–53.

von Nolcken, Christina. "Some Alphabetical *Compendia* and How Preachers Used Them in Fourteenth-Century England." *Viator* 12 (1981): 271–88.

Wailes, Stephen. "The Composition of Vernacular Sermons by Berthold von Regensburg." *Michigan Germanic Studies* 5 (1979): 1–24.

Wenzel, Siegfried. "Joyous Art of Preaching: or, the Preacher and the Fabliau." *Anglia* 97 (1979): 304–25.

Miscellaneous

Aho, James A. "Rhetoric and the Invention of Double Entry Bookkeeping." *Rhetorica* 3 (1984): 21–43.

Bird, Otto. "Formalizing of the Topics in Mediaeval Logic." *Notre Dame Journal of Formal Logic* 1 (1960): 138–49.

Boggess, William F. "Hermannus Alemannus's Rhetorical Translations." *Viator* 2 (1971): 227–50.

Bolgar, Robert R., ed. *Classical Influences on European Culture,* A.D. *500–1500.* Cambridge: Cambridge University Press, 1971.

Bonebakker, Seeger A. "Aspects of the History of Literary Rhetoric and Poetics in Arabic Literature." *Viator* 1 (1970): 75–95.

———. *Materials for the History of Arabic Rhetoric.* Naples: Istituto Orientale, 1975.

Clanchy, M. T. *From Memory to Written Record: England, 1066–1307.* Cambridge: Harvard University Press, 1979.

Colish, Marcia L. *The Mirror of Language: A Study in the Medieval Theory of Knowledge*. New Haven: Yale University Press, 1968.

de Rijk, Lambert Marie. *Logica Modernorum: A Contribution to the History of Early Terminist Logic*. 2 vols. Assen: Van Gorcum, 1962.

―――. *Die mittelalterlichen Traktate De modo opponendi et respondendi. Einleitung und Ausgabe der Einschlägigen Texte*. Beiträge zur Geschichte der Philosophie und Theologie des Mittelalters, Neue Folge, Band. 17. Münster Westfalen: Aschendorff, 1980.

Dickey, Mary. "Some Commentaries on the *De inventione* and *Ad Herennium* of the Eleventh and Early Twelfth Centuries." *MARS* 6 (1968): 1–41.

Evans, Gillian R. "'Argumentum' and 'argumentatio': The Development of a Technical Terminology up to c. 1150." *Classical Folia* 30 (1976): 81–93.

Fredborg, Karin M. "The Commentaries on Cicero's *De inventione* and *Rhetorica ad Herennium* by William of Champeaux." *CIMAGL* 17 (1976): 1–39.

―――. "Petrus Helias on Rhetoric." *CIMAGL* 13 (1974): 31–41.

Gibson, Margaret T. "Latin Commentaries on Logic before 1200." *Bulletin de philosophie médiévale* 24 (1982): 54–64.

Green-Pedersen, Niels-Jørgen. "The Doctrine of 'maxima propositio' and 'locus differentia' in Commentaries from the 12th Century on Boethius' 'Topics.' " *Studia Mediewistyczne* 18 (1977): 126–63.

―――. "On the Interpretation of Aristotle's *Topics* in the Thirteenth Century." *CIMAGL* 9 (1973): 1–46.

―――. *Tradition of the Topics in the Middle Ages: The Commentaries on Aristotle's and Boethius' 'Topics.'* Munich: Philosophia Vertag, 1984.

―――. "William of Champeaux on Boethius' *Topics* According to Orléans Bibl. Mun. 266." *CIMAGL* 13 (1974): 13–30.

Iwakuma, Y., ed. " 'Instantiae': A Study of Twelfth-Century Technique of Argumentation with an Edition of Ms. Paris BN Lat. 6674, f. 1–5." *CIMAGL* 38 (1981): 1–91.

Karaus, S. M. J. "Selections from the Commentary of Bartolinus de Benincasa de Canulo on the *Rhetorica ad Herennium*." Ph.D. dissertation., Columbia University, 1970.

Kustas, George L. "Function and Evolution of Byzantine Rhetoric." *Viator* 1 (1970): 55–73.

Leff, Michael C. "Boethius and the History of Medieval Rhetoric." *CSSJ* 25 (1974): 134–41.

Lewry, P. Osmond. "Rhetoric at Paris and Oxford in the Mid-Thirteenth Century." *Rhetorica* 1 (1983): 45–63.

Maguire, Henry. *Art and Eloquence in Byzantium*. Princeton: Princeton University Press, 1981.

Monfasani, John. *George of Trebizond: A Biography and a Study of His Rhetoric and Logic*. Columbia Studies in the Classical Tradition, 1. Leiden: E. J. Brill, 1976.

———. "Humanism and Rhetoric." In *Renaissance Humanism: Foundation, Forms, and Legacy*, vol. 3: *Humanism and the Disciplines*, edited by Albert Rabil, Jr., 171–235. Philadelphia: University of Pennsylvania Press, 1988.

Murphy, James J. "Two Medieval Textbooks in Debate." *Journal of the American Forensic Association* 1 (1964): 1–6.

O'Donnell, James J. *Cassiodorus*. Berkeley: University of California Press, 1979.

O'Donnell, J. Reginald. "The Commentary of Giles of Rome on the Rhetoric of Aristotle." In *Essays in Medieval History Presented to Bertie Wilkinson*, edited by Thayron A. Sandquist and Michael R. Powicke, 139–56. Toronto: University of Toronto Press, 1969.

———. "The Liberal Arts in the Twelfth Century with Special Reference to Alexander Nequam (1157–1217)." In *Arts libéraux et philosophie au moyen age*, 127–36. Montreal and Paris, 1969.

———. "The *Rhetorica Divina* of William of Auvergne: A Study in Applied Rhetoric." In *Images of Man in Ancient and Medieval Thought: Studia Gerardo Verbeke ab amicis et collegiis dicata*, edited by F. Bossier et al., 323–33. Louvain: Louvain University Press, 1976.

Pack, Roger A. "*Ars memorativa* from the Late Middle Ages." *Archives d'histoire doctrinale et littéraire du moyen age* 46 (1979): 221–75.

Press, Gerald A. "The Subject and Structure of Augustine's *De doctrina christiana*." *Augustinian Studies* 2 (1980): 99–124.

Reinsma, Luke. "Rhetoric in England: The Age of Aelfric, 970–1020." *CM* 44 (1977): 390–403.

Rickert, Edith. "Chaucer at School." *MP* 29 (1931): 257–74.

Roberts, M. "Rhetoric and Poetic Imitation in Avitus' [of Vienne] Account of the Crossing of the Red Sea." *Traditio* 39 (1983): 29–80.

Scaglione, Aldo D. *The Classical Theory of Composition from Its Origins to the Present: A Historical Survey*. University of North Carolina Studies in Comparative Literature, no. 53. Chapel Hill: University of North Carolina Press, 1972.

Speer, Richard. "John of Salisbury: Rhetoric in the *Metalogicon*." *CSSJ* 20 (1969): 92–96.

Stump, Eleonore A. "Boethius's Work on the Topics." *Vivarium* 12 (1974): 77–93.

———. "Dialectic." In *The Seven Liberal Arts in the Middle Ages*, edited by David L. Wagner, 125–46. Bloomington: Indiana University Press, 1983.

————. *Dialectic and Its Place in the Development of Medieval Logic*. Ithaca: Cornell University Press, 1989.

————. "Dialectic in the Eleventh and Twelfth Centuries: Garlandus Compotista." *History and Philosophy of Logic* 1 (1980): 1–18.

————. "Topics: Their Development and Absorption into Consequences." In *The Cambridge History of Later Medieval Philosophy from the Rediscovery of Aristotle to the Disintegration of Scholasticism, 1100–1600*, edited by Norman Kretzmann, Anthony Kenny, and Jan Pinborg, 273–99. Cambridge: Cambridge University Press, 1982.

Wallach, Luitpold. *Alcuin and Charlemagne: Studies in Carolingian History and Literature*. Cornell Studies in Classical Philology, no. 32. Ithaca: Cornell University Press, 1959.

Ward, John O. "Classical Rhetoric and the Writing of History in Medieval and Renaissance Culture." In *European History and Its Historians*, edited by Frank McGregor and Nicholas Wright, 1–10. Adelaide: Adelaide University Union Press, 1977.

————. "The Date of the Commentary on Cicero's *De inventione* by Thierry of Chartres (c. 1095–1160?) and the Cornifician Attack on the Liberal Arts." *Viator* 3 (1972): 219–73.

Weisheipl, James A., O.P. "Curriculum of the Faculty of Arts at Oxford in the Early Fourteenth Century." *MS* 26 (1964): 143–85.

Wetherbee, Winthrop. *Platonism and Poetry in the Twelfth Century: The Literary Influence of the School of Chartres*. Princeton: Princeton University Press, 1972.

Wippel, John F. "Quodlibetal Question as a Distinctive Literary Genre." In *Les genres littéraires dans les sources théologiques et philosophiques médiévales: Définition, critique, et exploitation. Actes du Colloque international de Louvain-la-Neuve, 25–27 Mai, 1981*, 67–84. Louvain-la-Neuve: Université Catholique de Louvain, 1982.

Witt, Ronald. "Medieval Italian Culture and the Origins of Humanism as a Stylistic Ideal." In *Renaissance Humanism: Foundation, Forms, and Legacy*, vol. 1: *Humanism in Italy*, edited by Albert Rabil, Jr., 29–70. Philadelphia: University of Pennsylvania Press, 1988.

Yates, Frances A. *Art of Memory*. Chicago: University of Chicago Press, 1966, 1974.

THE RENAISSANCE

Don Paul Abbott

In his *English Literature in the Sixteenth Century* (Oxford: Clarendon Press, 1954), C. S. Lewis offers the following confession to his readers:

> Rhetoric is the greatest barrier between us and our ancestors. If the Middle Ages had erred in their devotion to that art, the 'renascentia', far from curing, confirmed the error. In rhetoric, more than in anything else, the continuity of the old European tradition was embodied. Nearly all our older poetry was written and read by men to whom the distinction between poetry and rhetoric, in its modern form, would have been meaningless. The "beauties" which they chiefly regarded in every composition were those which we either dislike or simply do not notice. This change of taste makes an invisible wall between us and them. Probably all our literary histories, certainly that on which I am engaged, are vitiated by our lack of sympathy on this point. If ever the passion for formal rhetoric returns, the whole story will have to be rewritten and many judgements may be reversed. (16)

As Lewis may have foreseen, rhetoric has indeed "returned," and the history of Renaissance literature is being rewritten by individuals who are far more sympathetic to rhetoric than were scholars of Lewis's generation. In the six years that have elapsed since the first edition of *The Present State of Scholarship in Historical and Contemporary Rhetoric* this revisionism has continued at a steady pace. While by no means all treatments of Renaissance culture display sympathy toward rhetoric, much of the earlier animus has subsided. As a result, our knowledge of Renaissance rhetoric and its relation to Renaissance life is becoming more balanced, more detailed, and more sophisticated.

The purpose of this essay is not to provide a synoptic history of Renaissance rhetoric; several admirable surveys are available and are discussed below. Rather, the intent is to detail the "rewriting" or, more accurately, the rediscovery of the primacy of rhetoric in Renaissance art and intellect; to document what has been rediscovered and to suggest in what direction future discoveries might lie.

Even a survey of the scholarship of Renaissance rhetoric is a rather imposing task. After all, the Renaissance was a phenomenon of great geographical scope and temporal longevity. Moreover, rhetoric was a central preoccupation of a remarkable number of Renaissance thinkers. Contemporary scholarship necessarily reflects the international and multilingual nature of this subject. To make the task of surveying such a diverse body of material manageable, I will focus upon the Renaissance in England and rhetorical treatises in the English language. While it is obviously impossible to consider the Renaissance without an examination of Continental sources, space constraints preclude more than a brief account of recent scholarship on European rhetoric.

State of the Primary Texts

James J. Murphy has called Renaissance rhetoric the field of "a thousand and one neglected authors" (*Renaissance Eloquence*, 20). While of course not all of these authors are English, enough are that G. P. Mohrmann has identified 267 first editions printed in England in the sixteenth and seventeenth centuries (*Renaissance Eloquence*, 68–83). Rather than attempt to discuss over two hundred works, it is probably more useful and realistic to discuss the availability of certain basic texts. The bibliographies discussed in the following section provide comprehensive listings of Renaissance treatises.

Perhaps the most obvious obstacle to research in sixteenth- and seventeenth-century rhetoric is the scarcity of the original works. For example, only five copies of Henry Peacham's *The Garden of Eloquence* (1577) are extant. Even rarer is Abraham Fraunce's *The Arcadian Rhetorike* (1588), of which only two copies remain. There are, of course, practical alternatives to wandering about widely scattered rare-book rooms. A number of Renaissance treatises are to be found in modern editions and facsimile reprints. The most widely available modern editions are those rhetorical materials included among the collected works of well-known writers. Standard collections of the works of Erasmus, Hobbes, and Bacon all contain important rhetorical documents. Unfortunately, the number of rhetorics included in such collections is quite small. More typically, the works of rhetoricians appear in facsimile form.

Probably the most complete collection of such facsimiles is English Linguistics 1500–1800, edited by R. C. Alston and published by Scolar Press. This series comprises facsimile reprints of rhetorics, grammars, logics, dictionaries, and other language books published in England during those three centuries. Rhetorical works in this series include Angel Day, *The English Secretorie* (1586); George Puttenham, *The Arte of English Poesie* (1589); Abraham Fraunce, *The Arcadian Rhetorike* (1588);

John Smith, *The Mysterie of Rhetorique Unvail'd* (1657); Thomas Farnaby, *Index rhetoricus* (1625); Henry Peacham, *The Garden of Eloquence* (1577); Thomas Blount, *The Academie of Eloquence* (1654); Joshua Poole, *Practical Rhetorick* (1663); Richard Rainolde, *The Foundacion of Rhetorike* (1563); and William Dugard, *Rhetorices elementa* (1648). Each volume in this series is prefaced by a brief note discussing the text chosen for reproduction and describing the general characteristics of the work. The volumes contain no other scholarly apparatus. A similar series, although one containing fewer rhetorics, is The English Experience: Its Record in Early Printed Books Published in Facsimile. Relevant titles include Rainolde's *Foundacion of Rhetorike* and Thomas Wilson's *The Arte of Rhetorique* (1553).

There are also a number of nonserial facsimiles, most notable of which is perhaps Leonard Cox, *The Arte or Crafte of Rhetoryke* (1530?), edited with an introduction by Frederick Ives Carpenter (1899). Cox's work, the first English rhetoric, is extremely rare, and Carpenter's edition is becoming so. Fortunately, this edition of Cox has been reissued by two different presses (1969 and 1975). Other facsimiles with useful introductions include William G. Crane's 1954 edition of Peacham's *The Garden of Eloquence*; Francis R. Johnson's 1945 edition of Rainolde's *The Foundacion of Rhetorike*; and Dudley Fenner's *The Artes of Logike and Rhetorike* (1584) in Robert D. Pepper's *Four Tudor Books on Education* (1966). Facsimile editions of other important works (although with less detailed introductions) include Richard Sherry, *A Treatise of Schemes and Tropes* (1550), and Wilson, *The Arte of Rhetorique*.

In addition to the facsimiles, a small but growing number of modern critical editions of Renaissance rhetorics are available. Of these, Gladys Doidge Willcock and Alice Walker's 1936 edition of Puttenham's *The Arte of English Poesie* is prefaced by an especially thorough introduction to a particularly rhetorical poetic. Ethel Seaton's 1950 edition of Fraunce's *The Arcadian Rhetorike* and James W. Cleary's 1974 edition of John Bulwer's *Chirologia. . . . Chironomia* (1644) also include informative introductory material.

One of the most valuable recent editions is Lawrence Green's *John Rainolds's Oxford Lectures on Aristotle's Rhetoric* (1986). This volume makes available the earliest critical study of Aristotle's *Rhetoric* in England and the only surviving lectures from Renaissance Oxford. Green's introduction establishes the context of Rainold's life and scholarship as well as an analysis of the *Lectures*.

Another Englishman's account of Aristotelian rhetoric can be found in Thomas Hobbes's *Brief of the Arte of Rhetorique* (1673), published with the seventeenth-century English translation of Bernard Lamy's *Art of*

Speaking (1676) in *The Rhetorics of Thomas Hobbes and Bernard Lamy* (1986), edited by John Harwood. Harwood elected to join these two very different rhetorics together because of their importance in the history of rhetoric. Each work is prefaced by a separate introduction. The introduction to Hobbes offers an interesting interpretation of the *Brief* that attempts to show how Hobbes's "translation" made the *Rhetoric* as much Hobbes as Aristotle.

Thomas Wilson's *Arte of Rhetorique*, considered by many to be the first "complete" rhetoric in English, has been issued in a critical edition edited by Thomas J. Derrick. This volume is a much needed successor to the increasingly rare edition of G. H. Mair (1909). Unlike Mair's edition, which is based on the 1558 printing, Derrick has chosen to base his edition on the 1553 edition and the 1560 revision. The most significant contribution of the Derrick edition is his careful study of the texts of the various sixteenth-century editions of Wilson, which are discussed in a list of "Emendations" and in a "Historical Collation" of the texts. Derrick's edition also includes a "Biographical Introduction" and a "Critical Introduction."

One other modern edition deserves special notice: *The Book of the Honeycomb's Flow*, by Judah Messer Leon, edited and translated by Isaac Rabinowitz (1983). This work, written in Italy in the late fifteenth century, is a remarkable rhetorical treatise in which classical precepts and doctrines are employed to interpret the Hebrew Bible. Rabinowitz's translation is the first in any modern language, and his careful introduction illuminates the intellectual appeal and pervasive scope of Italian humanism. Rabinowitz deserves considerable credit for making this work accessible to the non-Hebraist.

In addition to facsimiles and modern editions, microform resources must be noted. The pioneer microfilm series is *British and Continental Rhetoric and Elocution*, prepared by the Speech Association of America (now Speech Communication Association) and distributed by University Microfilms. This project consists of 142 rhetorical treatises printed in England and Europe from the fifteenth through the nineteenth centuries. In addition to providing the work or works of some twenty-five English Renaissance authors, this series makes available the texts of Continental figures influential in Britain. These include Arnauld, Crésol, Lamy, Ramus, Talon, Melanchthon, Vossius, Sturm, Susenbrotus, and Vives. *BCRE* makes possible the examination of a large collection of texts, many of which are unavailable in any form save the original.

A second significant microform resource is *Renaissance Rhetoric: A Microfiche Collection of Key Texts* A.D. *1472–1602*, edited by James J. Murphy (1987). *Renaissance Rhetoric* includes among its sixty-two treatises such disparate works as Rudolf Agricola's *De inventione dialecta*, Ermolao Barbaro's *Rhetoricum Aristoteles libre tres*, Bartolomeo Cavalcanti's *La retorica*, Angel Day's *English Secretorie*, Antonious Gouveanus's *Pro Aristotele responsio, adversus Petri Rami calumnias*, Philip Melanchthon's *Elementorum rhetorices libre duo*, Cyprian Soarez's *De arte rhetorica*, and Gulielmus Traversanus's *Margarita eloquentia castigata*. This collection of rhetorics makes available a number of significant texts that are otherwise not easily accessible.

This combination of modern editions, facsimiles, and microfilms allows a reasonable review of the primary sources of Renaissance rhetoric. This is not to say that the situation is altogether satisfactory. Many works remain exclusively in rare-book rooms, facsimile editions often lack clarity, and translations from the Latin are few. A considerable improvement in the availability and reliability of these basic resources would surely result in greater quantity and quality of scholarship in Renaissance rhetoric.

Bibliographies

Basic bibliographic resources for the study of Renaissance rhetoric have improved tremendously in recent years. The standard bibliography is James J. Murphy, *Renaissance Rhetoric: A Short Title Catalogue* (1981), which provides both primary and secondary sources for the study of rhetoric from 1455 to 1700. Most notably, the bibliography includes alphabetical entries for an astonishing 867 authors of rhetorical treatises. Each entry provides the author's name, birth and death dates, applicable aliases, a list by short titles of relevant works, and a list of libraries holding these works. While *Renaissance Rhetoric: A Short Title Catalogue* lists works published in Europe as well as Britain, a special index identifies 195 books in English or printed in England. A second edition is in preparation and should appear in 1990. The revised bibliography will contain 50 percent more entries than the first edition. Thus *Renaissance Rhetoric: A Short Title Catalogue* presents dramatic testimony to the richness of Renaissance rhetoric.

A second recent bibliography is Charles Stanford, "The Renaissance," which is less comprehensive than *Renaissance Rhetoric: A Short Title Catalogue*. However, unlike Murphy, Stanford annotates all entries. Forty-one primary and 181 secondary sources compose this useful bibliography.

A third important bibliography is *Rhetoric, Style, Elocution, Prosody, Rhyme, Pronunciation, Spelling Reform*, volume 6 of the monumental *Bib-*

liography of the English Language from the Invention of Printing to the Year 1800 (1974) edited by R. C. Alston. The rhetorical works are arranged chronologically within three categories: "Rhetoric," "Pulpit Rhetoric," and "Elocution." These three sections include nearly five hundred entries.

A number of specialized bibliographies are also available, and these will be noted in the appropriate sections below.

Rhetoric and Humanism

Rhetoric was a central preoccupation of those Renaissance scholars we now call Humanists. Indeed, it is difficult to separate the study of rhetoric from the study of humanism. In assessing this relationship, a convenient starting point is Hanna H. Gray's oft-quoted "Renaissance Humanism: The Pursuit of Eloquence" (1963). In this essay Gray rather neatly synthesizes many of the rhetorical concerns of the Italian and northern humanists, which ultimately appear in English treatises. An essay of greater historical breadth is Paul Oskar Kristeller's "Philosophy and Rhetoric from Antiquity to the Renaissance," in his *Renaissance Thought and Its Sources* (1979). Kristeller attempts to distinguish Renaissance rhetoric from its classical and medieval antecedents and to identify defining characteristics of sixteenth-century rhetoric. Another work that documents the humanistic debt to antiquity is *The Classical Heritage and Its Beneficiaries* by R. R. Bolgar (1954). While this virtually encyclopedic work examines all aspects of the survival of classical culture, rhetoric itself is discussed in detail throughout.

A book more directly about rhetoric is Jerrold Seigel's *Rhetoric and Philosophy in Renaissance Humanism* (1968), in which Seigel demonstrates the pervasiveness of the Ciceronian model as the governing ideal of early Renaissance rhetoric. Nancy S. Struever, in *The Language of History in the Renaissance* (1970), details the close relationship between rhetoric and historiography. These two works on Florentine humanism by Seigel and Struever are essential for an understanding of the Italian origins of Renaissance rhetoric and an appreciation of the humanist influence on English theory.

Another important work on humanism that goes well beyond the Quattrocento is *Rhetoric, Prudence, and Skepticism in the Renaissance* (1985) by Victoria Kahn. In this book Kahn argues that the humanists conceived of a close relationship between practical reason and the practice of eloquence, that is, between prudence and rhetoric. She also argues that the rhetorical practice of the humanists has been given insufficient attention by modern scholars. Accordingly, about one-half of the book is devoted to a textual analysis of the rhetoric of Erasmus, Montaigne, and Hobbes, writers who exemplify the union of prudence and rhetoric.

An exceptional study of an individual humanist is John Monfasani's *George of Trebizond: A Biography and a Study of His Rhetoric and Logic* (1976). Monfasani identifies Trebizond's *Rhetoricum libre V* as "the first complete *Rhetoric* of the humanist movement" (261) and the only true *summa* of classical rhetoric since Quintilian's *Institutio oratoria*. Monfasani re-creates Trebizond's life, intellectual milieu, and his views on rhetoric and dialectic with remarkable lucidity. His work clearly shows how much we need to know about other major figures of Renaissance rhetoric. A more recent work by Monfasani is "Humanism and Rhetoric," in *Humanism in the Disciplines*, volume 3 of *Renaissance Humanism: Foundation, Forms, and Legacy* (1988). Despite the author's disclaimer that he "makes no attempt to be comprehensive" (172), the essay is remarkable for its combination of comprehensiveness and concision. Indeed, "Humanism and Rhetoric" must be regarded as the best brief introduction to this important historical relationship.

National Surveys and Comprehensive Studies

A growing number of works detail the place of rhetoric in the development of a national consciousness while recognizing that the Renaissance remained an international phenomenon. Foremost among these is Marc Fumaroli's *L'âge de l'éloquence* (1980). Fumaroli presents an extremely detailed account of a sixteenth-century debate in France between the Jesuits and the *"gallicans"* about the nature of rhetoric. This work is invaluable as an account of the crucial role of the Jesuits in the history of rhetoric, not only in France, but in Italy and Spain as well. A work of somewhat similar scope and conception is *Formación de la teoría literaria moderna* by Antonio García Berrio (1977 and 1980). Despite what the title might suggest, this work of two volumes and nearly one thousand pages is very much concerned with Renaissance rhetoric. The first volume is primarily concerned with the development of literary theory (rhetoric and poetic) in fifteenth- and sixteenth-century Europe, while the second volume concentrates on similar issues in Spain's Golden Age. Few other works can match the exhaustiveness and erudition presented by Fumaroli and García Berrio. For example, Bernard Weinberg's *A History of Literary Criticism in the Italian Renaissance* (1961), despite its magistral qualities, neglects rhetorical treatises and concentrates almost exclusively on poetic theory. There is a significant body of literature which assesses the role of rhetoric in other

European nations, as well as its place in non-European cultures. This material is succinctly presented by Brian Vickers in *In Defence of Rhetoric* (470–75), a book that will be discussed in detail below.

A number of works detail the development of rhetoric in England itself. One of the earliest attempts is in Donald Lemen Clark's *Rhetoric and Poetry in the Renaissance* (1922), a study of the influence of classical rhetoric on the criticism of poetry. This work includes a useful explanation of the classical distinction between rhetoric and poetic. Another early survey is Charles Sears Baldwin's *Renaissance Literary Theory and Practice* (1939). Baldwin's preoccupation with the triumph of classical models unfortunately causes him to dismiss any rhetorician who deviates from classicism. As a result, Thomas Wilson is the only English theorist discussed in detail. A work far more sympathetic to a plurality of theoretical positions is William Garrett Crane's *Wit and Rhetoric in the Renaissance* (1937). Chapter 7, "English Rhetorics of the Sixteenth Century," remains one of the best brief introductions to English Renaissance rhetorical treatises. J. W. H. Atkins, in his *English Literary Criticism: The Renascence* (1947), argues that earlier studies exaggerated the assimilation of classical doctrine by English critics and underestimated the influence of the Italian humanists.

Wilbur S. Howell's *Logic and Rhetoric in England, 1500–1700* (1956) has long been a standard history of English Renaissance rhetoric. The work is based upon the assumption that "logic and rhetoric are the two great arts of communication, and that the complete theory of communication is identified, not with one, not with the other, but with both" (4). Howell further assumes that logic and rhetoric are quite distinct from the third art of communication, poetic. The development of both logic and rhetoric is charted across two centuries. For rhetoric this charting begins with the classically derived "traditional rhetoric," which Howell divides into three patterns: "Ciceronian," "stylistic," and "formulary." The dominance of these traditional approaches was successfully challenged by the arrival of Ramistic rhetoric in the last quarter of the sixteenth century. Howell sees in the writing of seventeenth-century figures such as Descartes and Bacon the portent of a "new rhetoric." *Logic and Rhetoric in England, 1500–1700* is detailed, erudite, and essential reading for any serious student of Renaissance rhetoric. An interesting supplement to this book is Howell's "Renaissance Rhetoric and Modern Rhetoric: A Study in Change" in his *Poetics, Rhetoric, and Logic* (1975). In this essay Howell isolates what he regards as the essential distinctions between the Renaissance conception of rhetoric and the modern formulation of the discipline.

An alternative interpretation of Renaissance rhetoric is advanced by

Brian Vickers in the recently reissued *Classical Rhetoric in English Poetry* (1990). Vickers argues here and elsewhere that American historians of rhetoric in general, and Howell in particular, misinterpret Renaissance rhetoric because of a failure to understand the figures of speech. Accordingly, Vickers provides a rationale for the figures and, in contrast to Howell, denies the separability of rhetoric and poetic. Vickers advances the same argument with greater historical scope in "Rhetorical and Anti-Rhetorical Tropes: On Writing the History of Elocutio" (1981).

A different type of general work is *A Handbook to Sixteenth-Century Rhetoric* by Lee A. Sonnino (1968). This is very much a reference work and, unlike the other works discussed thus far, provides little in the way of a narrative account of Renaissance rhetoric. What is provided, instead, is an alphabetical listing by Latin name of the various figures of rhetoric. For each entry the reader is provided with definitions cited from classical and Renaissance texts followed by examples of the figures, again from primary texts. A shorter section listing figures by Greek terminology is also included. Latin, Greek, and Italian terms are cross-referenced. This handbook simplifies the often complicated task of mastering the multitude of figures so familiar to sixteenth-century rhetoricians.

One of the most comprehensive surveys of the field is *Renaissance Eloquence*, a collection of twenty-three papers edited by James J. Murphy (1983). Essays of particular relevance for the study of English rhetoric include Gerald P. Mohrmann, "Oratorical Delivery and Other Problems in Current Scholarship on English Renaissance Rhetoric" (including the appended "First Edition of Rhetorical Works Printed in Britain to A.D. 1700"); Richard J. Schoeck, "Lawyers and Rhetoric in Sixteenth Century England"; Heinrich F. Plett, "The Place and Function of Style in Elizabethan England"; Thomas O. Sloane, "Reading Milton Rhetorically"; and Brian Vickers, " 'The Power of Persuasion': Images of the Orator, Elyot to Shakespeare." This volume also includes essays on virtually all aspects of Renaissance rhetoric by Paul Oskar Kristeller, James J. Murphy, A. Kibedi Varga, Nancy Struever, Charles Trinkaus, John W. O'Malley, Marc Fumaroli, Hugh Davidson, W. Keith Percival, and others.

A very different kind of survey is Brian Vickers's *In Defence of Rhetoric* (1988), a perceptive and polemical account of rhetoric from its classical origins to its postmodern future. The first five chapters of this book may be the best short history of the subject now available. While medievalists will probably bridle at Vickers's interpretation of the "Medieval Fragmentation" of rhetoric followed by its "Renaissance Reintegration" (chapters 4 and 5), his treatment of the latter is, like Monfasani's "Rhetoric and Humanism," an extraordinary synthesis which captures the scope of Renaissance rhetoric without sacrificing the complexity of the issues involved. *In Defence of Rhetoric* is an excellent place to begin an examination of not only rhetoric in the Renaissance, but the entire history of the art.

The general studies discussed above can provide the reader with a very comprehensive view of rhetoric in the sixteenth and seventeenth centuries. But no survey, however thorough, can detail every aspect of a subject as expansive as Renaissance rhetoric. Specialized studies are, of course, necessary to supplement the surveys, and there is a rather large body of such scholarship. Because rhetoric was so pervasive in Renaissance culture, the special studies will be reviewed in the context of the relation of rhetoric to other disciplines and intellectual pursuits.

Rhetoric and Logic

Logic and rhetoric have always had a rather curious coexistence: a relationship that is at once both cooperative and competitive. Renaissance thinkers expended great energy in efforts to realign the functions of logic and rhetoric in order to make both arts more practical and productive. A historical introduction to these efforts, written from a logician's point of view, is provided by E. J. Ashworth, *Language and Logic in the Post-Medieval Period* (1974). This book includes a comprehensive bibliography of logical treatises published during the Renaissance.

One generally accepted consequence of the Renaissance reform of dialectic is that logic became more "rhetorical," that is, "topical." The basic study of the 'topoi' or 'loci' is Joan Marie Lechner's *Renaissance Concepts of the Commonplaces* (1962). Lechner sorts out the various definitions of this concept and traces its development from antiquity to the seventeenth century.

Rudolph Agricola inspired much of the logical reform of the Renaissance. An article of special relevance to such reforms in England is James R. McNally, "Prima pars dialecticae: The Influence of Agricolan Dialectic upon English Accounts of Invention" (1968). An excellent introduction to the Agricolan program is Marc Cogan's "Rodolphus Agricola and the Semantic Revolutions of the History of Invention" (1984). In this essay Cogan skillfully charts the various changes in the complex relationship between rhetoric and dialectic from Cicero's *Topica* to Agricola's *De inventione dialectica*.

The Agricolan reform of logic may be said to have culminated in the writings of the Frenchman Pierre de la Ramée, or, as he is known in

English, Peter Ramus, and the educational ideology known as Ramism. The dominant interpretation of the Ramist phenomenon is Walter J. Ong's *Ramus, Method, and the Decay of Dialogue* (1958). This work is a magisterial study of Ramism and its intellectual milieu. Ong offers accounts of the life of Ramus, medieval education, scholastic logic, and Agricola's dialectical reform. And all of this is prefatory to a detailed analysis of Ramism itself, including a chapter devoted to Ramist rhetoric. The work concludes by following the spread of Ramism from France into England, Germany, Switzerland, and Spain.

Also essential for the serious investigation of Ramism is Ong's *Ramus and Talon Inventory*, published conjointly with *Ramus, Method, and the Decay of Dialogue*. This bibliography lists over eight hundred editions of the works of Ramus and his "literary lieutenant," Omer Talon, as well as nearly four hundred attacks on and apologies for Ramism by a variety of writers. Also included in this volume is a short-title catalog of editions and printed compendia of Agricola's *Dialectical Invention*.

Several of Ong's essays on rhetorical subjects have been collected in his *Rhetoric, Romance, and Technology* (1971). Articles on Elizabethan rhetoric include "Oral Residue in Tudor Prose Style," "Tudor Writings on Rhetoric, Poetic, and Literary Theory," "Memory as Art," and "Ramist Method and the Commercial Mind."

Perhaps in part because of the admirable scholarship of Howell and Ong, Ramus is widely accepted as the central figure in Renaissance rhetoric. A contrary view is presented in a rather polemical manner by Norman E. Nelson in *Peter Ramus and the Confusion of Logic, Rhetoric, and Poetry* (1947). More recently, Vickers has argued that Ramus has been accorded too much importance in the history of rhetoric (*Classical Rhetoric in English Poetry*, 40–44).

One of the most thorough studies of Ramus since Ong's *Ramus, Method, and the Decay of Dialogue* is *Rhétorique et poétique au XVIe siècle en France: Du Bellay, Ramus et les autres* (1986) by Kees Meerhof. In this important book Meerhof details the interaction of rhetoric and poetic in an impressive variety of sixteenth-century artifacts. The first English translation of a work by Ramus since the sixteenth century is *Arguments in Rhetoric against Quintilian* (1549), translated by Carole Newlands with an introduction by James J. Murphy. The same team has completed a translation of Ramus's *Brutinae quaestiones* (*The Questions of Brutus about Cicero's "Orator"*) (1547) which should appear in print in 1991.

Peter Ramus has become an object of intense scholarly scrutiny which has inevitably resulted in a wealth of publications pertinent to Ramism. Fortunately, this research is critically summarized in two essays by Peter Sharrat: "The Present State of Studies on Ramus" (1972) and "Recent Work on Peter Ramus (1970–1986)" (1987). These two essays demonstrate both the versatility of Ramus's thought and the present vitality of Ramus studies. Sharrat has done a great service to all those interested in the phenomenon that was, and continues to be, Ramism.

Rhetoric, Poetics, and Drama

Rhetoric and literature are, in the Renaissance, often coterminous; rhetorical precept and literary production are so intertwined as to be virtually inseparable. This inseparability draws in large part from the Renaissance deference to classical authority. Several sources discussed in "National Surveys and Comprehensive Studies" chart the influence of classical rhetoricians on English literature. Another effort to assess the Renaissance debt to classical rhetoric is Annabel M. Patterson, *Hermogenes and the Renaissance* (1970). Patterson demonstrates that Hermogenes became, in the sixteenth century, an authority to rival Cicero and Quintilian and the rhetorician most responsible for propagating the concept of stylistic decorum. While this work is concerned with the influence of Hermogenes throughout Europe, his impact on Elizabethan literature is discussed at length. Considering the pervasiveness of decorum and related stylistic concepts, *Hermogenes and the Renaissance* is a book of broad applicability.

An influential interpretation of the literary consequences of Ramism can be found in Rosemond Tuve, *Elizabethan and Metaphysical Imagery* (1947). Tuve believes that Ramism increased the appeal of logic and the attendant concept of wit, thereby providing much of the impetus for metaphysical poetry. Others have challenged this thesis principally on the grounds that Ramism also promoted the plain style and must thereby be incompatible with metaphysical imagery. A convenient summary of these various interpretations of Ramism and poetry is Jackson I. Cope's chapter on "Ramist Implications," in his *The Metaphoric Structure of* Paradise Lost (1962).

In *Elizabethan and Metaphysical Imagery*, Tuve necessarily devotes considerable attention to figurative language, for it is impossible to study Renaissance rhetoric without encountering the figures of speech. One especially helpful guide to the multitude of figures, Sonnino's *Handbook to Sixteenth-Century Rhetoric*, has been discussed previously. A similar work is Warren Taylor, *Tudor Figures of Rhetoric* (1972). This reprint of Taylor's 1937 doctoral dissertation is less comprehensive than Sonnino's work, but it does offer certain features not found in the *Handbook*. In addition to a typical dictionary of figures, Taylor also supplies "A Guide for Determining the Names of the Figures" that describes the function of each figure and then provides the technical term. Another work largely devoted to the figures is Miriam Joseph's *Rhetoric in Shakespeare's Time* (1947). Joseph presents an overview of Renaissance compositional theories, examines Shakespeare's use of those theories, and concludes with a comparative analysis of the figures and the topics. Joseph contends that figurative rhetoric and topical logic are essentially the same, for the purpose of each is the amplification of meaning.

It is in the figures, perhaps, that the commonalities of rhetoric and poetic are most clearly revealed. A number of works attempt to clarify the relationship of these two arts. An early attempt is Herbert David Rix, *Rhetoric in Spenser's Poetry* (1940). To determine Spenser's reliance on rhetoric, Rix first catalogs the figures using terminology from Susenbrotus and Peacham together with examples from Spenser. Based on this inventory, Rix concludes that while Spenser occasionally used the figures for ornamentation, he more often employed them to achieve emotional or persuasive efficacy.

In *Ben Jonson's Poems* (1962), Wesley Trimpi demonstrates that Jonson, too, profited from the conscious use of rhetoric. Jonson, however, is an advocate of the plain style and hence is not heavily reliant on such figurists as Peacham or Puttenham. Rather, it is the Spanish humanist Juan Luis Vives who is Jonson's most important source. Trimpi demonstrates that key passages in the *Discoveries* are translated from Vives's *De ratione dicendi*. And it is the *Discoveries* that provides a rationale of the plain style that in turn governs the composition of Jonson's poems.

In *The Enduring Monument* (1962), O. B. Hardison, Jr., explores another aspect of the link between rhetorical theory and literary practice. Of the three genres of classical oratory—forensic, deliberative, and epideictic—Hardison maintains that only the last was fully assimilated into Renaissance literary criticism. This is because the functions of epideictic oratory, praise and blame, are also the end of many poetic genres. Hardison supports this thesis with an analysis of a wide variety of Renaissance poetry, and in so doing he illuminates the correspondence between epic and epideictic.

That relationship is also the subject of Brian Vickers's "Epideictic and Epic in the Renaissance" (1983). The key link between these two literary forms, argues Vickers, is ethics: "The most significant topic for literature, especially the epic, was the realm of human virtue and vice. Epideictic occupied its distinguished position because it had been moralized, as it were: from a very early date, praise (and with it fame) was held to be the proper and exclusive response to virtue only; blame, to vice. . . . rhetoric had aligned itself with philosophy, especially with ethics, so that the poet, like the orator, became the propagator of accepted moral systems" (502). Two recent works that examine the poet and the orator as propagators of moral systems are *In Praise of Aeneas: Virgil and Epideictic Rhetoric in the Early Italian Renaissance* (1989) by Craig Kallendorf and *Funeral Oratory and the Cultural Ideals of Italian Humanism* (1989) by John M. McManamon, S.J.

Just as poetic creation profited from rhetorical theory, the development of Renaissance drama was also guided, in part, by the rhetorical tradition. This development is detailed by Charles O. McDonald in *The Rhetoric of Tragedy* (1966). This work examines the influence of rhetorical instruction on the dramatic creativity of fifth-century B.C. Greece, first-century A.D. Rome, and sixteenth- and seventeenth-century England. In assessing the impact of rhetoric on tragedy, McDonald considers in detail Shakespeare's *Hamlet*, Marston's *Sophonisba* and *The Malcontent*, Chapman's *Bussy D'Ambois*, Tourneur's [?] *The Revengers Tragedie*, Webster's *The White Devil*, and Ford's *The Broken Heart*. McDonald concludes that these dramas derive their worldview and verbal technique from rhetorical instruction. The rhetorical influence on drama is also investigated by Joel B. Altman in *The Tudor Play of the Mind* (1978). Altman contends that the rhetorical *quaestio* and its attendant forms of inquiry inspired a large body of Elizabethan drama. That is to say, plays are questions, or more precisely "fictional realizations of questions" (3). Such a view of drama, says Altman, derives directly from the Elizabethan fondness for formal rhetoric. Drama as rhetorical inquiry applies not only to tragedy but also to comedy, court plays, and all variants of Elizabethan theater. Another rhetorical interpretation of Renaissance drama is Marion Trousdale, *Shakespeare and the Rhetoricians* (1982). Trousdale's concern is with the interaction of "the assumptions of rhetoric" and dramatic form. According to Trousdale, Agricola's place-logic, Erasmus's amplitude, and Puttenham's figures largely explain dramatic composition; therefore, an understanding of these forces makes possible a more meaningful reading of Shakespeare.

The influence of rhetoric upon the poets of the English Renaissance is clearly apparent in Thomas O. Sloane's *Donne, Milton, and the End of Humanist Rhetoric* (1985). Of these two great poets, Sloane argues that "Donne was more the humanist than Milton" because "Donne was more the rhetorician" (xi). That is, Donne was a humanist-rhetorician because of his affinity for *controversia* and the methods of forensic oratory. On the other hand, Milton, as a Ramist, avoided the judicial genre in favor of a one-sided *elocutio*. The poetry of Milton, therefore, marks the end of humanist rhetoric with its close association with forensic and controversial methods. This intriguing thesis is itself controversial. Sloane's identification of humanism with the judicial oratory is at odds with many scholars who argue for the epideictic as the typical Renaissance *genus*. Sloane's argument that Milton, as a Ramist, broke with sixteenth-century humanism is equally suggestive, but inconsistent with those who view Milton as both a humanist and a controversialist. Thus, Sloane has challenged certain interpretations of Donne and Milton while reaffirming the intimate connection between rhetoric and poetry in the Renaissance.

Another important, and even more sweeping, account of the interaction of poetry and rhetoric in the Renaissance is *Humanist Poetics: Thought, Rhetoric, and Fiction in Sixteenth-Century England* (1986) by Arthur F. Kinney. Kinney argues that the prose fiction of the Renaissance derives in large measure from the humanist rhetoric of the times. He supports this thesis with an examination of the works of Sir Thomas More, George Gascoigne, John Lyly, Robert Greene, Sir Philip Sydney, Thomas Nashe, and Thomas Lodge. Kinney believes that for each of these Renaissance texts there are one or more classical models that directly or indirectly inspired the author. So, for example, More found inspiration in Plato and Cicero, as well as Erasmus, and Lyly found it in the orators of the Second Sophistic. Kinney's *Humanist Poetics* demonstrates admirably how the classical doctrine of *imitatio* was crucial to the remarkable fictive creativity of the Tudor humanists.

Sacred Oratory

Rhetoric began in antiquity as the art of oratory, and despite the rise of printing and the increasing importance of writing in the Renaissance, the oration maintained its position as the dominant form of human expression. And one of the dominant forms of Renaissance oratory was the sermon. The logical point of departure for the study of this genre is Alan F. Herr, *The Elizabethan Sermon: A Survey and a Bibliography* (1940). This book begins with an introductory essay placing the sermon within the greater body of Elizabethan prose. Herr documents the popularity of preaching and describes the occasions of presentation, methods of delivery, and structure of the sermon. The second portion of the book is a bibliography of sermons printed in England up to 1610, including about 1,200 sermons printed in 513 separate publications. Herr claims, rather convincingly, that this list includes the great majority of sermons printed in Elizabethan England.

A more analytic study of the sermon is J. W. Blench, *Preaching in England in the Late Fifteenth and Sixteenth Centuries* (1964). Blench devotes successive chapters to the preacher's scriptural interpretation, the form of the sermon, style, classical allusions, preaching themes, and the influence of these themes on poetry and drama. Each chapter is developed chronologically, tracing the particular topic through the sermons of the pre-reformation Catholics, early reformers, preachers of Mary's reign, and the Elizabethan preachers. Taken together, the works of Herr and Blench present a comprehensive account of preaching in the Elizabethan age.

An account of a later age is presented by W. Fraser Mitchell in *English Pulpit Oratory from Andrewes to Tillotson* (1932). Mitchell first examines the theory of sermonizing, regarding preaching as a branch of rhetoric and a product of the "rhetorical bias" in English education. He then turns from theory to practice and surveys the preaching of Anglo-Catholics, Anglicans, Cambridge Platonists, Latitudinarians, and preachers of the Restoration. From theory and practice Mitchell proceeds to criticism, arguing that secular criticism was largely responsible for the evolution of preaching in this period. The work has a thorough bibliography, which includes a forty-page listing of "Representative English Sermons of the Seventeenth Century." *English Pulpit Oratory from Andrewes to Tillotson* remains the standard survey of late Renaissance preaching.

A more specialized work on preaching is *Increase and Multiply: Arts-of-Discourse Procedure in the Preaching of Donne*, by John S. Chamberlin (1976). While Donne is the ultimate object of this study, Chamberlin's concerns go well beyond the practice of an individual preacher. He attempts to explain how a preacher elaborates a scriptural text by using all the arts of discourse—grammar, dialectic, and rhetoric.

The most important recent addition to the literature in this area is Debora K. Shuger's *Sacred Rhetoric: The Christian Grand Style in the English Renaissance* (1988). Shuger contends that not only has Renaissance rhetoric in general been neglected, but the sacred rhetoric of the age especially so. She maintains that the rhetorical treatises of the Renaissance were divided between treatises that were either essentially sacred or essentially secular in orientation. The secular works have received more scholarly attention because they appear more "modern." Yet for much of the Renaissance these sacred rhetorics were the dominant mode of preaching. These sacred rhetorics advocated what Shuger calls the "Christian Grand Style": a style that is vivid, figurative, and, above all, passionate. This style is modeled after the grand style of antiquity and represents, therefore, the theological confirmation of ancient rhetorical precepts. Shuger's *Sacred Rhetoric* demonstrates how the ancient and pagan art of rhetoric was finally and irrevocably integrated into a Christian world.

Rhetoric and Education

The conspicuous presence of rhetoric in Renaissance literature is convincing evidence of the efficacy of rhetorical training in the sixteenth and seventeenth centuries. Preachers, poets, and playwrights could employ rhetorical techniques with great skill because they had been taught to do so. While many of the books discussed in the preceding two sections devote as much as a chapter to rhetorical education, more complete treatments are available. An important early work is William H. Woodward's *Studies in Education during the Age of the Renaissance* (1906). Woodward describes in detail the pedagogical philosophies and practices of such teachers and rhetoricians as Agricola, Erasmus, Budé, Vives, Melanchthon, and many others. Foster Watson's *The English Grammar Schools to 1660* (1908) is another early work that retains its usefulness. Because the instructional aim of these schools was the writing and speaking of Latin, the grammatical was often inseparable from the rhetorical.

The advantages of a rhetorical education can be most clearly seen in T. W. Baldwin's *William Shakspere's Small Latine and Lesse Greeke* (1944). Although Shakespeare may not have actually attended a grammar school, he was, argues Baldwin, inevitably affected by the intellectual environment such schooling created. In the second volume of this 1,500–page work, seven chapters are devoted to the rhetorical training Shakespeare might have received. Baldwin concludes that such training in large part explains Shakespeare's extraordinary accomplishments with language.

Milton was another careful student of rhetoric, as Donald Lemen Clark documents in *John Milton at St. Paul's School* (1948). The goal of this work is to demonstrate the influence of classical rhetoric on Milton's prose and poetry. To do so Clark reconstructs the curriculum Milton would have followed at St. Paul's School, a course of studies that might be described as a Roman education tinted with Ramism. Clark speculates that Milton's rhetoric text may have been Talon's *Rhetorica* or a similar work by Butler or Farnaby and that this early exposure to Ramism shaped Milton's poetry.

From Humanism to the Humanities (1986) by Anthony Grafton and Lisa Jardine represents significant new scholarship on Renaissance education. Grafton and Jardine concentrate not so much on the humanists' well-known philosophical and theoretical statements about education as on the less familiar educational practices used in the humanists' classrooms. This approach results in several self-contained case studies of educational practices including the school of Guarino, female humanists, humanism in the universities, and "Northern methodical humanism." One question the authors wish to answer is why humanism replaced scholasticism as the dominant educational program in Europe. Grafton and Jardine deny that this change is the simple triumph of virtue over vice, as it is often described, for in many ways scholasticism was better suited to the needs of Europe than was humanism. Their explanation is essentially a political one: "The education of the humanists was made to order for the Europe of the Counter-Reformation and of late Protestant orthodoxy. . . . Scholasticism bred too independent an attitude to survive. In the Renaissance, as in other periods, in sum, the price of collaboration in the renewal of art and literature was collaboration in the constriction of society and polity" (xiv).

A key player in the transition from humanism to the humanities was, not surprisingly, Peter Ramus. According to Grafton and Jardine, Ramism shared with its competitors the "assumption that the aim of classical education is to produce effective writers and active participants in civic life, rather than original scholars and philosopher kings" (197). The result of this pragmatic program was the fragmentation of humanism into a loose association of "value-free" disciplines that we now recognize as the humanities.

Another recent work that explores the role of rhetoric in Western education is *A Short History of Writing Instruction from Ancient Greece to Twentieth-Century America* (1990), edited by James J. Murphy. This "short history" is probably the first attempt to trace the relationship of rhetoric and writing from the advent of literacy to the present. *A Short History of Writing Instruction* includes a chapter on the Renaissance by Don Paul Abbott. Abbott concentrates on the English Grammar School and examines the close link between oral and written word and the preeminence of imitation as an instructional method in those institutions.

Rhetoric and Science

The rise of science and its effect on English prose have long been a dominant concern of seventeenth-century rhetorical scholarship. This concern began with the influential work of Morris W. Croll, who argued that about 1600 a new prose style emerged as a result of the "Anti-Ciceronian" movement. Anti-Ciceronianism is seen by Croll as a continuation of the classical plain style, which became, in the seventeenth century, the rhetorical expression of science. This thesis is developed by Croll in a series of essays published between 1914 and 1931 and now collected in *Style, Rhetoric, and Rhythm* (1966). A rather different explanation of this stylistic evolution is presented by Richard Foster Jones in several essays written in the thirties and later assembled in *The Seventeenth Century* (1951). Jones dates the emergence of modern prose at about 1660 and believes this change is a direct result of the scientific spirit. Hence modern prose is neither a continuation of the plain style of antiquity nor consistent with Anti-Ciceronianism. In *The Senecan Amble* (1951), George Williamson extends Croll's thesis by arguing that the writings of Seneca provided the model for the new style of the seventeenth century. A more recent account of this problem can be found in Robert Adolph, *The Rise of Modern Prose Style* (1968). Adolph analyzes the debate between Croll and Jones and adopts a position closer to Jones's interpretation. Adolph contends that neither Anti-Ciceronianism nor science was the decisive influence on stylistic development, but rather the "new utilitarianism" of the age was chiefly responsible for the emergence of modern prose.

The work of Croll, Jones, and others helped establish the opinion that English scientists, represented by members of the Royal Society, were hostile to rhetoric and opposed to all but the plainest styles. This view is strongly challenged by Brian Vickers in "The Royal Society and English Prose Style: A Reassessment" (1985). The principal evidence of the scientific opposition to rhetoric is supplied by Thomas Sprat's *History of the Royal Society* (1667). Sprat has been so misinterpreted, says Vickers, that "the study of English seventeenth century prose has yet to recover from the errors of Jones, George Williamson, and Morris Croll, all of whom imposed on prose style categories or labels which had no historical justification, and which neither defined the styles they purported to characterize nor succeeded in distinguishing one from another" (15). These errors of interpretation were caused primarily by a misreading of Sprat's text. Jones had assumed that Sprat was attacking all rhetoric and all language, whereas Vickers argues that Sprat was condemning only extravagant language and specious rhetoric. More significantly, Jones also failed to appreciate the nature of the controversy about style in seventeenth-century England. Vickers contends that the disputes about style were really moments in much larger conflicts about social, political, and religious issues. Thus the Royal Society's attack on rhetoric is actually an indictment of its opponents' rhetoric, in particular, that of religious dissenters and alchemists. In Vickers's reassessment, then, rhetoric was not under wholesale assault by the Royal Society, but was, in fact, valued by the scientists of the seventeenth century.

The key figure in the alliance of science and style was, of course, Sir

Francis Bacon. Beginning with Karl R. Wallace's *Francis Bacon on Communication and Rhetoric* (1943), there have been numerous books exploring various aspects of Bacon's influence on language. Wallace's work remains the most comprehensive treatment of Bacon as a rhetorical theorist. Drawing on such concepts as the "colors of good and evil," the "anti-theta," the "formulae," and "apothegms," Wallace is an admittedly "conservative" scholar and consequently renders Bacon as a rather classical rhetorician. Brian Vickers, in *Francis Bacon and Renaissance Prose* (1968), approaches Bacon as a stylist rather than as a theorist of rhetoric. Vickers believes that the power of Bacon's prose derives largely from his "symmetrical syntax" and his mastery of imagery. Lisa Jardine documents Bacon's debt to the dialectical reformation of the sixteenth century in *Francis Bacon: Discovery and the Art of Discourse* (1974). Although the focus of this book is on Bacon as a logician, Jardine includes chapters on "Methods of Communication" and "Bacon's View of Rhetoric." Jardine, in contrast to the interpretation of Wallace and others, concludes that Baconian rhetoric is essentially ornamental and figurative. James Stephens, in *Francis Bacon and the Style of Science* (1975), examines Bacon's indebtedness to Aristotelian thought. Stephens believes that the Baconian position represents a break with the rhetorical tradition, yet, ironically, Bacon relied on Aristotle to help create a new rhetoric.

The Future of Renaissance Rhetoric

Not so long ago James J. Murphy wrote that "Renaissance rhetoric must surely be one of the most-mentioned and least studied subjects in modern scholarship" (*Renaissance Eloquence*, 29). Fortunately, that observation is far less accurate now than it was in 1983. The serious study of Renaissance rhetoric is beginning to overtake the casual references. While the "passion for formal rhetoric" that dismayed C. S. Lewis has not altogether returned, the place of rhetoric in the modern academy continues to expand. The study of Renaissance rhetoric, in particular, has benefited from the growing interest both in the history of rhetoric and in the renewed inquiry into humanism. These two developments obviously intersect in the study of Renaissance rhetoric. It is increasingly unusual, though not unheard of, for any serious literary, cultural, or educational study of the Renaissance to ignore the intellectual contributions of rhetoricians.

One indication of the new maturity of this field is the extent of the scholarship that was excluded from this chapter. It was necessary, in the interests of concision, to omit a large number of excellent studies. For example, *Rhetorica*, the journal of the International Society for the History of Rhetoric, has published essays on the Renaissance in nearly every issue, and most of these could not be included here. While the necessity to exclude so many studies caused me considerable discomfort, it is surely a good sign that the scholarship in Renaissance rhetoric cannot be easily surveyed.

There is, of course, much that remains to be done. In the first edition of *The Present State* I lamented the shortage of critical editions and English translations of basic texts. Despite recent editions of Rainolds, Hobbes, Cox, and others, this problem remains a serious one. In particular, the paucity of English translations has made it difficult to evaluate fully the contributions of the northern European humanists to the development of English rhetoric. Comparatively little is known about the writings of Melanchthon, Sturm, Susenbrotus, Vives, or Vossius. Yet all of these writers were known in England and were sources of vernacular rhetorics. If more were known about these men and their ideas, the task of determining the influence of Ramism in England would be less difficult. After all, most of these figures preceded Ramus and spread similar doctrines about rhetoric and logic. Indeed, it might be most appropriate, for the sixteenth century at least, to examine the development of English rhetoric in concert with the study of northern European humanism.

Another unmet goal, but one that eventually must be achieved, is the completion of a truly comprehensive history of Renaissance rhetoric. With regard to Britain, Howell's *Logic and Rhetoric in England, 1500–1700* comes very close to this goal, but even it is incomplete insofar as the literary dimensions of rhetoric are excluded. Nor is there a Continental history that transcends national boundaries and literatures. There is, as yet, no work comparable in scope to George Kennedy's *The Art of Persuasion in Greece* (Princeton: Princeton University Press, 1963) and *The Art of Rhetoric in the Roman World* (Princeton: Princeton University Press, 1972) or to James J. Murphy's *Rhetoric in the Middle Ages* (Berkeley: University of California Press, 1974). Such a comprehensive history, when it comes, will help scholars to see Renaissance rhetoric as an intellectual mosaic, rather than as bits and pieces of antiquarian information.

I am confident the necessary editions, translations, specialized studies, and broad histories will be forthcoming, for the study of Renaissance rhetoric is clearly accelerating. The Renaissance was concerned with the recovery of texts and finding ways to make those texts meaningful in new situations. This process of recovery is, of course, what the contemporary study of rhetoric is about. Rhetoric is no longer "the greatest barrier between us and our ancestors," but neither has the barrier been completely removed. If we can continue to learn what rhetoric did for our ancestors, we will know with greater certainty what it can do for us.

Bibliography

This bibliography is by no means complete. However, the citations are sufficient for a rather thorough introduction to the rhetoric of the Renaissance. For the convenience of the reader, the organization of the bibliography parallels that of the essay. Only those primary sources available in facsimiles or modern editions are listed. Citations for less common works can be found in the bibliographies included in section II. Common sources of facsimile reprints are abbreviated as follows:

SFR: Gainesville, Fla.: Scholars' Facsimiles and Reprints.

EngLing: English Linguistics 1500–1800: A Collection of Facsimile Reprints. Edited by R. C. Alston. Menston, Eng: Scolar Press.

EngEx: The English Experience: Its Record in Early Printed Books Published in Facsimile. New York: Da Capo Press.

Works identified by these abbreviations are all facsimile reproductions. Other editions are modern imprints.

I. Primary Sources

A. Collected Works

Bacon, Francis, *The Collected Works of Francis Bacon*. Edited by James Spedding, Robert Leslie Ellis, and Douglas Denon Heath. 14 vols. London: Longmans, 1857–1874.

British and Continental Rhetoric and Elocution. Sixteen microfilm reels. Ann Arbor: University Microfilms, 1953.

Erasmus, Desiderius. *Collected Works of Erasmus. Literary and Educational Writings 2: De Copia, De Ratione Studii*. Edited by Craig R. Thompson. Toronto: University of Toronto Press, 1978.

Hobbes, Thomas. *The English Works of Thomas Hobbes of Malmsbury*. Edited by Sir William Molesworth. 11 vols. London: J. Bohn, 1839–1845.

Murphy, James J., ed. *Renaissance Rhetoric: A Microfiche Collection of Key Texts A.D. 1472–1602*. Elmsford, N.Y.: Microforms International, 1987.

B. Individual Treatises

Blount, Thomas, *The Academie of Eloquence* (1654). EngLing, no. 296, 1971.

Bulwer, John. *Chirologia: or the Natural Language of the Hand (and) Chironomia: or the Art of Manual Rhetoric* (1644). Edited by James W. Cleary. Carbondale: Southern Illinois University Press, 1974.

Cox, Leonard, *The Arte or Craft of Rhetoryke* (1530?). Edited by Frederic

Ives Carpenter. 1899. Reprint: Folcroft, Pa.: Folcroft Press, 1969; Norwood, Pa.: Norwood Editions, 1975.

———. EngEx, no. 862, 1977.

Day, Angel. *The English Secretorie* (1586). Edited by Robert O. Evans. SFR, 1967.

———. EngLing, no. 29, 1967.

Dugard, William. *Rhetorices elementa* (1648). EngLing, no. 365, 1972.

Farnaby, Thomas. *Index rhetoricus* (1625). EngLing, no. 240, 1970.

Fenner, Dudley. *The Artes of Logike and Rhetorike* (1584). In *Four Tudor Books on Education*, edited by Robert D. Pepper, 151–80. SFR, 1966.

Fraunce, Abraham. *The Arcadian Rhetorike* (1588). Edited by Ethel Seaton. Oxford: Basil Blackwell, 1950.

———. EngLing, no. 176, 1969.

Hawes, Stephen. *The Pastyme of Pleasure* (1517). Edited by William Edward Mead. London: Oxford University Press, 1928.

Hobbes, Thomas. *Brief of the Arte of Rhetorique*. In *The Rhetorics of Thomas Hobbes and Bernard Lamy*. Edited by John Harwood. 1986.

Hoskins, John. *Directions for Speech and Style* (1599?). Edited by Hoyt Hudson. Princeton: Princeton University Press, 1935.

Leon, Judah Messer. *The Book of the Honeycomb's Flow*. Edited and translated by Isaac Rabinowitz. Ithaca: Cornell University Press, 1983.

Peacham, Henry. *The Garden of Eloquence* (2d ed., 1593). Edited by William G. Crane. SFR, 1954.

———. EngLing, no. 267, 1971.

Poole, Joshua. *Practical Rhetorik* (1663). EngLing, no. 341, 1972.

Puttenham, George. *The Art of English Poesie* (1589). Edited by Gladys Doidge Willcock and Alice Walker. Cambridge: Cambridge University Press, 1936.

———. EngLing, no. 110, 1968.

Rainolds, John. *John Rainolds's Oxford Lectures on Aristotle's Rhetoric*. Edited and translated by Lawrence D. Green. 1986.

Rainolde, Richard. *The Foundacion of Rhetorike* (1563). Edited by Francis R. Johnson. SFR (New York), 1945.

———. EngEx, no. 91, 1969.

———. EngLing, no. 347, 1972.

Ramus, Peter. *Arguments in Rhetoric against Quintilian* (1549). Translated by Carole Newlands and James J. Murphy. DeKalb: University of Northern Illinois Press, 1983.

Sherry, Richard. *A Treatise of Schemes and Tropes* (1550). Edited by Herbert W. Hildebrandt. SFR, 1961.

Smith, John. *The Mysterie of Rhetorique Unvail'd* (1657). EngLing, no. 205, 1969.

Vives, Juan Luis. *Vives: On Education: A Translation of the De Tradendis Disciplinis* (1531). Translated by Foster Watson, 1913. Totowa, N.J.: Rowman and Littlefield, 1971.

Wilson, Thomas. *The Arte of Rhetorique* (1553). Edited by G. H. Mair. Oxford: Clarendon Press, 1909.

———. Edited by Robert Hood Bowers. SFR, 1962.

———. EngEx, no. 206, 1969.

———. Edited by Thomas J. Derrick. New York: Garland Press, 1982.

II. Bibliographies

Alston, R. C. *A Bibliography of the English Language from the Invention of Printing to the Year 1800*. 20 vols. Vol. 6: *Rhetoric, Style, Elocution, Prosody, Rhyme, Pronunciation, Spelling Reform*. Ilkley: James Press, 1974.

Murphy, James J. *Renaissance Rhetoric: A Short Title Catalogue of Works on Rhetorical Theory from the Beginning of Printing to A.D. 1700, with Special Attention to the Holdings of the Bodleian Library, Oxford. With a Select Basic Bibliography of Secondary Works on Renaissance Rhetoric*. New York: Garland, 1981.

Stanford, Charles L. "The Renaissance." In *Historical Rhetoric: An Annotated Bibliography of Selected Sources in English*, edited by Winifred Bryan Horner, 111–84. Boston: G. K. Hall, 1980.

III. Rhetoric and Humanism

Bolgar, R. R. *The Classical Heritage and Its Beneficiaries*. Cambridge: Cambridge University Press, 1954.

Gray, Hanna H. "Renaissance Humanism: The Pursuit of Eloquence." *Journal of the History of Ideas* 24 (1963). Reprinted in *Renaissance Essays from the Journal of the History of Ideas*, edited by Paul O. Kristeller and Philip P. Wiener, 192–216. New York: Harper and Row, 1968.

Kahn, Victoria. *Rhetoric, Prudence, and Skepticism in the Renaissance*. Ithaca: Cornell University Press, 1985.

Kristeller, Paul Oskar. *Renaissance Thought and Its Sources*. Edited by Michael Mooney. New York: Columbia University Press, 1979.

Monfasani, John. *George of Trebizond: A Biography and a Study of His Rhetoric and Logic*. Columbia Studies in the Classical Tradition, 1. Leiden: E. J. Brill, 1976.

———. "Humanism and Rhetoric." In *Renaissance Humanism: Foundation, Forms, and Legacy*, vol. 3: *Humanism and the Disciplines*, edited by

Albert Rabil, Jr., 171–235. Philadelphia: University of Pennsylvania Press, 1988.

Seigel, Jerrold. *Rhetoric and Philosophy in Renaissance Humanism: The Union of Eloquence and Wisdom, Petrarch to Valla.* Princeton: Princeton University Press, 1968.

Struever, Nancy S. *The Language of History in the Renaissance: Rhetoric and Historical Consciousness in Florentine Humanism.* Princeton: Princeton University Press, 1970.

Yates, Frances A. *The Art of Memory.* Chicago: University of Chicago Press, 1966.

IV. National Surveys and Comprehensive Studies

Atkins, J. W. H. *English Literary Criticism: The Renascence.* London: Methuen, 1947.

Baldwin, Charles Sears. *Renaissance Literary Theory and Practice: Classicism in the Rhetoric and Poetic of Italy, France, and England, 1400–1600.* Edited with introduction by Donald Lemen Clark. New York: Columbia University Press, 1939.

Clark, Donald Lemen. *Rhetoric and Poetry in the Renaissance: A Study of Rhetorical Terms in English Renaissance Literary Criticism.* New York: Columbia University Press, 1922.

Crane, William Garrett. *Wit and Rhetoric in the Renaissance: The Formal Basis of Elizabethan Prose Style.* New York: Columbia University Press, 1937.

Fumaroli, Marc. *L'âge de l'éloquence: Rhétorique et "res literaria" de la Renaissance au seuil de l'époque classique.* Geneva: Librairie Droz, 1980.

García Berrio, Antonio. *Formación de la teoría literaria moderna.* 2 vols. Madrid: Cupsa, 1977; Murcia: University of Murcia, 1980.

Howell, Wilbur S. *Logic and Rhetoric in England, 1500–1700.* Princeton: Princeton University Press, 1956.

———. *Poetics, Rhetoric, and Logic: Studies in the Basic Disciplines of Criticism.* Ithaca: Cornell University Press, 1975.

Murphy, James J., ed. *Renaissance Eloquence: Studies in the Theory and Practice of Renaissance Rhetoric.* Berkeley: University of California Press, 1983.

Sonnino, Lee A. *A Handbook to Sixteenth-Century Rhetoric.* New York: Barnes and Noble, 1968.

Vickers, Brian. *Classical Rhetoric in English Poetry.* 1970. Reprint: Carbondale: Southern Illinois University Press, 1990.

———. *In Defence of Rhetoric.* Oxford: Clarendon Press, 1988.

———. "Rhetorical and Anti-Rhetorical Tropes: On Writing the History of Elocution." In *Comparative Criticism: A Year Book*, edited by E. S. Schaffer, 3:105–32, 316–22. Cambridge: Cambridge University Press, 1981.

Weinberg, Bernard. *A History of Literary Criticism in the Italian Renaissance.* 2 vols. Chicago: University of Chicago Press, 1961.

V. Specialized Studies

A. Rhetoric and Logic

Ashworth, E. J. *Language and Logic in the Post-Medieval Period.* Boston: D. Reidel, 1974.

Cogan, Marc. "Rodolphus Agricola and the Semantic Revolutions of the History of Invention." *Rhetorica* 2 (1984): 163–94.

Lechner, Sister Joan Marie, O.S.U. *Renaissance Concepts of the Commonplaces: An Historical Investigation of the General and Universal Ideas Used in All Argumentation and Persuasion with Special Emphasis on the Educational and Literary Tradition of the Sixteenth and Seventeenth Centuries.* New York: Pageant Press, 1962.

McNally, James R. "Prima pars dialecticae: The Influence of Agricolan Dialectic upon English Accounts of Invention." *RQ* 21 (1968): 166–77.

————. "Rudolph Agricola's *De inventione dialecticae libri tres*: A Translation of Selected Chapters." *SM* 34 (1967): 393–422.

Meerhof, Kees. *Rhétorique et poétique au XVIe siècle en France: Du Bellay, Ramus et les autres.* Leiden: E. J. Brill, 1986.

Nelson, Norman E. *Peter Ramus and the Confusion of Logic, Rhetoric, and Poetry.* University of Michigan Contributions in Modern Philology, no. 2. Ann Arbor: University of Michigan Press, April 1947.

Ong, Walter, S.J. *Ramus, Method, and the Decay of Dialogue: From the Art of Discourse to the Art of Reason.* Cambridge: Harvard University Press, 1958.

————. *Ramus and Talon Inventory: A Short-Title Inventory of the Published Works of Peter Ramus (1515–1572) and of Omer Talon (ca. 1510–1562) in their Original and in their Variously Altered Forms with Related Material: 1. The Ramist Controversies: A Descriptive Catalogue. 2. Agricola Check List: A Short-Title Inventory of Some Printed Editions and Printed Compendia of Rudolph Agricola's "Dialectical Invention" ("De inventione dialectica").* Cambridge: Harvard University Press, 1958.

————. *Rhetoric, Romance, and Technology: Studies in the Interaction of Expression and Culture.* Ithaca: Cornell University Press, 1971.

Sharrat, Peter. "The Present State of Studies on Ramus." *Studi Francesi*, no. 47–48 (1972): 201–13.

————. "Recent Work on Peter Ramus (1970–1986)." *Rhetorica* 5 (1987): 7–58.

B. Rhetoric, Poetics, and Drama

Altman, Joel B. *The Tudor Play of the Mind: Rhetorical Inquiry and the Development of Elizabethan Drama*. Berkeley: University of California Press, 1978.

Cope, Jackson I. "Ramist Implications." In his *The Metaphoric Structure of* Paradise Lost, 27–49. Baltimore: Johns Hopkins University Press, 1962.

Hardison, O. B., Jr. *The Enduring Monument: A Study of the Idea of Praise in Renaissance Literary Theory and Practice*. Chapel Hill: University of North Carolina Press, 1962.

Joseph, Sister Miriam, C.S.C. *Rhetoric in Shakespeare's Time: Literary Theory of Renaissance Europe*. 1947. Reprint: New York: Harcourt, Brace & World, 1962.

Kallendorf, Craig. *In Praise of Aeneas: Virgil and Epideictic Rhetoric in the Early Italian Renaissance*. Hanover, N.H.: University Press of New England, 1989.

Kinney, Arthur F. *Humanist Poetics: Thought, Rhetoric, and Fiction in Sixteenth-Century England*. Amherst: University of Massachusetts Press, 1986.

McDonald, Charles O. *The Rhetoric of Tragedy: Form in Stuart Drama*. Amherst: University of Massachusetts Press, 1966.

McManamon, John M., S.J. *Funeral Oratory and the Cultural Ideals of Italian Humanism*. Chapel Hill: University of North Carolina Press, 1989.

Patterson, Annabel M. *Hermogenes and the Renaissance: Seven Ideas of Style*. Princeton: Princeton University Press, 1970.

Rix, Herbert David. *Rhetoric in Spenser's Poetry*. Pennsylvania State College Studies, no. 7. State College: Pennsylvania State College, 1940.

Sloane, Thomas O. *Donne, Milton, and the End of Humanist Rhetoric*. Berkeley: University of California Press, 1985.

Taylor, Warren. *Tudor Figures of Rhetoric*. Whitewater, Wis.: Language Press, 1972.

Trimpi, Wesley. *Ben Jonson's Poems: A Study of the Plain Style*. Palo Alto: Stanford University Press, 1962.

Trousdale, Marion. *Shakespeare and the Rhetoricians*. Chapel Hill: University of North Carolina Press, 1982.

Tuve, Rosemond. *Elizabethan and Metaphysical Imagery: Renaissance Poetic and Twentieth-Century Critics*. Chicago: University of Chicago Press, 1947.

Vickers, Brian. "Epideictic and Epic in the Renaissance." *NLH* 14 (1983): 497–537.

C. Sacred Oratory

Blench, J. W. *Preaching in England in the Late Fifteenth and Sixteenth Centuries: A Study of English Sermons 1450–c. 1600.* Oxford: Basil Blackwell, 1964.
Chamberlin, John S. *Increase and Multiply: Arts-of-Discourse Procedure in the Preaching of Donne.* Chapel Hill: University of North Carolina Press, 1976.
Herr, Alan F. *The Elizabethan Sermon: A Survey and a Bibliography.* 1940. Reprint: New York: Octagon Books, 1969.
Mitchell, W. Fraser. *English Pulpit Oratory from Andrewes to Tillotson: A Study of Its Literary Aspects.* 1932. Reprint: New York: Russell & Russell, 1962.
Shuger, Debora K. *Sacred Rhetoric: The Christian Grand Style in the English Renaissance.* Princeton: Princeton University Press, 1988.

D. Rhetoric and Education

Abbott, Don Paul. "Rhetoric and Writing in Renaissance Europe and England." In *A Short History of Writing Instruction from Ancient Greece to Twentieth-Century America,* edited by James J. Murphy, 95–120. Davis, Calif.: Hermagoras Press, 1990.
Baldwin, T. W. *William Shakspere's Small Latine and Lesse Greeke.* 2 vols. Urbana: University of Illinois Press, 1944.
Bland, D. S. "Rhetoric and the Law Student in Sixteenth-Century England." *SP* 54 (1957): 506–8.
Clark, Donald Lemen. *John Milton at St. Paul's School: A Study of Ancient Rhetoric in English Renaissance Education.* New York: Columbia University Press, 1948.
Grafton, Anthony, and Lisa Jardine. *From Humanism to the Humanities: Education and the Liberal Arts in Fifteenth- and Sixteenth-Century Europe.* Cambridge: Harvard University Press, 1986.
Watson, Foster. *The English Grammar Schools to 1660: Their Curriculum and Practice.* 1908. Reprint: London: Frank Cass, 1968.
Woodward, William H. *Studies in Education during the Age of the Renaissance 1400–1600.* 1906. Reprint: Cambridge: Cambridge University Press, 1924.

E. Rhetoric and Science

Adolph, Robert. *The Rise of Modern Prose Style.* Cambridge: MIT Press, 1968.

Croll, Morris W. *Style Rhetoric, and Rhythm: Essays by Morris W. Croll.* Edited by J. Max Patrick and Robert O. Evans, with John M. Wallace and R. J. Schoeck. Princeton: Princeton University Press, 1966.

Jardine, Lisa. *Francis Bacon: Discovery and the Art of Discourse.* Cambridge: Cambridge University Press, 1974.

Jones, Richard Foster. *Ancients and Moderns: A Study of the Battle of the Books.* Washington University Studies—New Series. Language and Literature—no. 6. St. Louis, 1936.

———. *The Seventeenth Century: Studies in the History of English Thought and Literature from Bacon to Pope.* Palo Alto: Stanford University Press, 1951.

———. *The Triumph of the English Language: A Survey of Opinions Concerning the Vernacular from the Introduction of Printing to the Restoration.* Palo Alto: Stanford University Press, 1953.

Stephens, James. *Francis Bacon and the Style of Science.* Chicago: University of Chicago Press, 1975.

———. "Rhetorical Problems in Renaissance Science." *PR* 8 (1975): 213–29.

Vickers, Brian. *Francis Bacon and Renaissance Prose.* Cambridge: Cambridge University Press, 1968.

———. "The Royal Society and English Prose Style: A Reassessment." In *Rhetoric and the Pursuit of Truth: Language Change in the Seventeenth and Eighteenth Centuries*, by Brian Vickers and Nancy S. Struever, 3–76. Los Angeles: Clark Memorial Library, 1985.

Wallace, Karl R. *Francis Bacon on Communication and Rhetoric or: The Art of Applying Reason to the Imagination for the Better Moving of the Will.* Chapel Hill: University of North Carolina Press, 1943.

Williamson, George. *The Senecan Amble: A Study in Prose Form from Bacon to Collier.* 1951. Reprint: Chicago: University of Chicago Press, 1966.

4

THE EIGHTEENTH CENTURY

Winifred Bryan Horner
and Kerri Morris Barton

Introduction

Our description of the scholarship in eighteenth-century rhetoric closely resembles the report from the first edition of this book because the research continues to be scarce and primarily limited to description. However, we are optimistic about the potential and persuaded of the need for continuing scholarly attention to an age so full of rhetorical activity. In this essay, we will first briefly outline the period before turning to our report on the scholarship and to our suggestions for future work.

The eighteenth century was an important turning point in the history of intellectual thought, and that turning point is clearly evidenced in the rhetoric of the period. The eighteenth century marks the end of a long tradition of rhetoric that had its beginning in Greece in the fifth century B.C. and that for twenty centuries dominated philosophic thought and the established institutions of church and government. It also marks the start of a new tradition that branched out into the varied fields of study that we know in modern scholarship as logic, semiotics, literary criticism, oral interpretation, and linguistics, to name only a few.

Scholars speak of the "decline" of rhetoric in the eighteenth century, but actually it was a decline in name only. Rhetoric as the study of human communication survived under other names, and as the basic concepts changed focus the terminology changed as well. The actual effects of these changes were far-reaching as rhetoric spread over a number of disciplines in the nineteenth- and twentieth-century academic communities.

One of the major changes in eighteenth-century rhetoric was the shift in interest from oral to written language. In an upwardly mobile society, the new merchant class conducted many of its affairs by letter. Consequently, the emphasis in education and rhetoric was bound to be on written language, with important effects on literature, some of which are still not fully understood. A second closely allied change was the separation of poetry and rhetoric. In the first half of the eighteenth century, scholars still saw poetry as part of rhetoric, but after 1850 poetry was isolated. Another change in rhetorical practice arising out of the new nationalism, primarily at the Scottish universities, was the use of English models rather than classical ones. This practice eventually brought about the rise of English studies. The emphasis was on a practical education. Another change that originated in the Renaissance and matured in the eighteenth century was the shift from logic as learned communication to logic as a system of inquiry. At the same time the scientific method forced the shift from deductive to inductive reasoning.

Of all the changes, the most significant was the shift from rhetoric's emphasis on speakers and the generative aspects of texts to an emphasis on readers and their interpretations of texts. Resulting in part from the epistemological and philosophical movements of the period, this shift in focus eventually led to the great critical theories of the late nineteenth and twentieth centuries.

In the eighteenth century, rhetoric was not the business of literary scholars and schoolteachers alone. It was the business of all people of learning. One cannot see the names of Joseph Priestley, Adam Smith, Robert Hartley, Thomas Sheridan, and Edmund Burke as authors of rhetorical treatises and dismiss the subject as unimportant or speak of "decline." Rhetoric was the business of the great thinkers of the period, and in eighteenth-century rhetoric one must think in terms of basic and important change.

Certainly eighteenth-century rhetoric, particularly as it developed in Scotland, had profound effects on education, not only in Scotland but in the United States and eventually in England as well. Rhetoric within the belletristic movement, under such men as George Campbell and Hugh Blair, has shaped our study of literature and composition today.

The important changes that occurred in rhetorical theory in the eighteenth century and their long-term effects are reflected in the origin and development of the words *literature* and *psychology*. The first occurrence of the word *literature*, cited in the *Oxford English Dictionary*, in the modern sense of "writing which has claim to consideration on the ground of beauty of form or emotional effect," was 1812, and the editors note, "This sense is of very recent emergence in both France and England." The first citation for the word *psychology* is 1693, and the second is 1748 from David Hartley's *Observations on Man*, in which he defined it as "the theory of the Human Mind."

The words in their modern sense were nonexistent before the eighteenth century because the concepts of literature and psychology as we know them now simply did not exist. It is the study of the mind as applied to literature—story and poetry as they developed in writing—that formed the new rhetorical theory of the eighteenth century. It was these two developing concepts, literature and psychology, that made the century so important, not only in rhetoric but in all humanistic studies.

In this essay, we will begin by considering the state of the primary works of rhetoric and continue with a description of the general secondary scholarship for the period. The next section will cover the epistemological and psychological theories as background for a consideration of the four main movements—Neo-Classicism; The Old Rhetoric, which will cover Logic and Stylistic Rhetoric; Elocution; and Belletristic Rhetoric. Each section on the main movements will include the primary figures, their works, and the secondary scholarship. We will not consider the Continental rhetorics of the period, and we will include only English-language scholarship about the period. In conclusion, we will consider possibilities for future directions in scholarship.

The State of the Primary Works

Except for new editions of previously published works and a newly discovered manuscript, the state of the primary works has changed little in the past six or seven years. Many of the minor rhetorical works of the eighteenth century survived through just one or two printings and are now available only in rare-book rooms in the larger libraries. Occasionally one can find old copies of books from the period still on library shelves. One of the authors discovered a 1773 edition of John Herries's *The Elements of Speech* in the open stacks of the University of Missouri–Columbia library. Its fairly new binding disguised the value of the edition.

In 1978 James Irvine provided a bibliography that details the manuscripts available in the Scottish archives on eighteenth-century rhetoric and moral philosophy lectures. This was followed in 1987 by his bibliography of George Campbell manuscripts. However, since libraries will not lend items from their rare-book collections on interlibrary loan, often the only source for many of these materials is microfilm or microprint. *The Eighteenth-Century British and Continental Rhetoric and Elocution Microfilms* (hereafter abbreviated as *BCRE*), published by the University Microfilms in Ann Arbor, Michigan, in 1953, contains a large number of eighteenth-century works. Another source of microfilm materials is the *Eighteenth-Century Sources for the Study of English Literature and Culture* (hereafter abbreviated as *ECS*), a collection of works relevant to the literary, artistic, and cultural milieu of eighteenth-century England, published in 1979 by Micrographics, 11, Keswick, Virginia. A third source is the microprint series *Early American Imprints 1639-1800* (hereafter abbreviated as *EAI*), which is based on a bibliography by Charles Evans (1941-1959). It is a monumental collection of microprints that includes editions of every existent book, pamphlet, and broadside printed in the United States between 1639 and 1800.

Although these micro materials make otherwise difficult to obtain treatises more readily available to students and scholars, they can be difficult to work with. The print is faded and some manuscripts are incomplete with pages missing, and one does not know if this is a flaw in the original text or whether it occurred in the reproduction process. Finally, micro materials are a poor substitute for the original for the scholar who needs to read closely. Consequently, scholars have welcomed the fine modern editions and facsimile reprints. Lord Kames's *Elements of Criticism* is available in a facsimile edition (1970) published by Georg Olms Verlag. But the series that finally saves eighteenth-century British rhetoric from relative obscurity is the Southern Illinois University Press Series Landmarks in Rhetoric and Public Address, edited by David Potter. Students and scholars interested in eighteenth-century rhetoric would do well to start with these editions and their excellent introductions by outstanding scholars. Included are the lectures of John Lawson; Adam Smith; George Campbell, in a 1988 edition; Joseph Priestley; and Hugh Blair. Unfortunately, the last two are now out of print, but the other editions are still available. Dennis R. Bormann has discovered a previously unknown lecture by Campbell, the *Cura Prima*, which is reproduced in the *Quarterly Journal of Speech* (1988). In addition, the Clarendon Press offers an edition of Smith's *Lectures on Rhetoric and Belles Lettres* (1983) as part of the Glasgow Edition of the Works and Correspondence of Adam Smith. It is edited by J. C. Bryce and is based on the original notes, but with normalized punctuation and grammar.

The lectures of some eighteenth-century rhetoricians are available only through manuscripts. Thus we have only Eric Wm. Skopec's "Thomas Reid's Rhetorical Theory: A Manuscript Report" (1978) for information on the unpublished manuscript of Thomas Reid's lectures on rhetoric, and for William Leechman, who lectured at the University of Glasgow from 1743 to 1766, we have only Herman Cohen's report (1968) of a student's notes of his lectures. The only record that we have of Adam Smith's lectures is also from student notes. Since prizes were awarded in the Scottish universities for the best sets of student notes, and since most professors dictated their lectures, these notes are quite accurate. They are carefully done in clear handwriting, with title pages and tables of contents. They serve as reliable sources, but, of course, are not available to the ordinary scholar or student.

The forthcoming *Eighteenth-Century Short Title Catalogue* will include everything published in the English language in the eighteenth century in Great Britain and the country's possessions. With headquarters in the British Library, the catalog has been collected from libraries all over the world. It should provide a reliable listing of books on rhetoric published during the century. The North American editor is Henry Schneider. If more of the primary materials were readily available, the study of eighteenth-century rhetoric might well take on new excitement.

General Works

The single most important general study for eighteenth-century rhetoric continues to be Wilbur Samuel Howell's *Eighteenth-Century British Logic and Rhetoric* (1971). Its analyses of the major works on logic and rhetoric of the eighteenth century make it indispensable for any student of the period. Howell analyzes individual works in great detail; for example, his treatment of John Ward's lectures at Gresham College covers forty-one pages. He describes Gresham College and Ward's history of the college, then examines Ward's position in the eighteenth century and the influence of his lectures, *A System of Oratory*, both within their own time and within the English rhetorical tradition as a whole. He describes in great detail Ward's treatment of *inventio, dispositio*, and *elocutio*, or style, and concludes with short analyses of Ward's lectures on pronunciation and memory. He ends his detailed discussion of Ward's *A System of Oratory* by documenting the work's reprintings, but he concludes, "When it first appeared in 1759, it already belonged not to its time or to the immediate future but to the past" (124). Such full treatment is accorded to all of the texts Howell mentions, and he covers most of the major works of rhetoric and logic for the period.

Howell's introductory essays to each chapter can be read by themselves as an overview of eighteenth-century logic and rhetoric. The second and third chapters treat the old logic and the old rhetoric of the period. The introduction to chapter 4 is an account of the elocutionary movement, the first pages of chapter 5 outline seven dominant traits of the new logic, and chapter 6 discusses the six points of opposition to the old rhetoric held by the new rhetoricians. In chapter 7, Howell summarizes his discussion of eighteenth-century rhetoric and logic by reviewing the main trends of the time.

Although Stephen H. Browne's "The Gothic Voice in Eighteenth-Century Oratory" arises from an investigation of "Fox's East India Bill," a speech by Edmund Burke, his comments have provocative implications for the rhetoric of the century and for the historical writing about the century. Scholars have, of course, always struggled with labels by which to characterize the eighteenth century. Browne proposes that instead of labels we explore rhetoric in terms of the "voices" that express this age and suggests that gothicism shaped much of eighteenth-century oratory through its "themes, images, and strategies of appeal" (227). Browne's use of voice offers a fitting and particularly rhetorical approach to historiography. "A given voice—provisionally defined here as the individuated and public expression of a general aesthetic sensibility—will accordingly be understood as a mode of representation. The Gothic voice, for example, may be treated as giving expression not only to issues and arguments, but to the expectations of the audience to which it speaks. To describe an age of oratory in terms of a significant voice, therefore, is to affirm the rhetorical unity of language and auditor" (228). Browne's is an important and distinctive study.

A lengthy overview of the rhetoric of the period, but from an entirely different perspective, is found in chapters 7–11 of Robert T. Oliver's *The Influence of Rhetoric in the Shaping of Great Britain* (1986). Oliver discusses speeches by Edmund Burke and others based on their political significance in the history of Great Britain, arguing, "The history of public speaking in Great Britain is an account of individual influence. It portrays the persuasive leadership of men, and some few times of women, who used their exceptional skill in speech to point the way for their fellow countrymen through times of uncertainty and morasses of difficulties" (304). Oliver's assessment of the speeches is helpful because it both considers the speeches in their political context and indicates the effectiveness of the speeches as evidenced by the actions they helped produce. He establishes a standard by which to judge oratory—not always considered by rhetoricians—and the consequences of spoken language.

Richard B. Sher's *Church and University in the Scottish Enlightenment: The Moderate Literati of Edinburgh* (1985) examines the "culture of the literati of eighteenth-century Scotland," in which many of the rhetorics of the period were produced. He seeks to place the Scottish Enlightenment "within an international framework of values and beliefs while still allowing for the uniqueness of the Scottish experience" (11). Sher considers not only the intellectual history of the period but also the cultural history at large, an important and helpful approach.

Two other authors who give an excellent and shorter overview of eighteenth-century rhetoric are James L. Golden and Edward P. J. Corbett in their introduction to *The Rhetoric of Blair, Campbell, and Whately* (1968). This book has been reprinted by Southern Illinois University Press with updated bibliographies (1990). The first three pages provide a succinct but informative view of rhetoric from Corax through Francis Bacon. The authors see the eighteenth century as the beginning of the period of modern or new rhetoric and outline four responses to the classical tradition. The first held that there was no need to alter the teachings of Aristotle, Cicero, and Quintilian; the second was the development of the elocutionary movement; and the third was the rise of belletristic rhetoric. The "most revolutionary response," according to these authors, was the "emergence of the psychological-philosophical theories of public address" (9). In discussing this response, Golden and Corbett review the epistemological theories embodied in the works of John Locke, Francis Hutcheson, David Hume, David Hartley, Thomas Reid, and Adam Smith. They review the theory of ideas developed by Locke, which led him to question the value of the syllogism. His support and that of Hume for faculty psychology and the doctrine of associationism had serious implications for the rhetorical theories of Campbell, Blair, and Whately. Locke, Hume, and Hartley concentrated on mental faculties, while Hutcheson focused on moral faculties. The philosophy of common sense advocated by the Scottish School of Philosophy, primarily by Thomas Reid, is also explained. This short overview is a succinct description of the epistemological ideas of the age that were so important for the development of the new rhetoric. Golden and Corbett conclude with the response of Campbell, Blair, and Whately to these four trends.

A short introductory article covering the latter half of the century is Douglas Ehninger's "Dominant Trends in English Rhetorical Thought, 1750–1800" (1952). Like Golden and Corbett, Ehninger identifies the dominant trends as classicism, psychological-epistemological theories of discourse, elocutionism, and belletristic rhetoric, and he discusses the primary proponents of each movement. The article is useful as an introduction to the period, but its brevity necessarily limits it. A new work that discusses the period broadly is Winifred Bryan Horner's "The Roots of Writing Instruction" (1990), a helpful discussion of the Dissenting Academies in the universities in England and Scotland.

Paul G. Bator provides insight into the establishing of the Regius Chair of Rhetoric and Belles Lettres at Edinburgh, suggesting that the chair was created because of political rather than educational concerns: "a select group of ministers belonging to what was known as the Moderate party, shifted among themselves for ecclesiastical and educational positions of power and authority" (58).

A dissertation that covers the same period is Harold F. Harding's "English Rhetorical Theory, 1750–1800" (1937). It contains a thorough bibliography of school textbooks, essays, lectures, and other treatises on rhetoric and a section on the connections between rhetoric and literary criticism. However, Harding's thesis that eighteenth-century rhetoricians were largely unaware of the philosophical and aesthetic theories of the day is open to serious question.

A work of general importance, particularly for the student of English literature, is P. W. K. Stone's *The Art of Poetry 1750–1820* (1967). Again, this work covers the second half of the period, but it reviews the relationship, not widely recognized, between eighteenth-century poetry and rhetoric. Stone maintains that the eighteenth-century "art of poetry" was, in fact, derived from rhetorical ideas on the nature of language and the relationship between the writer and his reader. He traces the broadening of the concept of rhetoric during the period until it can no longer be distinguished from literary theory or criticism. It was this joining of classical rhetoric with empirical philosophy that resulted in rhetoric becoming a theory of criticism during the latter half of the eighteenth century.

Finally, Horner's bibliography of eighteenth-century rhetoric (1980) lists the primary works of the period and the secondary scholarship. All entries are annotated. The primary works are listed chronologically, and the annotations can be read as an overview of the period. The introduction summarizes the principal movements and classifies the primary works according to the major trends of the century.

Eighteenth-Century Epistemology and Philosophy

During the eighteenth century, there were developments in philosophic thought that had serious and enduring consequences on the rhetoric and literature of the period. These ideas, growing out of the empiricism of Locke, Berkeley, and Hume, profoundly affected English and American education, and these effects are still apparent in the second half of the twentieth century. Though Thomas Reid may be a minor figure in the current of philosophic thought, his philosophy of common sense has exerted a major influence on educational philosophy for over two hundred years.

A clear understanding of eighteenth-century rhetoric and discourse during the second half of the century must rest on an understanding of the psychological and philosophical theories of the day, for it was out of these that the theories of rhetoric and the concept of taste as the human faculty of artistic judgment developed. For this reason, the major figures and their works are included here.

John Locke's *Essay Concerning Human Understanding*, published in 1690, soon became the major influence in English education. With its emphasis on sensation and reflection, it changed the way people viewed the world and the way rhetoricians viewed discourse. Its importance in eighteenth-century thought cannot be overestimated. Together with David Hume's *A Treatise of Human Nature* (1739–1740) and his *An Enquiry Concerning the Human Understanding* (1748), it reduced the world to the limits of the human mind and its contents. Edward P. J. Corbett discusses the influence of John Locke in his "John Locke's Contribution to Rhetoric" (1982), and John J. Richetti explores the "rhetorical movements" of Locke's *Essay* in chapter 2 of his *Philosophical Writing: Locke, Berkeley, Hume* (1983). In addition, Elizabeth Hedrick explores the effects that Locke's views of language had on Samuel Johnson's *Dictionary* (1987).

Out of this school came the work of David E. Hartley, *Observations on Man, His Frame, His Duty, and His Expectations* (1749), which introduced the doctrine of the association of ideas first developed by David Hume in *An Enquiry*. Hartley was not an innovator; he was a compiler. He was also a doctor, and his work is a mixture of physiology and psychology. For the eighteenth century, the study of the mind was new; psychology was the new "ology" of the period. Following Hartley, Joseph Priestley was the primary exponent of associationism in the field of rhetoric.

Faculty psychology was derived from the work of Christian Wolff, a German, who wrote *Psychologia Empirica* in 1732 and *Psychologia Rationalis* in 1734. In these works, he suggested that the mind is divided into sections with separate and distinct capacities. The idea had no scientific basis, but modern left brain/right brain research gives support to this view of the human mind. Faculty psychology was widely influential, especially on the work of George Campbell (1776) and Hugh Blair (1783).

Common-sense philosophy, developed in Aberdeen, is usually associated with Thomas Reid and had its fullest development in his *An Inquiry into the Human Mind, on the Principles of Common Sense* (1764). This work answered the skepticism of Locke and Hume, and in it Reid asserted that all philosophy must finally be rooted in common sense. Knowledgeable people must finally believe in their senses and know that the things they see, hear, and touch are real. From this basis of common sense there arises a human agreement as to the nature of the world. An excellent overview of this Scottish philosophy is that of S. A. Grave (1960).

A general overall treatment of these psychological and philosophical approaches to language is Gordon McKenzie's *Critical Responsiveness: A Study of the Psychological Current in Later Eighteenth-Century Criticism* (1949). McKenzie describes the psychological approaches to literary criticism that became current in the latter half of the eighteenth century and the shift in emphasis from the external work of art to the literary experience of the reader. This shift is represented in the eighteenth-century interest in the concept of taste, the faculty of artistic appreciation. All the major figures in the second half of the eighteenth century devoted parts of their treatises on rhetoric to this concept. Walter Jackson Bate traces the sources of taste and its influence on romanticism in his *From Classic to Romantic: Premises of Taste in Eighteenth-Century England* (1946). An article by D. W. Jefferson, "Theories of Taste in the Eighteenth Century" (1938–1943), outlines three theories of taste that were current in the period. Herman Cohen (1958) summarizes Hugh Blair's theory of taste and compares it to those of Lord Kames, Edmund Burke, and Sir Joshua Reynolds. John Waite Bowers (1961) also compares Blair's theory of taste—unfavorably—with those of Edmund Burke and Immanuel Kant, asserting that Blair's theory is without value, because it changes with each age. Another comparative treatment is that of Phil Dolph, who in "Taste and *The Philosophy of Rhetoric*" (1968) relates Campbell's view to those of other eighteenth-century figures. Taste is an obsolete concept and in modern speech is usually preceded with *in bad*. Nevertheless, for the eighteenth century it was useful and important in the analysis and evaluation of art of all kinds. The word is no longer in use, but the eighteenth-century concept has grown and thrived within the realm of critical theory.

Neo-Classical Rhetorics

The classical tradition was strong in the first half of the eighteenth century. There were numerous Latin editions of the works of Quintilian, Longinus, and the *Ad Herennium*, as well as Aristotle's *Rhetoric*. From the Continent, there were *L'Art de Parler* by Bernard Lamy and François Fénelon's *Dialogues sur Eloquence*, both of which had their English translations. Fénelon was translated by William Stevenson in

1722, and there is a modern translation by Wilbur Samuel Howell with an excellent introduction (1951). The two major English neo-classical works of the century, John Lawson's *Lectures Concerning Oratory Delivered in Trinity College, Dublin* and John Ward's *A System of Oratory, Delivered in a Course of Lectures, Publicly Read at Gresham College*, were published in 1758 and 1759 in London.

The first is available in an excellent facsimile edition published by Southern Illinois University Press (1972). Lawson delivered these lectures at Trinity College, Dublin, where he held the Erasmus Smith Chair for nine years. They went through four printings in the eighteenth century. In publishing his lectures, Lawson established a custom followed by other eighteenth-century rhetoricians at other colleges—a custom that makes these lectures available to us today. The lectures are clearly in the Ciceronian tradition and embrace the full canon in a reaction to rhetoric as only stylistic ornamentation. Lawson was openly hostile to some of the ideas of his day and especially to the development of the elocutionary movement.

The introduction to the facsimile edition by E. Neal Claussen and Karl R. Wallace provides a biography of Lawson and some information on the lectures themselves. In summarizing the eight characteristics of the lectures, the authors state: "The Lectures were firmly established upon faculty psychology, but only as it is consistent with ancient usage" (xlii). Ray E. Keesey's "John Lawson's Lectures Concerning Oratory" (1953) provides a good description of the lectures' content, and he, like Claussen and Wallace, agrees that Lawson's work offered little that was new. The lectures were, in fact, not widely influential in eighteenth-century thought. Howell, however, in *Eighteenth-Century British Logic and Rhetoric* (1971), makes a convincing case that Lawson combined elements from both the old and the new rhetorics and includes him with Hume, Priestley, Blair, and Witherspoon in a discussion of what he calls the "Discordant Consensus" (613–94).

John Ward published his two-volume *A System of Oratory, Delivered in a Course of Lectures Publicly Read at Gresham College* in London in 1759. It was a work of 879 pages that Douglas Ehninger in "John Ward and His Rhetoric" (1951) regarded as the fullest restatement of the classical canon in the English language. These fifty-four lectures were published a year after their author's death but never went into a second edition. They are available on microfilm in *ECS*, roll 1, and in *BCRE*, reel 6, item 88. Adelbert Edward Bradley, Jr., in two articles derived largely from his 1955 dissertation on John Ward, analyzes Ward's treatment of *dispositio* and *inventio* (1957, 1959).

In "John Ward and His Rhetoric" Ehninger maintained that John

Ward's work exerted almost no influence on later rhetoricians, but in an important article on the influence of Ward on American rhetoric (1960), Ronald F. Reid argues that the statutes governing the Boylston Professor of Rhetoric and Oratory at Harvard were based on Ward's System. He traces the direct influence of Ward on Joseph McKean, but maintains that McKean's successor in the Boylston Chair, Edward T. Channing, "wrote in the tradition of the creative rhetorics of Campbell and Blair" (344). Thus, Reid concludes that McKean stands as a transitional figure in American rhetoric in somewhat the same manner that Ward does in English rhetoric.

A final note in the neo-classical tradition should be made of John Holmes's *The Art of Rhetoric Made Easy: In Two Books*, published in 1755 before either Lawson's or Ward's works. Written primarily for youth in grammar schools, it offers nothing new and closely follows the classical tradition. In 1786 it was combined with John Stirling's *A System of Rhetoric* and was influential for many years after its first printing. Less scholarly than the works of Ward or Lawson, Holmes and Stirling's treatise was widely circulated in both England and the United States, with its last edition in 1849 in Philadelphia. It is available on microfilm in the *BCRE*, reel 5, item 45.

The Old Rhetoric: Logics and Stylistic Rhetorics

There are two threads in eighteenth-century rhetoric that are remnants of important seventeenth-century trends. The first is the stylistic rhetorics that reduced rhetoric to a single office; the second is the logics that saw rhetoric as a theory of learned communication. During the eighteenth century, logic was finally separated from rhetoric as it became a theory of inquiry rather than a theory of communication. Nevertheless, during the first half of the period there were at least three logical treatises that still viewed logic as learned communication in the seventeenth-century tradition. Although not important in the intellectual thrust of eighteenth-century rhetoric, these works were popular and widely circulated and cannot be ignored.

A treatise that held to the old view of logic and that had at least five editions in Europe in the eighteenth century was Jean Pierre de Crousaz's *La Logique*, translated into English by John Henley in 1724 as *A New Treatise of the Art of Thinking*. Isaac Watts's *Logick; Or the Right Use of Reason in the Enquiry after Truth* (1725) defines logic as "the art of using reason well in our inquiries after Truth, and the Communication of it to others" (13). It went through numerous editions in England and America, and the 1789 Philadelphia sixteenth edition is available on microprint in the *EAI* series. It stands as one of the most popular textbooks of the eighteenth century.

A third important logic in the old tradition is William Duncan's "The Elements of Logick" (1748). In "The Declaration of Independence and Eighteenth-Century Logic" (1961), Wilbur Samuel Howell demonstrates the influence of this work on Thomas Jefferson and the Declaration of Independence. Like Watts's, Duncan's book went through many printings in England, Scotland, and the United States. First published anonymously in Dodsley's *The Preceptor*, it had eight London editions between 1748 and 1793.

All of these authors saw logic and rhetoric as closely related; however, by the end of the century, logic had become a theory of discovery—a method of inquiry in the new age of science—and had embarked on a life of its own separated from its rhetorical base.

The truncating of rhetoric into a system of figures of speech, so common in Renaissance rhetoric, was still evident in the eighteenth century, and books that were little more than a listing of schemes and tropes were still in circulation. Two of these are Anthony Blackwall's *An Introduction to the Classics* (1718) and Thomas Gibbons's *Rhetoric* (1767). No scholar of the eighteenth century can be unaware of the wide currency of these stylistic rhetorics, but by the end of the century they had begun to lose favor.

Elocution

General Works

When rhetoric was reduced to the fifth canon, which in the Latin doctrine was *pronuntiatio* or *actio*, it was finally reduced to voice and gesture. (Howell discusses these terms in *Eighteenth-Century British Logic and Rhetoric*, 147–51.) Developing, it is commonly assumed, as a result of criticism of public speaking, especially pulpit oratory, elocution came to hold a place of importance in lectures and handbooks both inside and outside the school curricula for well over two hundred years. As late as the 1920s, children in the United States and Great Britain studied elocution. Strange as the practice may seem now, the art of delivery with emphasis on accent, pitch, voice modulation, pause, timing, and gesture became, for many people in the eighteenth century, the whole of rhetoric. The textbooks that developed out of this movement seem ridiculous to modern scholars, but they were quite serious to the eighteenth-century student.

Probably the best discussion of the books and figures associated with the elocutionary movement is that in Howell's *Eighteenth-Century British Logic and Rhetoric* (143–203). The sources of the movement have interested a number of scholars, and Howell's "Sources of the Elocutionary Movement in England, 1700–1748" (1959) is incorporated into his book. He maintains that the movement grew out of the neoclassical rhetoric and was not consistent with the new rhetorics of the eighteenth century. Frederick W. Haberman, in "English Sources of American Elocution" (1954), acknowledges that the movement came out of the plea for improved public speaking but argues that voice and gesture were measurable physical phenomena and as such were appropriate matters for study in an age of science. G. P. Mohrmann also makes this point in his "The Language of Nature and Elocutionary Theory" (1966). Mohrmann, however, explores the roots of the elocutionary movement and discounts the idea that it arose out of criticisms of public address. Such criticisms, he maintains, had been mounted since the time of Cicero. He asserts that the method of science explains the methods of the elocutionists but not their intense interest in delivery. Mohrmann sees elocutionism as a natural outgrowth of the accepted epistemology and psychology of the period, tracing it particularly to the belief in natural language and Thomas Reid's common-sense philosophy. In another article (1965), Mohrmann argues for the influence of Kames on the elocutionary movement. In his *Elements of Criticism*, Kames either directly or indirectly, according to Mohrmann, foretold "all those postulates that were basic to elocutionary theory" ("Kames and Elocution," 203). Mohrmann further emphasizes the close personal and professional relationship between Thomas Sheridan and Kames, who had assisted in sponsoring Sheridan's lectures in Edinburgh in 1861. Finally, John Walker, Gilbert Austin, and lesser figures in the elocutionary movement openly acknowledged Kames's influence.

Warren Guthrie's "The Development of Rhetorical Theory in America, 1635–1850–V" (1951) provides, as background, an overview of the elocutionary movement in England, and his 1947 article titled "The Development of Rhetorical Theory in America, 1635–1850" discusses the influence of John Mason and Thomas Sheridan on rhetoric in six American colleges. Charles A. Fritz, in "From Sheridan to Rush: The Beginnings of English Elocution" (1930), also notes the influence of Joshua Steele, Thomas Sheridan, and John Walker on elocution as it was taught in American schools.

An article by Giles Wilkeson Gray, "What was Elocution?" (1960), defends eighteenth-century elocution theories and states, "The opprobrium heaped upon both theory and practice, at least as far as the originators of that theory, or those theories, may be concerned, has been undeserved" (1). Gray maintains that elocution fell from grace as it became divorced from content and associated only with reading—finally degenerating into "statue-posing" and "bird calls."

Walter J. Ong, S.J., in his 1972 review of Howell's *Eighteenth-Century British Logic and Rhetoric*, connects the rise of elocutionism with the demise of orality and rhetoric and the beginning of a literate society. He maintains, "The elocutionist movement . . . shows in striking ways how the oral management of knowledge, threatened ever since the invention of writing, was by now thoroughly debilitated. . . . By the close of the eighteenth century, orality as a way of life was in effect ended, and with it the old-time world of oratory, or, to give oratory its Greek name, rhetoric" (641). Ong's discussion is certainly the best conceived explanation of elocutionism.

Primary Works and Secondary Scholarship

Michel Le Faucheur's *Traitté de l'action de l'orateur*, first printed in 1657 at Paris, received its first English translation in 1702, and an anonymous pamphlet based on this translation, *Some Rules for Speaking and Action* (London, 1715), had five English editions. This publication marked the beginning of the elocutionary movement in England. Howell discusses subsequent translations of this work in his *Eighteenth-Century British Logic and Rhetoric* (164–81), and it is clear that it came out under at least three separate titles, *An Essay upon the Action of an Orator* (1702), *The Art of Speaking in Public or an Essay on the Action of an Orator* (1727), and *An Essay upon Pronunciation and Gesture* (1750). *The Art of Speaking in Public* is available on microfilm, *BCRE*, reel 4, item 42. John Mason's short treatise, *An Essay on Elocution or Pronunciation* (1748), only thirty-nine pages long, is one of the first English works on elocution. Now available on microfilm (*ECS*, roll 87), it went through four editions, the last in 1757.

Two other typical pamphlets of the period are the anonymous *An Essay on the Action Proper for the Pulpit* (1753) and James Burgh's *The Art of Speaking* (1761). The first, often attributed to John Mason and therefore often indexed under his name, treated *actio* alone, dividing it into the soon to become familiar voice and gesture. It had only one edition and offered practical advice to preachers. James Burgh's longer treatise was written for younger students and had eighteen editions, eleven of them American. Frederick W. Haberman states that Burgh "was read by Sheridan, paraphrased by Walker, anthologized by Scott, pirated by an American publisher, quoted by Austin, and recalled in one way or another by elocutionists for over a century" ("English Sources of American Elocution," 114). The nature of these "recalls" is discussed below.

Probably the best known figure in the elocutionary movement of the eighteenth century was Thomas Sheridan, father of the better-known Richard Sheridan, political figure, dramatist, and author of *The Rivals* and *The School for Scandal*. Thomas Sheridan was an actor in Dublin and London, but his main role was as an educator. His three-volume *British Education*, published in London in 1756, urges the revival of the lost art of oratory. He published three works on elocution, the most important of which is *A Course of Lectures on Elocution Together With Two Dissertations on Language* (1762), now available on microfilm (*BCRE*, reel 7, item 67). Sheridan delivered his lectures, according to Howell (*Eighteenth-Century British Logic and Rhetoric*, 233), at Oxford, Cambridge, London, Bath, Belfast, and Edinburgh. There were eighteen eighteenth-century editions with sections on articulation, accent, emphasis, pauses and stops, tones, and gestures. In the dissertations on language, Sheridan outlined his plan "to refine, ascertain, and reduce" the English language to a standard.

Sheridan is one of the few members of the elocutionary movement to excite much scholarly interest. He is often treated unsympathetically in biographies of his son, Richard Sheridan, but two accounts of his life put him in a more favorable perspective. One is Wallace A. Bacon's "The Elocutionary Career of Thomas Sheridan (1719–1788)" (1964), and the other is W. Benzie's *The Dublin Orator: Thomas Sheridan's Influence on Eighteenth-Century Rhetoric and Belles Lettres* (1972). Bacon discusses Sheridan's early life and theater career and his *British Education*, in which Sheridan argues "with missionary zeal" for oratory as a panacea. Bacon also covers Sheridan's relations with Samuel Johnson, who dubbed him Sherry-Derry, as well as Sheridan's *Lectures* and *Dictionary*. W. Benzie's book, which analyzes the major works mentioned above, demonstrates the farsightedness of Sheridan's views on education and emphasizes his influence on modern lexicography. Benzie establishes Sheridan as a member of the Natural School of elocution, as opposed to James Burgh, who is classified as the first member of the Mechanical School to issue instructions on how to express various states of emotion. Burgh treats pity in the following manner: "Pity, a mixed passion of love and grief, looks down upon distress with lifted hands; eyebrows drawn down; mouth open; and features drawn together" (*The Art of Speaking*, 24).

Joshua Steele, whose *An Essay Towards Establishing the Melody and Measure of Speech to be Expressed and Perpetuated by Peculiar Symbols* appeared in 1775, and John Walker, whose *Elements of Elocution* was published in 1781, were also members of the Mechanical School. Both works are available on microfilm (*BCRE*). Walker's widely circulated

text gives careful instructions for expressing certain passions by placement of hands and feet as well as by eye, nose, head, and eyebrow
movements. Steele presents a complicated notation system, somewhat
similar to musical notation, for recording intonation and rhythm patterns. In his 1953 article, John B. Newman argues for the influence of
Steele in the development of the Walker-Rush elocutionary movement
in America. Certainly this school found its culmination in the work of
Gilbert Austin in the nineteenth century.

One of the few disputes in eighteenth-century rhetorical scholarship
involves what came to be called "the burglarizing of James Burgh." The
dispute was initiated in a 1952 article by Wayland M. Parrish in which
he maintained that John Walker only reprinted with very slight revisions most of James Burgh's descriptions of the passions. In a 1965
article, Jack Hall Lamb defended Walker against additional charges of
plagiarizing from Steele, and in 1969 David H. Grover defended Walker
on all counts, maintaining that he acted as a synthesizer and compiler.
In 1976, Mary C. Murphy refuted Parrish's accusation against Walker
and maintained that Thomas Sheridan's essay on elocution, included in
the introduction to *A Rhetorical Grammar* (1781), is a direct copy of
James Burgh's *The Art of Speaking*. Murphy further maintained that
Thomas Sheridan, unlike Walker, who acknowledges Burgh, "took
credit for the essay by referring to himself in the Preface as 'I' and 'the
author'" (141).

A work that should be noted as influential in the United States is
Noah Webster's *An American Selection of Lessons in Reading and Speaking*,
first published in 1785. It contained a section on elocution and had a
wide circulation in the United States as a textbook. Charles Evans's
bibliography lists forty editions.

Belletristic Rhetoric

In the second half of the eighteenth century, rhetorical theory was
dominated by six men: Edmund Burke; Joseph Priestley; Henry Home,
Lord Kames; Adam Smith; George Campbell; and Hugh Blair. These
men introduced a new rhetoric and were influential in shifting the
emphasis from the creative act to the interpretive act and in opening
the way for the study of English literature in the nineteenth century.
This rhetoric marked the beginning of the theories of literary criticism
that developed so richly in the nineteenth and twentieth centuries.
Literary criticism would not have been possible without the new rhetoric, which, in turn, would never have come about without the philo-

sophical and psychological theories of the day. The eighteenth century opened up new realms in humanistic thought.

The works of these six men are all preserved and appear in modern editions. Kames, Priestley, and Blair are published in facsimile editions, and the Southern Illinois University Press edition of Campbell's *Philosophy of Rhetoric* is the first modern one of that important work. The lectures of Adam Smith (1762–1763) come down to us only through a set of student notes, which do not cover the full year. In an appendix to the Southern Illinois University Press edition, T. I. Rae explains that from the handwriting, the lectures appear to be notes taken by a student, "written at speed in the lecture room, and not a fair copy" (195). However, J. C. Bryce, editor of the Glasgow Edition of Smith's *Lectures*, asserts that two students were responsible for the notes and that they were transcribed outside class and based on in-class notations. Bryce "rule[s] out the possibility that the pages we have were written while the students listened" both because of the manuscript itself and because of Smith's reputed dislike of student note-taking (3–4).

The editors' introductions to the available editions of eighteenth-century belletristic rhetoric vary widely and will be discussed later. Four of the six sets are lectures first delivered in the city of Edinburgh, and their authors, Kames, Smith, Campbell, and Blair, were leaders in the Scottish Enlightenment. Edmund Burke was a Londoner, and Priestley was a lecturer at Warrington Academy in northwest England. Finally, many of them are better known for activities other than rhetoric, as I indicate below. It was an age in which the study of rhetoric was the concern of everyone, and these men made important contributions to that study.

Edmund Burke

Edmund Burke, noted statesman and conservative, was a figure of consequence in English political circles of the eighteenth century. He protested the restraint of trade and urged British reconciliation with the American colonies. Born in Ireland, he supported Irish interests as well. His treatise, *A Philosophical Enquiry into the Origin of our Ideas of the Sublime and the Beautiful*, which he started writing before he was nineteen, was published in 1756 when he was only twenty-seven. A second edition appeared in 1757 to which was added "An Essay on Taste." The work had forty-five editions, the last in 1958, edited with an introduction by James T. Boulton.

Burke defines taste as "that faculty or faculties of the mind, which are affected with, or which form a judgment of, the works of imagination and the elegant arts" (5). Burke represents his contemporaries in this view, but Herman Cohen points out that Burke does not specifically view taste as applied only to rhetoric (1958). It is for him a faculty for the appreciation of all the arts. Since Burke's career as a rhetor and a diplomat overshadows his career as a rhetorician, the secondary scholarship tends to concern itself with those aspects of his life. Consequently, his "Essay on Taste" is often treated only peripherally in its relationship to his other major works. Stephen H. Browne, however, discusses Burke's *Letter to a Noble Lord* and his "Fox's East India Bill" in terms of their rhetorical importance. The *Letter* demonstrates Burke's stance as a synthesis, which "negotiates . . . between philosophy's private and rhetoric's public realm" ("Edmund Burke's *Letter*," 216), and "Fox's East India Bill" expresses a gothic voice, characteristic of the century, as we discussed earlier. There is still little scholarship on Burke that focuses on his rhetorical contributions.

Joseph Priestley

Joseph Priestley, best known as the discoverer of oxygen, is important in the history of rhetorical theory for his *A Course of Lectures on Oratory and Criticism* (1777). Priestley delivered these lectures in 1762 at the age of twenty-nine at Warrington Academy, one of the important English dissenting academies. In his preface, Priestley supports the doctrine of the association of ideas and applies it to criticism. He acknowledges his debt to Lord Kames and John Ward but argues against the Scottish philosophy of common sense. Although Priestley included a section on elocution in his classroom lectures, it is not part of the published work. The lectures have had only five printings.

These lectures are described by Howell (*Eighteenth-Century British Logic and Rhetoric*, 632–47) and discussed in a lengthy introduction to the Southern Illinois University Press facsimile edition by Vincent M. Bevilacqua and Richard Murphy (1965). The introduction covers Priestley's life and works and the background of the lectures. Called upon to teach at Warrington Academy, according to his biographers, Priestley had no great fondness for his subject of language and belles lettres. He composed his lectures by drawing on a number of materials current at the time, including the lectures of John Ward, John Lawson, and Lord Kames. Therefore, the lectures are eclectic, with additions from Priestley's own ideas, particularly on associationism, which he readily applied to his subject.

In "Campbell, Priestley, and the Controversy Concerning Common Sense" (1964), Bevilacqua delineated the common sense/associationism controversy and the effect of that controversy on the rhetorical system of Priestley. A dissertation on Priestley by Ross Stafford North

(1957) examines Priestley's views on language and rhetoric in relation to eighteenth-century philosophic thought. Unfortunately, North does not appear to have done any additional work on Priestley.

Henry Home, Lord Kames

Henry Home, Lord Kames, was described by one critic as "having a finger in every bowl of porridge in Scotland" (Bushnell, "Lord Kames and Eighteenth Century Scotland," 252). His influence has already been noted in connection with Thomas Sheridan and Adam Smith. Certainly he was important in the age of enlightenment in Scottish thought and in the shift to literary criticism and belles lettres in rhetorical history.

Bevilacqua's dissertation (1961) presents a full account of Kames's rhetorical theory. He asserts that Kames saw human nature as the unifying principle for his rhetoric. Much of the dissertation appears in other articles by Bevilacqua listed in this bibliography. A more readily available source of information is Helen Whitcomb Randall's "The Critical Theory of Lord Kames" (1940–1941). Written prior to the discovery of Adam Smith's lecture notes, Randall's work cannot take into account the influence of Kames on Smith, but it provides a biography of Kames, a thirty-five-page analysis of *Elements of Criticism*, and a useful outline of the book's history with quotes from current reviews and letters. Appendixes contain an index of books and authors cited in Kames's work and a list of editions.

Arthur E. McGuinness's *Henry Home, Lord Kames* (1970) is a good summary of the man's life and work. Chapter 3 covers the *Elements*, and chapter 4 considers the alterations that Kames made in traditional rhetorical theory. Howell, in *Eighteenth-Century British Logic and Rhetoric*, does not give much attention to the *Elements of Criticism*, and Robert Voitle's introduction to the facsimile edition (1970) is brief. Randall's discussion is still the most thorough of this man who is known as the father of literary criticism.

Adam Smith

Adam Smith is best known to the world as an economist and only secondarily as a rhetorician. Smith lectured on rhetoric and belles lettres in the city of Edinburgh from 1748 to 1751. He then moved to the University of Glasgow, where he was professor of logic for one year and professor of moral philosophy until 1763. He appears to have delivered the same set of lectures in both professorships. His lectures on rhetoric are not available to us in their full form since Adam Smith ordered that they be destroyed before his death. Fortunately, in 1961, an edition of a student's notes was published with an introduction by John Lothian. The edition was hailed as one of the most valued discoveries of our time, but its impact, whether from imperfect copy or lack of interest, has been disappointing. The edition is incomplete (see discussion under The State of the Primary Works above) and difficult to work with since the individual lectures are only numbered with no titles to indicate their content. Bryce's introduction to the Glasgow Edition of the *Lectures* details the history of the manuscript and the content of the lectures and offers a contrast to Lothian's introduction.

Howell, in *Eighteenth-Century British Logic and Rhetoric* gives us additional insight into Smith's lectures as seen through the eyes of three of his contemporaries, John Millar, James Woodrow, and Hugh Blair, and further demonstrates their importance in the Scottish enlightenment (537–75). Lord Kames urged Smith to deliver these lectures in Edinburgh, and Smith was followed in that lectureship by Robert Watson, who left to continue the lectures at the University of St. Andrews, and by Hugh Blair, who was subsequently appointed first Regius Professor of Rhetoric and Belles Lettres at the University of Edinburgh. Thus Adam Smith's lectures set the pattern. Howell concludes, "Smith's rhetorical theory is remarkable for its originality, its validity, and its timeliness" (575).

Among Smith's biographers, there was speculation that he burned his lectures because they had been largely taken over by Hugh Blair. In his introduction to Blair's *Lectures*, Harold F. Harding asserts that plagiarism was not an issue but acknowledges that Blair was influenced by Smith in combining the study of belles lettres with that of rhetoric.

Two articles by Bevilacqua furnish excellent material both on the origins of Smith's lectures in eighteenth-century thought and on their influence on Lord Kames and Hugh Blair. "Adam Smith's Lectures on Rhetoric and Belles Lettres" (1965) is a careful analysis of the lectures and makes the point, now generally accepted, that "young Smith appears to have been the teacher and Blair and Kames the students" (59). The other article is "Adam Smith and Some Philosophical Origins in Eighteenth-Century Rhetorical Theory" (1968). In both articles Bevilacqua stresses that Smith reflected eighteenth-century thought more than classical theory and gave impetus to the Scottish belles lettres movement. Smith adapted a stylistic-belletristic view of rhetoric based on eighteenth-century views of ethics, aesthetics, and criticism.

Michael Carter (1988) and J. Michael Hogan (1984) offer less traditional readings of Smith's *Lectures*. Carter reconsiders the assumption that invention was absent from Smith's view of rhetoric, examining "Smith's explicit treatment of arrangement and style, which show that the belletristic version of these two rhetorical arts derived partly from invention" ("The Role of Invention in Belletristic Rhetoric," 4). Hogan asserts the importance of historiography in Smith's *Lectures*, nine of which are devoted to the topic, and notes that Smith advocates " 'indirect description' in historiography—a method emphasizing the emotions and sentiments of historical actors" ("Historiography and Ethics in Adam Smith's Lectures on Rhetoric," 77). Smith's view contradicts the notion of objectivity assumed by historians of his day.

There is one dissertation on "Adam Smith and Belles Lettres" (University of Mississippi, 1966) by Frank Morgan, Jr.

George Campbell

George Campbell's *The Philosophy of Rhetoric* (1776) is one of the most important rhetorical treatises in the eighteenth century. It was reprinted numerous times and used as a textbook in American colleges well into the nineteenth century. Its direct influence was impressive, but its indirect influence on theories of composition and rhetoric is immeasurable. Its "ends of discourse" still shape twentieth-century composition readers. A 1981 article by John Hagaman outlines the influence of *The Philosophy of Rhetoric* on contemporary invention. The *Philosophy* is available in a modern edition in the Southern Illinois University Press Landmark series with a new introduction by Lloyd F. Bitzer (1988).

Bitzer points out the importance of Campbell's concept of rhetoric as a "general art of discourse" (xiv). He discusses the features of common-sense philosophy, taking in turn Campbell's views on phenomenalism, empiricism, skepticism, sensationalism, and naturalism as well as his theory of human nature. Bitzer's new introduction also includes a description of Campbell's religious views and an assessment of their relevance to this theory of rhetoric (xlvii-li).

Campbell is well covered in rhetorical scholarship, although, with the exception of Howell's excellent account in *Eighteenth-Century British Logic and Rhetoric* (577–612), Hagaman's work cited above, and two other essays discussed below, much of the secondary scholarship is from the sixties. An excellent perspective on Campbell is in the introduction by Golden and Corbett to *The Rhetoric of Blair, Campbell, and Whately* (1968), mentioned earlier under the discussion of general works.

Bitzer has written one article on the influence of David Hume's philosophy on Campbell (1969) and another on Campbell's Doctrine of Evidence as depending on common-sense philosophy (1960). Dennis R. Bormann, in "Some 'Common Sense' about Campbell, Hume, and

Reid" (1985), refutes Bitzer's claim that Hume influenced Campbell, detailing the context within which Campbell wrote and emphasizing that the rhetorician was viewed by contemporaries as a member of the common-sense group, which was clearly opposed to Hume's skepticism.

Clarence W. Edney has also written a number of articles on Campbell, and his "George Campbell's Theory of Logical Truth" (1948) discusses Campbell's logic. Howell takes up the same subject in his discussion of Campbell's view of the syllogism (*Eighteenth-Century British Logic and Rhetoric*, 401–8). Bevilacqua, in two articles titled "Campbell, Vico, and the Rhetorical Science of Human Nature" (1983), contrasts Campbell's views of rhetoric with Vico's, suggesting that Campbell's philosophy tends toward the scientific. He concludes "that to study rhetoric narrowly as a scientific rather than as an imaginative poetic concern" is to view it incompletely (8).

George Campbell has probably aroused more scholarly interest than any other figure in eighteenth-century rhetoric besides Hugh Blair, and a lively dispute about whether he was a true innovator or only another rhetorician in the classical tradition took place in scholarship in the late 1960s. Douglas Ehninger initiated the discussion with his dissertation (Ohio State, 1949) and two articles from that work (1955, 1963) in which he asserts that Campbell, as well as Blair and Whately, was an anticlassicist and actually reversed that trend in eighteenth-century theory by placing the emphasis on the hearer rather than on the speaker or text. In "George Campbell and the Classical Tradition" (1963), Douglas McDermott supports Ehninger's 1963 position by saying, "In linking rhetoric with the psychological principles of the human mind Campbell may indeed, be said to bring us into new country" (409).

The spring 1968 *Journal of the Western Speech Association* was devoted to a symposium on "The Rhetorical Theory of George Campbell." This issue includes four papers written by Dominic La Russo, Herman Cohen, G. P. Mohrmann, and Phil Dolph, edited with an introduction by Ernest Ettlich. La Russo takes issue with Ehninger and McDermott by asserting that *The Philosophy of Rhetoric* "might well be characterized as an eclectic work which is a product not of a great and original mind, but rather the shadow of a zeitgeist that reflects a social and intellectual transition" (86). Ehninger answered La Russo in the fall 1968 issue by reasserting his 1963 position that Campbell is revolutionary as the first influential rhetorician to point the science in a new direction, taking as his starting point the mental processes of the listener. The other two papers in the symposium treat the psychological and philosophical bases of Campbell's rhetoric.

In 1983 the *Rhetoric Society Quarterly* published a series of responses called "The Most Significant Passage in George Campbell's *Philosophy of Rhetoric,*" including short essays of two to five pages by Lloyd F. Bitzer, Don M. Burks, Herman Cohen, John Hagaman, and Howard Ulman. Each of the writers focuses on the psychological theories and motivations of Campbell's rhetoric and offer informative, but brief, explications of passages from the *Rhetoric.*

Stuart C. Brown and Thomas Willard explore the role of audience in Campbell's rhetoric in their "George Campbell's Audience: Historical and Theoretical Considerations" (1990), proposing that "Campbell's philosophical and religious background led him to take particular interest in the way that rhetoric could explain the workings of the mind, and how to use language to affect other minds, to propose, in fact, one of the first modern instances of audience awareness" (page numbers not available).

Hugh Blair

In his "Editor's Introduction" to the Southern Illinois University Press facsimile edition of Hugh Blair's *Lectures on Rhetoric and Belles Lettres* (1965), Harold F. Harding remarks that there were "scores of thousands of copies" of these lectures "printed over scores of years" (v). Certainly Hugh Blair was by far the most influential of the eighteenth-century Scottish rhetoricians and his work the most widely disseminated, not only in Scotland but in England and the United States as well. The lectures were published in 1783 and reprinted, abstracted, condensed, edited, adapted, and reissued in textbooks for over one hundred years on both sides of the Atlantic. More than any other person, Blair turned the compass of rhetoric in new directions; more than any other name, his is associated with those new directions.

The best introduction to Blair is Harold F. Harding's introduction to the facsimile edition. He discusses the relationship between Blair and Adam Smith and investigates the suggestion by John Rae, Smith's biographer, that Blair's lectures are only a reproduction of Smith's. In this introduction, Harding puts to rest the presumption that Smith burned his lectures to save the reputation of his friend. He points out the similarities in the two sets of lectures, but concentrates on the notable differences. He gives Smith credit for combining the study of rhetoric and belles lettres, an idea followed by all of Smith's successors and one that had important educational repercussions. Harding asserts that it is natural that Blair's lectures gained fame for him since he "spent a lifetime teaching his subject, practicing it, and, indeed, trying to save souls by it" (xxv). Smith's lecture notes, however, "come down to us two centuries later as a literary curiosity." Harding concludes his essay with the statement that Blair was neither "original, comprehensive, nor profound," but that his popularity continued unabated in American classrooms until 1828 (xxv).

Warren Guthrie (1948) and Clarence W. Edney (1954) trace the influence of Blair on American rhetoric, and both maintain that American rhetoric was dominated by Blair and Campbell until the middle of the nineteenth century. Robert M. Schmitz has provided a book-length study of Blair (1948), valuable for its list of editions, adaptions, and anthologies of Blair's works, but it precedes John Lothian's discovery of the Adam Smith notes and therefore is of limited value. Don Paul Abbott, in "The Influence of Blair's *Lectures* in Spain" (1989), reminds us of the importance of Blair not only in Britain and America, but on the Continent as well. Blair's lectures were translated into Spanish and used as a university text in Spain for over twenty-five years.

James L. Golden is the most authoritative voice on Hugh Blair, and his introduction with Edward P. J. Corbett to *The Rhetoric of Blair, Campbell, and Whately* (1968) furnishes an excellent picture of Hugh Blair in the context of the eighteenth century. Golden, together with Ehninger, has written two articles, one on the extrinsic sources (1956), the other on the intrinsic sources of Blair's popularity (1955). Blair's lectures were delivered for twenty-four years in Edinburgh, went through more than seventy editions, and were translated into French, Italian, Spanish, and German. These two articles seek a rationale for this popularity.

A recent discussion of Blair appears in "The Most Significant Passage in Hugh Blair's *Lectures on Rhetoric and Belles Lettres*," compiled by Lois Einhorn (1987) and based on a panel at the Speech Communication Association convention. The article includes short essays, none longer than four pages, by Herman Cohen, Edward P. J. Corbett, S. Michael Halloran, Charles W. Kneupper, Eric Skopec, and Barbara Warnick. Kneupper's essay is the most innovative of the group, suggesting the importance of Blair's work for modern readers and recommending that we "inquire what they can mean to us theoretically, humanistically, heuristically, and rhetorically today" (Einhorn, 296). Specifically, Kneupper explores the importance of the metaphor of "transfusion" in Blair's sixth lecture (294).

Future Directions

Scholarship in eighteenth-century historical rhetoric for the past six years is characterized both by its paucity and by its narrow approach. Two levels of historical inquiry, recovery and description, predominate, and a third level, scholarly conversation, is noticeably absent.

(See Stephen North's discussion in chapter 3 of *The Making of Knowledge* for a similar critique of this phenomenon.) Recovery, a basic level of research, has been done well and with many important implications. Scholars have spent much of their time recovering documents, recording their existence in bibliographies, and preparing corrected editions for wider dissemination. This kind of work in particular is invaluable. Without reliable texts and a sound knowledge of what documents and artifacts exist, no valid interpretive or theoretical work can begin. Another level, that of describing and interpreting texts and artifacts, has also occupied historians of rhetoric. Through interpretations and descriptive essays, scholars establish theories, suggest possibilities and trends, and follow traditions. In fact, most of the secondary citations in this essay are devoted to interpretation and description. Many of the important works (such as Howell's *Eighteenth-Century British Logic and Rhetoric*) construct narrative accounts that clarify a time period or text. These necessary and important levels of work have established the foundation for scholarly discussion, from which writers can wrestle with the larger issues and exchange strong discourse. This kind of exchange is, however, missing in the scholarship, and our discussion of future directions arises out of this context. First, we will consider historical recovery; second, interpretation and description; and, third, scholarly dialogue.

It is exciting when previously unknown texts are uncovered. Dennis Bormann's publication of George Campbell's *Cura Prima* (1988) is evidence that this work continues and evidence, perhaps, that historians never finish completely with recovery. Bormann and John M. Lothian before him are truly "scholar adventurers," whose success is furnished by providence and persistence. We can hardly suggest what unknown texts or artifacts are waiting for detection. A different kind of recovery, however, is demonstrated in Roy Porter's "The Language of Quackery in England, 1660–1800" (1987), which explores the language used by "quacks," medical practitioners who sold their abilities in the open market, and discusses the "language of salesmanship and the culture of health in early modern England" (78–79). This may seem, at first, an inconsequential essay on the periphery of rhetorical concerns, but we suggest that Porter has highlighted an important and heretofore unexplored aspect of eighteenth-century rhetoric—popular rhetorics, not the rhetorics of the institution or of the educated person, but of the mass of humanity. As classical rhetoricians have explored the importance of the sophists and as twentieth-century scholars are interested in television, advertising, and other genres, perhaps scholars of the eighteenth century should uncover the popular, and perhaps more pervasive, rhetorics of that period.

As demonstrated by the significantly few new bibliographical citations included in this essay, there is still necessary work to be done in the area of the interpretation of texts. As Horner suggested in the first edition of this work, there is much that needs consideration and exploration. Certainly the shift in the eighteenth century from a study of the speaker and the text to a study of the reader and the interpretation of the text deserves close scrutiny. This shift occurred also in the study of music. How did the invention of print, the dissemination of books, and the rise of the universities affect this shift? Any student interested in human communication cannot help but be intrigued by the shift from oral to written language in rhetorical theory in the eighteenth century. As we've already suggested, students of this period need to consider the effects of increased literacy and even of the preoccupation with style on the people of the day. How did these changes affect the culture? And how did the culture at large affect these rhetorics? What subversive rhetorics, if any, ran counter to received opinions of the day and how were these transacted? Scholars are more attentive to tracing the strands of classical, usually Aristotelian, rhetorics in the eighteenth century, but have not, for instance, traced the sophistic notion of *dissoi logoi*. What other rhetorical traditions, besides the Aristotelian, are found in the eighteenth century?

Scholars have been virtually inattentive to this period since the 1960s. This suggests something about our practice of writing and interpreting the history of eighteenth-century rhetoric. We should explore historiographical questions, then, in response to this dearth of scholarship. Why do we resist these rhetorics? What epistemologies and ethics and ideologies do eighteenth-century thinkers sanction that we resist? And, as Kneupper mused, how can these ideas inform our own work?

Until we explore these questions and others about the rhetoric of the eighteenth century, we will be unable to bring our monologues into the parlor of academic conversation and exchange. We must accumulate a body of strong and variegated scholarship in order to create interest in an age that is clearly and abundantly rich with possibility. Scholars such as Howell, Golden and Corbett, and others have laid too solid and important a foundation for us to abandon the construction of eighteenth-century rhetorical histories.

Bibliography

Primary Works

Anon. *The Art of Speaking in Public or an Essay on the Action of an Orator.* London, 1727.

——. *An Essay on the Action Proper for the Pulpit.* London, 1753.

——. *An Essay upon Pronunciation and Gesture, Founded upon the Best Rules and Authorities of the Ancients.* London, 1750.

——. *An Essay upon the Action of an Orator; As to his Pronunciation and Gesture, Useful both for Divines and Lawyers, and necessary for all Young Gentlemen, that study how to Speak well in Publick.* London, 1702.

Blackwall, Anthony. *An Introduction to the Classics.* London, 1718. Reprinted with revisions and additions in Robert Dodsley, The Preceptor. London, 1748.

Blair, Hugh. *Lectures on Rhetoric and Belles Lettres.* 2 vols. London and Edinburgh, 1783. Reprinted in facsimile: Harold F. Harding, ed. 2 vols. Southern Illinois University Press Series, Landmarks in Rhetoric and Public Address, edited by David Potter. Carbondale: Southern Illinois University Press, 1965.

Burgh, James. *The Art of Speaking.* London, 1761.

Burke, Edmund. *A Philosophical Enquiry into the Origin of our Ideas of the Sublime and the Beautiful,* 1757. Edited with an introduction and notes by James T. Boulton. Notre Dame: University of Notre Dame Press, 1958.

Campbell, George. *The Philosophy of Rhetoric.* London, 1776. Reprinted: New Edition, London, 1850. New Edition reprinted in facsimile: Lloyd F. Bitzer, ed. Southern Illinois University Press Series, Landmarks in Rhetoric and Public Address, edited by David Potter. Carbondale: Southern Illinois University Press, 1988.

Crousaz, Jean Pierre de. *A New Treatise of the Art of Thinking; Or, a Compleat System of Reflections, Concerning the Conduct and Improvement of the Mind.* 2 vols. London, 1724.

Duncan, William. "The Elements of Logick." In Robert Dodsley, *The Preceptor.* London, 1748.

Gibbons, Thomas. *Rhetoric.* London, 1767.

Hartley, David E. *Observations on Man, His Frame, His Duty, and His Expectations.* London, 1749.

Holmes, John. *The Art of Rhetoric Made Easy: In Two Books.* London, 1755.

Home, Henry, Lord Kames. *Elements of Criticism.* 3 vols. Edinburgh, 1762. Reprinted in facsimile: 3 vols. Anglistica and Americana, A

Series of Reprints Selected by Bernhard Fabian et al. Hildesheim and New York: Georg Olms Verlag, 1970.

Hume, David. *An Enquiry Concerning the Human Understanding*. London, 1748.

———. *A Treatise of Human Nature*. 3 vols. London, 1739–1740.

Lawson, John. *Lectures Concerning Oratory Delivered in Trinity College, Dublin*. London, 1758. Reprinted in facsimile: E. Neal Claussen and Karl R. Wallace, eds. Southern Illinois University Press Series, Landmarks in Rhetoric and Public Address, edited by David Potter. Carbondale: Southern Illinois University Press, 1972.

Locke, John. *Essay Concerning Human Understanding*. London, 1690.

Mason, John. *An Essay on Elocution or Pronunciation*. London, 1748.

Priestley, Joseph. *A Course of Lectures on Oratory and Criticism*. London, 1777. Reprinted in facsimile: Vincent M. Bevilacqua and Richard Murphy, eds. Southern Illinois University Press Series, Landmarks in Rhetoric and Public Address, edited by David Potter. Carbondale: Southern Illinois University Press, 1965.

Reid, Thomas. *An Inquiry into the Human Mind, on the Principles of Common Sense*. London and Edinburgh, 1764.

Sheridan, Thomas. *A Course of Lectures on Elocution Together with Two Dissertations on Language*. London, 1762.

Smith, Adam. *Lectures on Rhetoric and Belles Lettres Delivered in the University of Glasgow by Adam Smith Reported by a Student in 1762–63*. Edited by John M. Lothian. Southern Illinois University Press Series, Landmarks in Rhetoric and Public Address, edited by David Potter. Carbondale: Southern Illinois University Press, 1977.

———. *Lectures on Rhetoric and Belles Lettres*. Edited by J. C. Bryce. Glasgow Edition of the Works and Correspondence of Adam Smith, edited by A. S. Skinner. New York: Clarendon Press, 1983.

Steele, Joshua. *An Essay Towards Establishing the Melody and Measure of Speech to be Expressed and Perpetuated by Peculiar Symbols*. Piccadilly, 1775.

Walker, John. *Elements of Elocution. Being the Substance of a Course of Lectures on the Art of Reading: Delivered at several Colleges in the University of Oxford*. London, 1781.

Ward, John. *A System of Oratory, Delivered in a Course of Lectures Publicly Read at Gresham College*. 2 vols. London, 1759.

Watts, Isaac. *Logick; Or the Right Use of Reason in the Enquiry after Truth*. London, 1725.

Webster, Noah. *An American Selection of Lessons in Reading and Speaking*. Philadelphia, 1785. Reprinted: 3d ed., Greatly Enlarged. Philadelphia, 1787.

Secondary Works

Abbott, Don Paul. "The Influence of Blair's Lectures in Spain." *Rhetorica* 7 (Summer 1989): 275–89.

Ayling, Stanley. *Edmund Burke: His Life and Opinions*. London: John Murray, 1988.

Bacon, Wallace A. "The Elocutionary Career of Thomas Sheridan (1719–1788)." *SM* 31 (March 1964): 1–53.

Bass, Jeff D. "An Efficient Humanitarianism: The British Slave Trade Debates, 1791–1792." *QJS* 75 (1989): 152–65.

Bate, Walter Jackson. *From Classic to Romantic: Premises of Taste in Eighteenth-Century England*. Cambridge: Harvard University Press, 1946.

Bator, Paul G. "The Formation of the Regius Chair of Rhetoric and Belles Lettres at the University of Edinburgh." *QJS* 75 (1989): 40–64.

Benzie, W. *The Dublin Orator: Thomas Sheridan's Influence on Eighteenth-Century Rhetoric and Belles Lettres*. Leeds Texts and Monographs, n.s., edited by A. C. Cawley and R. C. Alston. Leeds: University of Leeds School of English, 1972.

Bevilacqua, Vincent M. "Adam Smith and Some Philosophical Origins of Eighteenth-Century Rhetorical Theory." *MLR* 63 (1968): 559–68.

———. "Adam Smith's Lectures on Rhetoric and Belles Lettres." *SSL* 3 (July 1965): 41–60.

———. "Campbell, Priestley, and the Controversy Concerning Common Sense." *SSJ* 30 (Winter 1964): 79–98.

———. "Campbell, Vico, and the Rhetorical Science of Human Nature." *RSQ* 13 (1983): 5–12.

———. "Philosophical Assumptions Underlying Hugh Blair's Lectures on Rhetoric and Belles Lettres." *WS* 31 (Summer 1967): 150–64.

———. "Philosophical Influences in the Development of English Rhetorical Theory: 1748 to 1783." *Proceedings of the Leeds Philosophical and Literary Society, Literary and Historical Section* 12 (April 1968): 191–215.

———. "Philosophical Origins of George Campbell's Philosophy of Rhetoric." *SM* 32 (March 1965): 1–12.

———. "The Rhetorical Theory of Henry Home, Lord Kames." Ph.D. dissertation, University of Illinois at Urbana-Champaign, 1961.

———. "Two Newtonian Arguments Concerning 'Taste.'" *PQ* 47 (October 1968): 585–90.

Bevilacqua, Vincent, and Richard Murphy. "Editors' Introduction." In *A Course of Lectures on Oratory and Criticism*, by Joseph Priestley, lix–lxix. Carbondale: Southern Illinois University Press, 1965.

Bitzer, Lloyd F. "Editor's Introduction." In *The Philosophy of Rhetoric*, by

George Campbell, vi–li. Carbondale: Southern Illinois University Press, 1988.

———. "Hume's Philosophy in George Campbell's Philosophy of Rhetoric." *PR* 2 (Summer 1969): 139–66.

———. "A Re-Evaluation of Campbell's Doctrine of Evidence." *QJS* 46 (April 1960): 135–40.

Bitzer, Lloyd F., et al. "The Most Significant Passage in George Campbell's Philosophy of Rhetoric." *RSQ* 13 (1983): 13–27.

Blakemore, Steven. "Burke and the Fall of Language: The French Revolution as Linguistic Event." *ECSt* 17 (Spring 1984): 284–307.

Bormann, Dennis R. "George Campbell's Cura Prima on Eloquence—1758." *QJS* 74 (1988): 35–51.

———. "Some 'Common Sense' about Campbell, Hume, and Reid: The Extrinsic Evidence." *QJS* 71 (1985): 395–421.

Boulton, James T. "Editor's Introduction." In *A Philosophical Enquiry into the Origin of our Ideas of the Sublime and the Beautiful*, by Edmund Burke, xv–cxxvii. Notre Dame: University of Notre Dame Press, 1958.

Bowers, John Waite. "A Comparative Criticism of Hugh Blair's Essay on Taste." *QJS* 47 (December 1961): 384–89.

Bradley, Adelbert Edward, Jr. "John Ward's Theory of Rhetoric." Ph.D. dissertation, Florida State University, 1955.

———. "The *Inventio* of John Ward." *SM* 26 (March 1959): 56–63.

———. "John Ward's Concept of *Dispositio*." *SM* 24 (November 1957): 258–63.

Brown, Stuart C., and Thomas Willard. "George Campbell's Audience: Historical and Theoretical Considerations." In *A Sense of Audience in Written Communication*, edited by Gesa Kirsch and Duane Roen. Beverly Hills, Calif.: Sage, 1990.

Browne, Stephen H. "Edmund Burke's Letter to a Noble Lord: A Textual Study in Political Philosophy and Rhetorical Action." *CM* 55 (September 1988): 215–29.

———. "The Gothic Voice in Eighteenth-Century Oratory." *CQ* 36 (Summer 1988): 227–36.

Bryce, J. C. "Introduction." In *Lectures on Rhetoric and Belles Lettres*, by Adam Smith, 1–37. New York: Clarendon Press, 1983.

Bushnell, Nelson S. "Lord Kames and Eighteenth Century Scotland." *SSL* 10 (April 1973): 241–54.

Carter, Michael. "The Role of Invention in Belletristic Rhetoric: A Study of the Lectures of Adam Smith." *RSQ* 18 (Summer 1988): 3–13.

Clark, Gregory. "Timothy Dwight's Moral Rhetoric at Yale College, 1795–1817." *Rhetorica* 5 (Spring 1987): 149–61.

Claussen, E. Neal, and Karl R. Wallace. "Editor's Introduction." In

Lectures Concerning Oratory Delivered in Trinity College, Dublin, by John Lawson, ix–liii. Carbondale: Southern Illinois University Press, 1972.

Cohen, Herman. "Hugh Blair's Theory of Taste." *QJS* 44 (October 1958): 265–74. Reprinted in *Readings in Rhetoric*, edited by Lionel Crocker and Paul A. Carmack, 333–49. Springfield, Ill.: Charles C. Thomas, 1965.

————. "The Mirror Image: Eighteenth Century *Elocutio* and the New Philosophy." *WS* 26 (Winter 1962): 22–27.

————. "William Leechman's Anticipation of Campbell." *WS* 32 (Spring 1968): 92–99.

Corbett, Edward P. J. "John Locke's Contribution to Rhetoric." In *The Rhetorical Tradition and Modern Writing*, edited by James J. Murphy, 73–84. New York: Modern Language Association, 1982.

Covino, William A. *The Art of Wondering: A Revisionist Return to the History of Rhetoric*. Portsmouth, N.H.: Boynton/Cook, 1988.

Dolph, Phil. "Taste and *The Philosophy of Rhetoric*." *WS* 32 (Spring 1968): 104–13.

Edney, Clarence W. "English Sources of Rhetorical Theory in Nineteenth-Century America." In *A History of Speech Education in America*, edited by Karl R. Wallace, 80–104. New York: Appleton-Century-Crofts, 1954.

————. "George Campbell's Theory of Logical Truth." *SM* 15 (1948): 19–32.

————. "Hugh Blair's Theory of Dispositio." *SM* 23 (March 1956): 38–45.

Ehninger, Douglas. "Campbell, Blair, and Whately: Old Friends in a New Light." *WS* 19 (October 1955): 263–69.

————. "Campbell, Blair, and Whately Revisited." *SSJ* 28 (Spring 1963): 169–82. Reprinted in *Readings in Rhetoric*, edited by Lionel Crocker and Paul A. Carmack, 359–73. Springfield, Ill.: Charles C. Thomas, 1965.

————. "Dominant Trends in English Rhetorical Thought, 1750–1800." *SSJ* 18 (September 1952): 3–12. Reprinted in *Readings in Rhetoric*, edited by Lionel Crocker and Paul A. Carmack, 297–307. Springfield, Ill.: Charles C. Thomas, 1965.

————. "George Campbell and the Revolution in Inventional Theory." *SSJ* 15 (May 1950): 27–76.

————. "George Campbell and the Rhetorical Tradition: A Reply to La Russo." *WS* 32 (Fall 1968): 276–79.

————. "John Ward and His Rhetoric." *SM* 18 (March 1951): 1–16.

Ehninger, Douglas, and James Golden. "The Intrinsic Sources of Blair's Popularity." *SSJ* 21 (Fall 1955): 12–30.

Einhorn, Lois, comp. "The Most Significant Passage in Hugh Blair's Lectures on Rhetoric and Belles Lettres." *RSQ* 17 (Summer 1987): 281–304.

Ettlich, Ernest [Earl], Dominic La Russo, Herman Cohen, G. P. Mohrmann, and Phil Dolph. "Symposium: The Rhetorical Theory of George Campbell." *WS* 32 (Spring 1968): 84–113.

Fritz, Charles A. "From Sheridan to Rush: The Beginnings of English Elocution." *QJS* 16 (February–November 1930): 75–88. Reprinted in *Readings in Rhetoric*, edited by Lionel Crocker and Paul A. Carmack, 319–32. Springfield, Ill.: Charles C. Thomas, 1965.

Golden, James L. "Hugh Blair: Minister of St. Giles." *QJS* 38 (April 1952): 155–60.

Golden, James L., and Edward P. J. Corbett. *The Rhetoric of Blair, Campbell, and Whately*. New York: Holt, Rinehart and Winston, 1968, 1980. With updated bibliographies. Carbondale: Southern Illinois University Press, 1990.

Golden, James L., and Douglas Ehninger. "The Extrinsic Sources of Blair's Popularity." *SSJ* 22 (Fall 1956): 16–32.

Grave, S. A. *The Scottish Philosophy of Common Sense*. Oxford: Clarendon Press, 1960.

Gray, Giles Wilkeson. "What was Elocution?" *QJS* 46 (February 1960): 1–7.

Grover, David H. "John Walker: The 'Mechanical' Man Revisited." *SSJ* 34 (Summer 1969): 288–97.

Guthrie, Warren. "The Development of Rhetorical Theory in America, 1635–1850: Domination of the English Rhetorics." *SM* 15 (1948): 61–71.

———. "The Development of Rhetorical Theory in America 1635–1850–V: The Elocution Movement—England." *SM* 18 (March 1951): 17–30. Reprinted in *The Province of Rhetoric*, edited by Joseph Schwartz and John A. Rycenga, 255–74. New York: Ronald Press Co., 1965.

———. "The Development of Rhetorical Theory in America, 1635–1850: The Growth of the Classical Tradition, 1730–1785." *SM* 14 (1947): 38–54.

Haberman, Frederick W. "English Sources of American Elocution." In *A History of Speech Education in America*, edited by Karl R. Wallace, 105–26. New York: Appleton-Century-Crofts, 1954.

Hagaman, John. "On Campbell's Philosophy of Rhetoric and Its Relevance to Contemporary Invention." *RSQ* 21 (Summer 1981): 145–55.

Harding, Harold F. "Editor's Introduction." In *Lectures on Rhetoric and Belles Lettres*, by Hugh Blair, viii–xl. Carbondale: Southern Illinois University Press, 1965.

———. "English Rhetorical Theory, 1750–1800." Ph.D. dissertation, Cornell University, 1937.

Hargis, Donald E. "James Burgh and The Art of Speaking." *SM* 24 (November 1957): 275–84.

Hedrick, Elizabeth. "Locke's Theory of Language and Johnson's Dictionary." *ECSt* 20 (Summer 1987): 422–45.

Hogan, J. Michael. "Historiography and Ethics in Adam Smith's Lectures on Rhetoric, 1762–1763." *Rhetorica* 2 (Spring 1984): 75–91.

Hooker, Edward Niles. "The Discussion of Taste, from 1750 to 1770." *PMLA* 49 (1934): 577–92.

Horner, Winifred Bryan. "The Eighteenth Century." In *Historical Rhetoric: An Annotated Bibliography of Sources in English*, edited by Winifred Bryan Horner, 187–226. Boston: G. K. Hall, 1980.

———. "The Roots of Writing Instruction: Eighteenth- and Nineteenth-Century Britain." *RR* 8 (Spring 1990): 322–45. Reprinted as "Writing Instruction in Great Britain: Eighteenth and Nineteenth Centuries" in *A Short History of Writing Instruction from Ancient Greece to Twentieth-Century America*, edited by James J. Murphy, 121–49. Davis, Calif.: Hermagoras Press, 1990.

Howell, Wilbur Samuel. "Adam Smith's Lectures on Rhetoric: An Historical Assessment." *SM* 36 (November 1969): 393–418. Reprinted with revisions in *Essays on Adam Smith*, edited by Andrew S. Skinner and Thomas Wilson, 11–43. Oxford: Clarendon Press, 1975.

———. "The Declaration of Independence and Eighteenth-Century Logic." *WMQ*, 3d ser., 18 (October 1961): 463–84. Reprinted in *A Casebook on the Declaration of Independence*, edited by Robert Ginsberg, 194–215. New York: Crowell, 1967. Also reprinted in Wilbur Samuel Howell, *Poetics, Rhetoric, and Logic: Studies in the Basic Disciplines of Criticism*, 163–90. Ithaca and London: Cornell University Press, 1975.

———. *Eighteenth-Century British Logic and Rhetoric*. Princeton: Princeton University Press, 1971.

———. *Fénelon's Dialogues on Eloquence: A Translation with an Introduction and Notes*. Princeton: Princeton University Press, 1951.

———. "John Locke and the New Rhetoric." *QJS* 53 (December 1967): 319–33.

———. "Sources of the Elocutionary Movement in England, 1700–1748." *QJS* 45 (February 1959): 1–18. Reprinted with considerable expansion in his *Eighteenth-Century British Logic and Rhetoric*, 143–203. Princeton: Princeton University Press, 1971.

Irvine, James R. "George Campbell: Manuscripts in Scottish Archives." *RSQ* 17 (Winter 1987): 101–3.

————. "Rhetoric and Moral Philosophy: A Selected Inventory of Lecture Notes and Dictate in Scottish Archives 1700–1900." *RSQ* 8 (Fall 1978): 159–64.

Jefferson, D. W. "Theories of Taste in the Eighteenth Century." *Proceedings of the Leeds Philosophical and Literary Society, Literary and Historical Section* 5 (1938–1943): 1–9.

Keesey, Ray E. "John Lawson's Lectures Concerning Oratory." *SM* 20 (March 1953): 49–57. Reprinted in *Readings in Rhetoric*, edited by Lionel Crocker and Paul A. Carmack, 283–96. Springfield, Ill.: Charles C. Thomas, 1965.

Lamb, Jack Hall. "John Walker and Joshua Steele." *SM* 32 (November 1965): 411–19.

La Russo, Dominic. "Root or Branch? A Re-examination of Campbell's 'Rhetoric.'" *WS* 32 (Spring 1968): 85–91.

Lehmann, William C. *Henry Home, Lord Kames, and the Scottish Enlightenment: A Study in National Character and in the History of Ideas.* The Hague: Martinus Nijhoff, 1971.

Lothian, John M. "Introduction." In *Lectures on Rhetoric and Belles Lettres Delivered in the University of Glasgow by Adam Smith Reported by a Student in 1762–63*, by Adam Smith, xi–xl. Carbondale: Southern Illinois University Press, 1971.

Lynn, Steven. "Johnson's Rambler and Eighteenth-Century Rhetoric." *ECSt* 19 (Summer 1986): 461–79.

McDermott, Douglas. "George Campbell and the Classical Tradition." *QJS* 49 (December 1963): 403–9. Reprinted in *Readings in Rhetoric*, edited by Lionel Crocker and Paul A. Carmack, 349–58. Springfield, Ill.: Charles C. Thomas, 1965.

McGuinness, Arthur E. *Henry Home, Lord Kames.* New York: Twayne Publishers, 1970.

McKenzie, Gordon. *Critical Responsiveness: A Study of the Psychological Current in Later Eighteenth-Century Criticism.* University of California Publications in English, 20 (1949).

————. "Lord Kames and the Mechanist Tradition." *Essays and Studies.* University of California Publications in English, 14 (1943): 93–121.

Mohrmann, G. P. "George Campbell: The Psychological Background." *WS* 32 (Spring 1968): 99–104.

————. "Kames and Elocution." *SM* 32 (June 1965): 198–206.

————. "The Language of Nature and Elocutionary Theory." *QJS* 52 (April 1966): 116–24.

Murphy, Mary C. "Detection of the Burglarizing of Burgh: A Sequel." *CM* 43 (June 1976): 140–41.

Newman, John B. "The Role of Joshua Steele in the Development of Speech Education in America." *SM* 20 (March 1953): 65–73.

North, Ross Stafford. "Joseph Priestley on Language, Oratory, and Criticism." Ph.D. dissertation, University of Florida, 1957.

North, Stephen M. *The Making of Knowledge in Composition Studies: Portrait of an Emerging Field.* Upper Montclair, N.J.: Boynton/Cook Publishers, 1987.

Oliver, Robert T. *The Influence of Rhetoric in the Shaping of Great Britain.* Newark: University of Delaware Press, 1986.

Ong, Walter J., S.J. "Review of Eighteenth-Century British Logic and Rhetoric." *WMQ* 29 (October 1972): 637–43.

Parrish, W[ayland] M. "The Burglarizing of Burgh, or the Case of the Purloined Passions." *QJS* 38 (December 1952): 431–34.

Perrin, Porter Gale. "The Teaching of Rhetoric in the American Colleges before 1750." Ph.D. dissertation, University of Chicago, 1936.

Porter, Roy. "The Language of Quackery in England, 1660–1800." In *The Social History of Language*, edited by Peter Burke and Roy Porter, 73–103. New York: Cambridge University Press, 1987.

Randall, Helen Whitcomb. "The Critical Theory of Lord Kames." *Smith College Studies in Modern Languages* 22 (1940–1941).

Reid, Ronald F. "John Ward's Influence in America: Joseph McKean and the Boylston Lectures on Rhetoric and Oratory." *SM* 27 (November 1960): 340–44.

Richetti, John J. *Philosophical Writing: Locke, Berkeley, Hume.* Cambridge: Harvard University Press, 1983.

Rizvi, S. N. A. *The Sociology of the Literature of Politics: Edmund Burke.* Salzburg, Austria: Institut für Anglistik und Amerikanistik, 1982.

Sandford, William P. *English Theories of Public Address, 1530–1828.* Columbus, Ohio: H. L. Hedrick, 1931.

Schmitz, Robert M. *Hugh Blair.* New York: King's Crown Press, 1948.

Sher, Richard B. *Church and University in the Scottish Enlightenment: The Moderate Literati of Edinburgh.* Princeton: Princeton University Press, 1985.

Skopec, Eric Wm. "The Theory of Expression in Selected Eighteenth-Century Rhetorics." In *Explorations in Rhetoric*, edited by Ray E. McKerron, 119–36. Glenview, Ill.: Scott, Foresman and Co., 1982.

———. "Thomas Reid's Fundamental Rules of Eloquence." *QJS* 64 (October 1978): 400–408.

———. "Thomas Reid's Rhetorical Theory: A Manuscript Report." *CM* 45 (August 1978): 258–64.

Stone, P. W. K. *The Art of Poetry 1750–1820.* New York: Barnes and Noble, 1967.

Voitle, Robert. "Introduction." In *Elements of Criticism*, by Henry Home, Lord Kames, l:i–xiv. Hildesheim and New York: Georg Olms Verlag, 1970.

Walzer, Arthur E. "Logic and Rhetoric in Malthus's Essay on the Principle of Population, 1798." *QJS* 73 (February 1987): 1–17.

5

THE NINETEENTH CENTURY
Donald C. Stewart

Anyone attempting to generalize about nineteenth-century rhetoric—anyone, in fact, attempting to generalize about the rhetoric of any period—immediately encounters three significant problems: (1) how shall rhetoric in this period be defined; (2) how many "rhetorics" actually exist in the period; (3) to what geographical and national boundaries shall one limit discussion of the topic?

The third question is the least difficult for me to answer here. This chapter will, for the most part, be restricted to nineteenth-century rhetoric in Great Britain and the United States of America, but I intend to return to this matter in the section headed "Future Directions." The first and second questions are much more difficult to deal with because nineteenth-century rhetoric poses some special problems, the greatest of which is that it has apparently had no intellectual, philosophical, or theoretical center. The problem, in part, has been described by John Elliott Braun in a doctoral dissertation entitled "The Philosophical Roots of the Nineteenth-Century 'Repose' in Rhetoric, with Emphasis on the Idea of Communication in the Thought of Josiah Royce" (1977). He begins his abstract with the following observation: "Historians of rhetorical theory seem to be in implicit agreement that little of philosophical significance to rhetoric developed during much of the nineteenth century. Most analyses of modern theories of rhetoric either ignore the period completely, or assign it to slumbering 'repose.'"

Those who take this position, he says, argue that rhetoric in the nineteenth century didn't adapt itself to two predominant philosophical themes: Kantian subjectivity and Hegelian historicism. But he suggests that the "repose" may not have been what it seems and turns to the work of Franz Theremin, Sören Kierkegaard, Charles Sanders Peirce, and Josiah Royce as correctives.

James A. Berlin in his *Writing Instruction in Nineteenth-Century American Colleges* takes a much different position in defining rhetoric and "rhetorics" in the nineteenth century. Limiting his discussion to the rhetoric which informs writing instruction in nineteenth-century

American colleges, he argues that "every rhetoric . . . has at its base a conception of reality, of human nature, and of language. . . . it is grounded in a noetic field: a closed system defining what can, and cannot, be known; the nature of the knower; the nature of the relationship between the knower, the known and the audience; and the nature of language" (2). Using these criteria, he finds three distinctive systems in nineteenth-century rhetoric: classical, psychological-epistemological, and romantic. The first has its origins in the rhetoric of ancient Greece and Rome; the second in Scottish Common Sense Realism and the work of Hugh Blair and George Campbell; the third in the American transcendental movement and the work of Emerson and Thoreau. His arguments for the first two categories are strong; those for the third are on much shakier ground, particularly in his discussion of Emerson's influence on Fred Newton Scott of Michigan, a late nineteenth-century pioneer in his attempt to revitalize instruction in rhetoric. The problem, briefly, is that Berlin traces Scott's intellectual origins to Emerson when, in fact, they were in German transcendental philosophy, to which he was introduced by William Jones, first president of Indiana State University, when Scott was a student in the university's lab schools. Berlin's mistake is an understandable one because at the time he wrote his monograph these facts about Scott were not yet known.

Interestingly, Scott himself, although he lived until 1931, provides the most comprehensive definition of rhetoric by anyone who was formed intellectually by the nineteenth century. It occurs in the entry on rhetoric that he contributed to Dodd and Mead's *New International Encyclopedia* (1902–1904). In the first part of this article, the subject of which is rhetoric's etymology and scope, Scott says that rhetoric is "the science and art of communication in language" (763). It "properly belongs to that branch of knowledge which is concerned with the relations of men in society" and more specifically with the group of activities through which "men express themselves and convey their thoughts and feelings to their fellows" (773). He divides these activities in two ways: "(1) according to the medium employed in the process of thought conveyance, and (2) accordingly as the emphasis is thrown upon the individual or the social phase of the process. The first method of classification leads to the differentiation of the several arts; the second to the distinction of processes mainly self-expressive from processes mainly communicative" (763). Space limitations prohibit further amplification of Scott's remarks; interested readers should consult the entire entry.

I prefer to define, or perhaps more accurately to describe, nineteenth-century rhetoric in terms of its affinity with the preceptive tradition. With very few exceptions, the primary works cited here have something to do with aspects of invention, arrangement, style, memory, and delivery. It is immediately apparent to any historian of this period that rhetoric in the nineteenth century splintered into a number of strands, some of which underwent mutations and survived, others of which simply disappeared. I propose to identify these strands, to discuss briefly major representatives of each, to take up significant scholarship dealing with both trends and figures in the century, and, finally, to suggest the direction that future scholarship in this field might take.

At the outset, however, I must point out a continuing problem for scholars working in this field. With the exception of J. Jeffrey Auer and Jerald L. Banninga's edition of John Quincy Adams's *Lectures on Rhetoric and Oratory* (1962) and the Southern Illinois University Press's Landmark editions of Gilbert Austin's *Chironomia* (1966), Edward T. Channing's *Lectures Read to the Seniors in Harvard College* (1968), Thomas De Quincey's *Essays on Rhetoric* (1967), Richard Whately's *Elements of Rhetoric* (1963), and Chauncey Allen Goodrich's *Essays from Select British Eloquence* (1963), primary materials are scattered and in generally poor shape. Many are consigned to the rare-book rooms of the libraries which have them, and scholars must use interlibrary loans to acquire these books, even for a short period of time. Availability of materials thus becomes a problem, but not an insurmountable one.

I must add one other note regarding both the discussion of primary works and the bibliography of primary sources at the end of this chapter. The list of works is a *selected* one that represents the preceptive tradition in nineteenth-century rhetoric. Those seeking a longer list of primary works in the century should turn to the following sources: my chapter on nineteenth-century rhetoric in *Historical Rhetoric: An Annotated Bibliography of Selected Sources in English*; the list of primary sources at the end of James A. Berlin's *Writing Instruction in Nineteenth-Century American Colleges*; the bibliography of rhetoric in England and America in the nineteenth century that Berlin prepared for the summer 1981 issue of *Rhetoric Society Quarterly*; or Forrest Houlette's *Nineteenth-Century Rhetoric: An Enumerative Bibliography* (New York: Garland, 1989). The latter, by far the most complete bibliography of this material yet attempted, is still, according to the author, unfinished. A subsequent edition is planned in the near future. Some improvements could be made in the next edition: (1) provision of dates for *all* entries; (2) reorganization of the entries into a sequence beginning with books, proceeding to chapters in books, and finishing with articles; (3) addition of non-British and non-American sources.

The Primary Works

Turning to the field itself, then, one can detect the following strands of rhetorical theory and practice at various stages in the nineteenth century: (1) classical, (2) elocutionary, (3) psychological-epistemological, (4) belletristic, and (5) practical. I will examine the primary works for each in turn.

Classical Rhetoric

Classical rhetoric as a force in the everyday lives and vocations of people had, of course, been dead since the collapse of the Roman Empire, but the tradition established primarily by Plato, Aristotle, Cicero, and Quintilian had lived on, modified by succeeding ages through the eighteenth century. By the end of the eighteenth century, however, it was nearly defunct, and it survived in a highly visible manner only for about twenty years into the nineteenth century, primarily in the work of the first two holders of the Boylston Chair of Rhetoric at Harvard: John Quincy Adams and Joseph McKean. McKean did not leave any published lectures, but Adams did, in two volumes that never went into a second printing in his lifetime. They reflect Adams's knowledge of the classical tradition and his desire, despite the conflicting pull of political duties, to fulfill his responsibilities as specified in the articles establishing the Boylston Chair. Auer and Banninga, in their edition of Adams's *Lectures on Rhetoric and Oratory*, describe them "as the first attempt by an American to reunite rhetorical theory with classical doctrines" (1). Among the works Adams studied in preparing his lectures were Aristotle's *Rhetoric*; the anonymous *Rhetorica ad Herennium*; Quintilian's *Institutes of Oratory*; Cicero's *De Oratore, Orator*, and *Orations*; Plato's *Gorgias, Phaedrus,* and *Protagoras*; Hugh Blair's *Lectures on Rhetoric and Belles Lettres*; George Campbell's *Philosophy of Rhetoric*; John Walker's *Elements of Elocution*; Thomas Sheridan's *Lectures on Elocution*; John Lawson's *Lectures Concerning Oratory*; and Lord Kames's *Elements of Criticism*.

The sequence of lectures indicates clearly the nature of his topics. After an inaugural lecture, he took up an overview of the history of rhetoric and oratory, gave two lectures to objections against eloquence and the origin of oratory, then discussed the Roman rhetoricians, specifically Cicero and Quintilian. The history of rhetoric behind him, he concentrated, in the remainder of his lectures, on specific rhetorical topics: the concepts of status; topoi; demonstrative, judicial, deliberative, and pulpit oratory; the qualities of an orator; the parts of a discourse (introduction, narration of facts, argument, refutation, and conclusion); and finally matters of style, primarily figurative language. On the whole, the lectures are a restatement of classical doctrines, but two aspects of them are noteworthy. First, as already noted, they represent an attempt by an American familiar with the British rhetorics to break away from them. Second, Adams's emphasis on deliberative and judicial oratory reflects the preoccupations and needed competencies of those in an emerging democracy. The lectures were not much noted, however, because of the increasing popularity of the elocutionary movement, which reached its zenith in America in the first half of the nineteenth century.

Elocutionary Rhetoric

The most significant nineteenth-century works on elocution were Gilbert Austin's *Chironomia* (1806) and James Rush's *The Philosophy of the Human Voice* (1827). Austin, an Irish clergyman who conducted a school for the sons of Irish nobility, was a fine scholar with an educational mission: to elevate the study of delivery, particularly physical gesture, to a position equal to that shared by invention, arrangement, style, and memory. "Although the ancient writers have left various and complete systems of rhetoric, as far as relates to the four first divisions, viz. invention, disposition, elocution (that is, choice of language), and memory," he says in his preface to the work,

> and although modern writers have expounded, and detailed, and added to all these precepts, insomuch that in every language abundant instructions can be obtained in all that relates to these *four* divisions by every man who studies public speaking; and although within the British islands, in all these divisions, the public speakers have arrived at distinguished excellence; yet it is a fact, that we do not possess from the ancients, nor yet from the labours of our own countrymen, any sufficiently detailed and precise precepts for the *fifth* division of the art of rhetoric, namely, *rhetorical delivery*, called by the ancients *actio* and *pronunciatio*. . . . My object in this work is therefore to contribute my share of labour towards the completion of the rules for the better study and acquisition of rhetorical delivery, the *fifth* and least cultivated, but if we are to believe ancient authorities, not the least important division of the art. (ix–x)

Austin's book is distinguished in two respects. First, he dissected the physical actions of delivery in a way not previously done by developing an elaborate notational scheme for indicating, within an imaginary sphere, a speaker or actor's body, hand, and foot positions (his book contains 122 meticulously drawn sketches), and he gives specific directions for lawyers, preachers, politicians, and actors functioning in their respective spheres. Second, he intended his notational scheme to be a guide for subsequent readers as to the ways certain speeches, both in real life and onstage, were given. In his way, he was attempting to provide a historical record of public speaking similar to what is accomplished today with sophisticated video and audio equipment. All in all, Austin was a model teacher in that he combined knowledge of his subject, a historical sense of educational methods and purposes, and a willingness to experiment with new modes.

Rush is unique in that he was a medical doctor who wrote his book in the odd bits of time he was able to eke out of his medical practice over the course of three years. The book is characterized by clarity of purpose, attention to the minute details of voice use, and an ironic wit that expresses Rush's skepticism that teachers of elocution will pay any attention to, much less make use of, the insights in his book. General scholarly opinion is that his book was heeded, but only superficially by too many of those it was written to serve.

Rush states his purpose early and fully: "In the following essay, the reader will find an analysis of the human voice, which will enable an Elocutionist of any nation, to reduce to established form, the best modes of speech in his language. He will also find the outline of a system of principles that I have ventured to propose, upon a survey of those excellencies of utterance, which are accommodated to the temper and habits of the English ear; and which, in analogy with the above named arts, may be called the Ideal Beauty of speech" (xxiii–xxiv). He is quite clearly annoyed with those for whom "the high accomplishments in Elocution are supposed to be, universally, the unacquired gifts of genius, and to consist of powers and graces 'beyond the reach of art.' So seem the plainest services of arithmetic to a savage" (xxvi). In general, common sense, a passion for scientific accuracy, and scorn of romantic and imprecise language characterize Rush's introduction.

The body of the text contains very precise descriptions of the pitch, timbre, glides, and other sounds of the human voice with frequent use of musical terms and analogies to explain the concepts. Rush believed he had given elocution a scientific basis if its practitioners and teachers would only be willing to study his system and apply it, although he indicated frequently that he did not think they would. However, both Austin and Rush were far more influential than they thought they would be, and their works are still regarded as the finest treatises on elocution in the nineteenth century.

Psychological-Epistemological Rhetoric

A third strand of nineteenth-century rhetoric, the psychological-epistemological, is exemplified in Richard Whately's *Elements of Rhet-*

oric (1828). Whately is often linked with Blair and Campbell, the three of them generally being regarded as the most influential rhetoricians of the period between 1780 and 1880. There have been nearly three times as many scholarly articles published on Whately as on any other nineteenth-century rhetorical figure, and despite the fact that four individuals are responsible for most of these papers, Whately remains the only figure of the period about whom one can say that a body of scholarship has developed.

In the Southern Illinois University Press Landmarks edition of Whately's *Rhetoric*, Douglas Ehninger identified six significant characteristics of the book: (1) it is an ecclesiastical rhetoric with service of the Cross, not Caesar, in view; (2) it focuses persistently upon the "problems and methods of oral argumentation" (xii); (3) unlike Campbell's *Philosophy of Rhetoric*, its predecessor, it is a practical textbook, not a theoretical inquiry into the nature of communication; (4) it underwent continuous revision, its seven editions spanning a third of a century; (5) it is uneven, the sections on the nature of rhetoric, logic, and delivery being the strongest, those on persuasion and style the weakest; and (6) it rejects the elocutionary and belletristic traditions in rhetoric but endorses and carries to its logical completion the psychological-epistemological tradition.

> For while in denying rhetoric an investigatory method of its own Campbell and Priestley had made it exclusively a managerial science, these writers had left unformulated the principles and methods of "management" as they apply in the crucial area of invention.
>
> Accepting the challenge thus posed, Whately developed an inventional system aimed at systematizing the selection and application of cogent "reasons," just as the ancients had systematized the process of choosing an appropriate argumentative position and discerning the proofs inherent in it. (xxviii)

Recent essays by Lois J. Einhorn and Ray E. McKerrow have modified but not significantly changed Ehninger's analysis of this work.

Whately's book, while not dominating the field of rhetorical instruction throughout the rest of the nineteenth century, was a consistent force in the period. In 1980 James Berlin argued that Whately's ideas on rhetoric were among those shaping the composition course that developed in the late nineteenth century and persists today.

Belletristic Rhetoric

Belletristic rhetoric, that which focused primarily on style and the criticism of literature, is a fourth discernible strand in nineteenth-century rhetoric. It is significant because it contributed strongly to the movement that eventually established departments of English. I divide major works in this strand into two categories: those that are primarily theoretical and those that are essentially textbooks with a belletristic emphasis.

The figure of greatest stature in this area is clearly the English essayist Thomas De Quincey, whose five essays on rhetoric were first gathered together in 1889–1890 in David Masson's *The Collected Writing of Thomas De Quincey*. Fred Newton Scott in De Quincey's *Essays on Style, Rhetoric, and Language* (1893) and Helen Darbishire in *De Quincey's Literary Criticism* (1909) were the only other individuals to collect these essays before Frederick Burwick edited them for the Landmarks edition in 1967.

The essays are entitled "Rhetoric," "Style," "Language," "Conversation," and "A Brief Appraisal of the Greek Literature in Its Foremost Pretensions." Burwick notes several important features of the essays as a collected body of material on rhetoric. First, their emphasis is belletristic, not oratorical. Second, De Quincey developed the essays from his own idea of the nature of the informal essay, which, he said, began in a paradox and was developed with polemical skill. A paradox De Quincey defined as some truth which ran counter to general opinion.

> Thus in *Rhetoric* (1828), we find De Quincey correcting the popular misconceptions of rhetoric and basing his own definition on an interpretation of Aristotle that counters much scholarly opinion. The essay on *Style* (1840–41) opens with an argument against the British notion that manner and matter are separate entities in composition. The same argument is continued in *Language* (n.d.), where he also discusses misconceptions concerning the national attributes of languages. In *Conversation* (1847), the paradox is that conversation as a fine art depends not upon brilliant speech, but upon a rhetoric of sympathy and association. And in *A Brief Appraisal of the Greek Literature* (1838–39), he examines the negative aspects of Greek poetry, prose, and oratory often ignored in the general veneration of Grecian culture. (*Essays on Rhetoric*, xii)

Burwick makes one other observation of considerable significance about these essays, that there is a common philosophical and intellectual thread running through them. "De Quincey's signal contribution to the history of rhetoric is that he brought together for the first time the principal elements of Scottish associationism and German aesthetics" (xiii).

One should also note that De Quincey's essays are full of factual errors—his prodigious memory occasionally betrayed him—and genuinely entertaining writing. His account of German rhetoric (he likens it to the phenomenon of snakes in Iceland: there are none) and of the German sentence is a breath of fresh air to one accustomed to reading the more ponderous prose of solemn rhetoricians:

> Every German regards a sentence in the light of a package, and a package not for the mailcoach but for the waggon, into which his privilege is to crowd as much as he possibly can. Having framed a sentence, therefore, he next proceeds to *pack* it, which is effected partly by unwieldy tails and codicils, but chiefly by enormous parenthetic involutions. All qualifications, limitations, exceptions, illustrations, are stuffed and violently rammed into the bowels of the principal proposition. That all this equipage of accessaries is not so arranged as to assist its own orderly development no more occurs to a German as any fault than that in a package of shawls or carpets the colours and patterns are not fully displayed. To him it is sufficient that they are *there*. (*Essays on Rhetoric*, 122)

A small but controversial and influential theoretical work on rhetoric was Herbert Spencer's "The Philosophy of Style," which appeared unsigned in the *Westminster Review* in October 1852. In it he amplified his principle of the economy of style. The ultimate criterion of a good style, he said, is that it presents ideas so that they can be understood by the reader with the least possible mental effort. A style that calls attention to itself and is difficult causes the reader to expend mental energy better applied to assimilating the idea the words are expressing.

It is an intriguing hypothesis but one which occasionally led Spencer into chauvinistic remarks on a topic like the proper collocation of a substantive and its adjective. He argued, for example, that English's "the black horse" is superior to its French equivalent, "un cheval noir," because "cheval," coming first, generates certain pictures (perhaps brown, gray, or spotted horses) that have to be checked by the following "noir," whereas "black," preceding "horse," inclines the mind to be receptive to what black object follows. The naiveté of this kind of psychology is apparent and amusing to the sophisticated linguist today who is not so certain about the structure of the mind and of language acquisition and use as Spencer was more than a century ago. This naiveté was even noted by Fred Newton Scott in his 1892 edition of Spencer's essay.

Spencer, assuming the superiority of his principle of economy, however, went on to illustrate its validity and usefulness through the examples of inverted sentence forms, figures, and the brevity of poetry, which is what makes poetry superior to prose. He also put forth a principle of organic unity in composition, a unity derived from a great writer's intuitive perception of how often and in what circumstances to employ principles of economy. On this matter, Scott was to link

Spencer with Plato (otherwise very strange bedfellows), who stated the principle of organic unity in the *Phaedrus* when he said that a composition should have a body and the appropriate head and feet (see "Rhetoric Rediviva").

A third belletristic work, highly theoretical and little known but of far greater significance than has generally been recognized, was Gertrude Buck's doctoral dissertation under Fred Scott, published as *The Metaphor—A Study in the Psychology of Rhetoric* (1899). Albert R. Kitzhaber, the first person to conscientiously study Buck's paper, called it the only serious attempt in that era to solve "the essential problem of the nature and function of figurative language" ("Rhetoric in American Colleges: 1850–1900," 282). Drawing on the data of the experimental psychology of her time, Buck first attacked the assumption that metaphor was a response to the essential poverty of language, that it expressed a need for ornamentation in language. Her most provocative, and perhaps most profound, insight was that metaphor was not mechanical but organic, that it developed out of undifferentiated language into a clearly differentiated structure. She questioned traditional assumptions about the aesthetics of the metaphor, and she rejected the notion of mixed metaphors, which she said were never mixed in the mind of the person who produced them. Recognizing the shortcomings of the study, especially from a modern point of view, Kitzhaber concluded by observing, "Buck deserves much credit for her courage in brushing away the accumulated dust of well over two thousand years and for making an earnest attempt to attack the subject of metaphor from a wholly new point of view, bringing to bear on it the most recent and most pertinent information she could find, even though that knowledge was drawn from another discipline. In a period when rhetorical theory was becoming steadily more isolated from other fields of knowledge, Buck's attitude was unusually and commendably independent" (291). That "unusual and commendable independence," it is likely, was in no small measure attributable to the two individuals Buck acknowledges as having directed her work and given her the fundamental philosophic considerations in it: Scott and John Dewey.

Edward T. Channing's *Lectures Read to the Seniors in Harvard College* (1856) revealed how far the third Boylston Professor of Rhetoric had departed from the charge originally accepted by John Quincy Adams. Channing seems to have rejected much of classical rhetoric, in particular the topics for invention (he believed that no great thinker needed artificial aids to develop his subjects) and the essential function of rhetoric in an oral society. His first lecture clearly revealed his perception of the ancient orator as one who employed a variety of stratagems to accomplish his will with an undisciplined mob. The modern writer he perceived as one laboring in the quiet of his study writing for an unseen audience and moving them with sweet reason.

In Channing's defense it can be said that he sought to adapt rhetoric to the needs of his time, which meant, specifically, observing and experiencing human nature and adjusting rhetoric accordingly. His perceptions about human nature seem to have been strongly influenced by the Scottish philosopher Thomas Reid, who was also an influence on the work of Blair, Campbell, and Whately. Channing viewed rhetoric as a comprehensive art affecting all communication in language, and this conception determined the nature of his teaching. He was evidently a believer in faculty psychology, the notion that the mind was strengthened by exercise of its primary faculties, and he apparently thought that students would profit most from writing on provocative subjects of interest to them. In this respect he would be a thoroughly modern teacher of composition.

Despite the fact that Channing kept literary criticism as an after-class activity, a number of his lectures were of this kind, and it is noteworthy that his successor, Francis Child, gravitated immediately to literary scholarship and never looked back. The belletristic interests of the third Boylston professor had prepared the way for the fourth's eventually becoming Harvard's first professor of English.

Two belletristically oriented textbooks widely used in the nineteenth century deserve mention here. The first, Alexander Jamieson's *A Grammar of Rhetoric and Polite Literature* (1820), was divided into seven books: "Of Language and Style and the Foundation of Eloquence"; "Of the Structure of Language, or the Principles of General Grammar"; "Of the Nature and Structure of Sentences, the General Principles of Perspicuity, and the Harmony of Periods"; "Of Figures"; "On the Nature of Taste and the Sources of Its Pleasures"; "General Characters of Style"; and "Poetry." Book 1 contains a very romantic and unscientific account of the differences between primitive and modern language (an account essentially based on the doctrine of the perfectibility of man), and it even becomes somewhat humorous in its use of examples from the poems of Ossian to illustrate the highly metaphorical aspect of primitive languages. Book 2 is a predictable treatment of Latin-based grammar, a discussion of national, reputable, and present usage, which seems heavily indebted to Campbell, and of the virtues and faults of style, which comes straight from Blair. The discussion of sentence grammar in book 3 is unoriginal and Latinate, and the author's exposition of such topics as strength, harmony, and unity in sentences; figures of writing; taste; kinds of styles (dry, plain, neat, elegant, and flowery); and the directions for forming a good style reflect even more clearly his indebtedness to Blair, Campbell, and Lord Kames. Jamieson concentrates primarily on arrangement, style, and delivery, particularly on style, and ignores invention and memory. All in all, Jamieson's work does not have any fresh ideas about rhetoric, but the presentation must have been appealing to those who used it as a text. It went through nearly sixty editions in the nineteenth century.

Samuel P. Newman's *A Practical System of Rhetoric* (1827) was the first American text for written composition. Its emphasis is practical, and its subject is, primarily, style. Newman implies that previous books on rhetoric did not balance theory with practice, hence his decision to explain the rules for forming a good style, then to illustrate them with examples, and finally to ask students to apply the theory and practice they had supposedly learned.

The introduction of the book does take a modern view toward the priorities of good writing. First comes substance, then arrangement, then style. And Newman clearly implies that a major cause of bad writing is a lack of knowledge. But his book concentrates primarily on forming a good style from prose models, a time-honored practice, and his recommendations that students should be familiar with the best models of style and compose frequently and with care were not particularly original even at that time.

Practical Rhetoric

Of the last set of primary works to be discussed here, one can only say that while some or all are touched by the kinds of rhetorical theory already cited—classical, psychological-epistemological, or belletristic (since they are textbooks for written composition they would, by necessity, not be touched by the work of the elocutionists)—they come down to us as the ancestors of the most popular twentieth-century composition textbooks. They are the originators and carriers of a tradition in composition called "current-traditional" rhetoric by Daniel Fogarty, a tradition that Richard Young, more than a decade ago, said was under fire for its failure to adequately describe the composing process or deal effectively with invention (see "Paradigms and Problems: Needed Research in Rhetorical Invention").

A major work in this category is, of course, Alexander Bain's *English Composition and Rhetoric*, which went through several editions from the time of its first publication in 1866 into the 1890s. Bain, who was primarily a psychologist and logician but who occupied the chair of rhetoric at Aberdeen, saw his book as being more closely allied to the works of Blair, Campbell, and Whately than to recent books in the field. This is a curious observation because one might have a much more difficult time establishing a common link among these three than is superficially apparent. Blair is the spokesman for belletristic rhetoric and Campbell the godfather of psychological-epistemological rhetoric. Although Whately follows in Campbell's line, he differs from him on a number of important issues. Perhaps Bain sought association with his three predecessors because of their prestige. If he wanted to exert influence equal to theirs on the teaching of written composition, he certainly succeeded. More than any of his contemporaries, he established two features of composition teaching which have persisted with remarkable tenacity: the organic paragraph and the so-called forms of discourse—narration, description, exposition, and argument. Bain added a fifth category, poetry, which was employed only sometimes. Only in very recent years have the modes of discourse been challenged—by James Britton, Kitzhaber, and most recently Robert Connors, who catalogs their rise and fall—but they continue to persist, on the surface, at least, in many modern textbooks.

Bain's rules for paragraph construction are still being presented, particularly the concept of the topic sentence indicating the subject of a paragraph, his insistence that paragraphs should be formed around a single idea, and the notion that sentences within a paragraph should bear on this single idea. He rejected invention as part of rhetoric—the burden of finding subject matter belongs to other disciplines (perhaps those that are to provide the information dealt with in expository paragraphs: mathematics, natural philosophy, chemistry, physiology, natural history, and the human mind)—and even said that the English teacher cannot provide the student with a fund of expression.

Rhetoric he defined as the means whereby spoken or written language is made effective. Its ends are to inform, to persuade, and to please, and they correspond to the three departments of the mind: the understanding, the will, and the feelings. Clearly, this early and influential text was dominated by faculty psychology, but while that emphasis may have disappeared, Bain's forms of discourse and rules for paragraphing are with us yet. The most serious challenge to the latter was provided by Richard Braddock in 1974 (see "The Frequency and Placement of Topic Sentences in Expository Prose"), but many recent textbooks have still not assimilated fully the implications of Braddock's work.

David J. Hill's *The Science of Rhetoric* (1877), published slightly over a decade after the first edition of Bain's *Rhetoric*, differs from other composition texts of the era in that it is identified by its author as "a systematic presentation of laws of discourse for advanced classes," not as a beginning text. Hill rejected several contemporary notions of the nature and function of rhetoric. For example, he argued that Whately limited rhetoric by treating it as a branch of logic, Blair by making it a department of applied aesthetics, and Theremin by linking it to ethics. These are all incomplete perceptions of rhetoric, according to Hill. "The specific province of the rhetorician is to render given ideas effective in producing mental changes in others. Rhetoric treats of thought militant. Logic furnishes conceptions which are formally *true*; aesthetics, conceptions which are *beautiful*; ethics, conceptions which are *just*. Rhetoric takes these conceptions and establishes them in the mind of another" (3).

Hill then rejected the traditional categories of rhetoric. No useful rules for invention can be given, he believed; disposition (arrangement or organization) depends on the nature of the subject (the traditional five-part structure of the classical oration—introduction, narration of facts, argument, refutation, and conclusion—he found too mechanical to be useful and not adaptable to a variety of composing situations, a point with which I would agree); taste, beauty, and sublimity belong to aesthetics, not rhetoric; elocution is too important in itself to be taken up as a part of rhetoric; study of the history and origin of language is of little use to the person who must employ it for rhetorical purposes; the study of genres is not too productive; and terms such as *purity, propriety, precision, clearness,* and *vivacity* are too vague for his purposes.

At this point, one might well wonder just what Hill thought rhetoric was. In his text, although it appears to be dominated by the forms of discourse codified by Bain, Hill gave this answer: "The rhetorical process extends farther than the mere *presentation* of ideas; it is complete only when those ideas *are referred to the preexisting ideas* of the person addressed in such a manner that they will effect the desired change. All mental laws take place in accordance with certain laws. As an *art*, Rhetoric communicates ideas according to these laws; as a *science*, it discovers and establishes these laws. Rhetoric is, therefore, the science of the laws of effective discourse" (37). His book, then, is organized around laws of mind, of idea, and of form. Under laws of mind he discussed *reason, imagination,* and *memory*. The laws of idea he separated into ideas of individual objects and general notions. His law of form was essentially derived from Herbert Spencer's principle of economy, which Hill translated thus: "That form of language is most excellent which yields its contained idea with the least expenditure of mental energy" (147).

On the whole, the book is an attempt to establish rhetoric on a primitive psychological basis. In that sense, although the psychology

Hill accepted has long been rejected, the book anticipates modern work, particularly the linking of cognitive psychology and the composing process.

Adams Sherman Hill, the fifth Boylston Professor of Rhetoric and no relation to David Hill, exerted more influence on late nineteenth-century rhetorical theory and practice than he should have. He had taken two degrees from Harvard and was a practicing journalist when Charles William Eliot called him to return to his old school as an assistant to Francis Child. When Child was offered Harvard's first chair of English literature in 1876, Hill was elevated into the Boylston Chair. His *The Principles of Rhetoric and Their Application*, first published in 1878 and modified in the second edition of 1895, was the principal freshman rhetoric text at Harvard for more than thirty years. The book focused on principles of style, particularly word choice, and Hill's dogmatic judgments about usage and editorial correctness. In the 1895 edition he added sections on the forms of discourse because practically every textbook of that period was including them. Hill's book is well written, but it does not contain a single fresh idea about rhetoric, even for that era, and it severely limited the conception of what rhetoric should be. But it became one of a few books which shaped early twentieth-century perceptions of what the study of rhetoric should be (he excluded invention and did very little that was significant with arrangement)—essentially a study of style and editing—and thus contributed to the movement which, consciously or unconsciously, separated rhetoric as taught in the school from meaningful acts of communication in real life.

John Franklin Genung of Amherst, not so dogmatic as Hill, produced a small rhetoric in 1885 whose success prompted him to amplify it into *The Practical Elements of Rhetoric* of 1886, another of the late nineteenth-century texts that greatly influenced the teaching of composition in American schools in the early twentieth century. A point should be made at this time. I began talking about works that were influential in the history of nineteenth-century rhetoric. The term *rhetoric* is shifting to *composition* in this discussion of late nineteenth-century works, however, because rhetoric, as discussed in the treatises of Blair, Campbell, and Whately, for example, was ceasing to exist. What was left of the preceptive rhetorical tradition was carried on by the elocutionists—who were in the process of forming their own national professional organization in speech—and through the composition texts written by those in English departments who were much involved in the teaching of expository writing.

Genung split rhetoric into the study of style and invention. Style he defined as "the various rhetorical principles that are developed from grammars: how to use words and figures, and how to build them together so as to impart to the whole a desired power and quality. The sphere of the work of style is the construction of sentences and paragraphs" (7). Invention he tied to logic, to what I would call principles of arrangement—thesis statements, introduction, development, and conclusions—and to the forms of discourse he labeled narration, description, exposition, argument, and persuasion. He distinguished between argument developed through rigorous logic and practical persuasion, which one uses when the force of logic fails. In this work he acknowledged the influence of Bain.

Genung rejected invention as a process of generating material on a subject:

> The first stage, the finding of material by thought or observation, is the fundamental and inclusive office of invention, the distinctive power that we designate in the popular use of the term. Herein lies obviously, the heart and centre of literary production; it is what the writer finds, in his subject or in the world of thought, that gauges his distinction as an author. *Yet this is of all processes, the one least to be invaded by the rules of the text-book.* It is a work so individual, so dependent on the peculiar aptitude and direction of the writer's mind, that each one must be left for the most part to find his way alone, according to the impulse that is in him. . . . Such invention is incommunicable by teaching. (217; italics mine)

Genung's book is a congenial one, well written and devoid of the dogmatic tone that characterizes Hill's book, but it, too, does not contain a really fresh approach to the study of rhetoric. Yet it was a significant force in composition teaching for decades.

A contemporary of A. S. Hill's at Harvard, Barrett Wendell, made his contribution to the teaching of writing in *English Composition*, which consisted of a series of lectures given at the Lowell Institute in November and December 1890. The book has had an enduring influence on subsequent composition textbooks, both because of its organization and because of three concepts that emerged from it. Wendell defined style as "the expression of thought and feeling in the written word" and expressed his belief that modern style was the result of a struggle between good use and principles of composition. In discussing style he took up, in order, the word, the sentence, the paragraph, and the whole composition, a still popular pattern. "Each of these elements," he says, "I shall examine in detail, inquiring first how far it is affected by the paramount authority of good use and then how within the limits of good use it may be made, by means of the principle of composition or otherwise, to assume various forms and to perform various offices" (39, 40).

He developed another set of concepts, Unity, Coherence, and Mass (later converted to Emphasis by his contemporaries), the acquisition of which he felt contributed to clearness, force, and elegance in writing. It is quite clear that Wendell gave no thought to invention as the technique of generating ideas for writing, and his discussion of arrangement, particularly in the paragraph and the whole composition, is heavily indebted to Bain, whom he acknowledges.

Like Hill, Wendell exerted a tremendous influence on twentieth-century composition practice, and, indirectly, he influenced another trend that has had considerable vogue in later years. One of his students, Henry G. Pearson, was thoroughly taken with Wendell's method of teaching writing, but he wanted to make one significant change: to invert the order in which the topics were taken up. Pearson's *The Principles of Composition* (1897) has the basic Wendellian concepts, but he began with the whole composition and worked down, through the paragraph, to the sentence and then the word. Pearson thought this was psychologically sounder than the other method. So did Sheridan Baker of Michigan, who, in his *Practical Stylist* (1966), later amplified into *The Complete Stylist*, worked from the big end of the composition triangle to the small. Baker's book was extremely popular for at least ten years.

Two other works in the composition/rhetoric strand at the end of the nineteenth century deserve attention. The first, Edwin H. Lewis's *The History of the English Paragraph* (1894), was the only scholarly study of this unit of discourse in the period. Lewis studied seventy-three prose writers and came away with the following conclusions: (1) the paragraph emerged and gained popularity because it was more economical than the long periodic sentence; (2) writers have recognized, from the beginning, a unit of discourse longer than the sentence; (3) loose paragraphs (those in which the subject is stated first and then developed) have been more popular than those constructed differently; (4) William Tyndal was the first English writer to have any sense of the paragraph; (5) the average number of words per paragraph had not changed significantly at the time of his study; (6) the modern paragraph had been influenced by a medieval tradition that a paragraph distinguishes a stadium of thought.

The significance of the study was its attempt to define the paragraph in a scientific and scholarly way. Unfortunately, the paragraph theory of the textbooks became classroom gospel, and paragraph theory atrophied at the turn of the century. Only recently have scholars attempted some systematic and descriptive accounts of what the paragraph as a unit of discourse really is.

A second important work in this strand, Fred Newton Scott and Joseph Villiers Denney's *Paragraph-Writing* (1893), grew out of classroom exercises developed by the two when they were beginning their teaching careers at Michigan. Scott stayed in Ann Arbor for the rest of his life, but Denney went to Ohio State, where he had a distinguished career as professor of English, head of the department, and eventually dean of the College of Arts and Sciences. The first edition of *Paragraph-Writing* (1891) came out in response to the demand from teachers in preparatory schools and colleges. However, according to the authors, the book "goes farther. Its aim is to make the paragraph the basis of a method of composition, to present all the important facts of rhetoric in their application to the paragraph" (1893 ed., iii).

Scott and Denney promoted the idea of teaching the paragraph as a theme in miniature. There were two distinct advantages in this method, one for students, one for teachers. Scott's sister Harriet, principal of the Detroit Training School for Teachers, had reported that children learning to read comprehended a paragraph-group or sequence of sentences better than either single sentences out of context or longer units of discourse. Scott and Denney also argued that students had far less trouble producing a paragraph than a longer piece of discourse, even though in producing a paragraph they would be required to do all that the longer unit required. Thus, the paragraph, both for student comprehension and for production, seemed the ideal unit of discourse to work with. There was a practical benefit for teachers, also. They were caught in the middle of the back-to-basics movement of the era, and paper grading had become impossible. The paragraph proved to be a much more manageable assignment for teachers to grade, and many more could be assigned than themes.

In all of this, Scott and Denney were doing nothing particularly new to the modern composition teacher, and they acknowledged the influences of Bain, D. J. Hill. A. S. Hill, and Wendell, but they provided one chapter not found in discussions of paragraphs at that time: a section which tried to discover some psychological bases for paragraphing. They defined an essay as "the result of sustained movement of a writer's thought toward a definite goal" (96) but noted intermediate stages in this movement. These are the paragraph divisions, and they can occur in a variety of patterns, which Scott and Denney diagram. While not as sophisticated as some contemporary models (the Pitkin paragraph, for example), these efforts show these authors thinking along lines congenial to modern composition theorists but almost unique in their own time. Unfortunately, this section on the theory of the paragraph gives readers only the barest insight into the rich and comprehensive rhetoric program Scott was developing at Michigan, a program which would, in 1903, split away from the literature program and find its home in Michigan's newly formed Department of Rhetoric.

Secondary Works

Nearly a decade ago, I could say that "the most notable feature of scholarship in nineteenth-century rhetoric [was] its relative absence." That is no longer the case. Although the quantity of work now being produced on other historical periods is still much greater than that being produced on the nineteenth century, there is a growing and very solid body of scholarship in this field, and it is being produced in departments of English as well as speech.

I have identified nearly 160 pieces of scholarship, published from 1980 to the present, having some bearing on nineteenth-century rhetoric. Sixty-six of these are doctoral dissertations, five of them, by John Bayer, David Heddendorf, Susan Jarratt, Marshall Kremers, and Mark Waldo, being especially promising. Jarratt and Kremers have already mined their dissertations for published work which appears in the list of secondary sources following this essay. Equally encouraging has been the appearance of three new publications, *Pre/Text*, *Rhetorica*, and *Rhetoric Review*, which carry articles on the history of rhetoric. The bulk of nineteenth-century material still comes, however, from the speech journals, particularly the *Quarterly Journal of Speech* and the *Rhetoric Society Quarterly*. Occasional papers on the history of nineteenth-century rhetoric have appeared, however, in some rather unexpected places: *Victorian Poetry*, *Thoreau Journal Quarterly*, and the *Walt Whitman Quarterly Review*.

I see two extremely beneficial consequences of this sudden and promising increase in the scholarship on this period. First, more and more English teachers are rediscovering a part of their past from which they have been cut off for many decades. We are learning more every day about the birth of English and speech departments, the unfortunate separation of literature and composition and of instruction in speaking and writing, and the origins of methods of teaching writing which proved to be inefficient and ineffective for most of the twentieth century. Second, scholarship on this period is helping us to define rhetoric in it. In addition to studies of the preceptive tradition in the period and its major figures, we are seeing an increasing number of papers on the rhetoric of science, the feminist movement in the nineteenth century and its relationship to the abolitionist movement (a phenomenon which was duplicated in America in the 1960s when the civil-rights and women's movements found common ground), the rhetoric of the pre- and post–Civil War South, and the rhetoric of the preservationist movement. I will have more to say on this subject in "Future Directions."

From 1949 to the present there have been eight studies of note that attempted to generalize broadly about rhetoric in the nineteenth century. The fourth section of Warren Guthrie's "The Development of Rhetorical Theory in America, 1635–1850" deals with the emergence of an indigenous American rhetoric in the early nineteenth century as Americans were breaking away from the British. In 1954 John P. Hoshor amplified the thesis of the Guthrie study in "American Contributions to Rhetorical Theory and Homiletics." Ronald F. Reid and Paul E. Ried completed studies on Harvard's Boylston Chair of Rhetoric in 1959 and 1960, respectively, each of them concerned with the way changes in the holders of the chair reflected changing perceptions of rhetoric in the nineteenth century. Hal Rivers Weidner's doctoral dissertation, "Three Models of Rhetoric" (1975), traces the evolution of eighteenth- and nineteenth-century rhetorical theory from what he calls traditional (Aristotelian) to mechanical (Cambellian) to vitalistic (essentially an attitude favoring inspiration and rejecting the notion of one's developing conscious control of invention) and eventually to the practical rhetoric of the late nineteenth century. Albert R. Kitzhaber ("Rhetoric in American Colleges," 1953) and Harold Jordan ("Rhetorical Education in American Colleges and Universities," 1952) look specifically at individuals, events, and trends that occurred in the latter half of the century. James Berlin's *Writing Instruction in Nineteenth-Century American Colleges* (1984) is the newest addition to this group. To some extent Berlin amplifies Kitzhaber's dissertation, but he breaks significant new ground in attempting to establish epistemological bases for the strands of nineteenth-century rhetoric he identifies.

Interesting as all these studies are, and four are dissertations, my judgment is still that Kitzhaber provides the best overall picture of what happened in the nineteenth century. He traces the influence of the major British rhetoricians, particularly Blair, Campbell, and Whately, looks at developments early in the century, identifies those who did most to shape theory and practice in the latter half of the century—Bain, A. S. Hill, Wendell, Genung, and Scott (who is the only one identified by Kitzhaber as an original thinker)—and discusses significant rhetorical topics: the emergence and atrophying of paragraph theory, the four forms of discourse, and matters of style. So valuable has this work been to students of nineteenth-century rhetoric that, although it was completed in 1953, the Southern Methodist University Press is publishing it in the fall of 1990.

There has been a significant increase in the number and variety of topics having to do with nineteenth-century rhetoric. In the first edition I singled out only Frederick Haberman's (1954) and Marie Hochmuth and Richard Murphy's (1954) studies of elocution; Elbert Harrington's (1948) and Ernest Ettlich's (1966) essays on invention; and Virgil Baker's (1953), Kitzhaber's, and Robert Connors's (1981) examinations of the forms of discourse. To Harrington's and Ettlich's studies of invention we now add those of James A. Berlin and Sharon Crowley. To Baker's, Kitzhaber's, and Connors's examinations of the forms of discourse, we must add a fairly recent essay by Frank D'Angelo.

Representative of the scholarship developing around a number of other topics are essays on the rhetoric of science by Edward Block, John Angus Campbell, and Barbara Warnick; on protest and reform by Paul H. Boase and his collaborators; and on the women's movement by Karlyn Kohrs Campbell and Ellen Reid Gold. In addition one should note Robert Connors's essays on mechanical correctness and the rhetoric of explanation, Marie J. Secor's essay on style, and Nan Johnson's work on nineteenth-century Canadian rhetoric. Of greatest interest to those who are attempting to bridge the gap between literature and composition are Richard Dillman's essay on Thoreau's Harvard education in rhetoric and C. Carroll Hollis's study of the effects of nineteenth-century rhetorical education on Whitman's *Leaves of Grass*.

Richard Whately continues to be the only figure around whom a significant body of scholarship has developed, but some new pieces on figures already studied have appeared as well as new work on individuals not previously studied. Ray E. McKerrow has almost created a Whately industry, adding four essays to those he had already published on the author of *The Elements of Rhetoric*. William Covino's essay on Thomas De Quincey is a welcome addition to studies on that English essayist, Gerald P. Mulderig has produced a useful essay on Gertrude Buck, and Paul E. Ried has given us a new essay on John Quincy Adams and A. S. Hill, the first and fifth holders of the Boylston Chair at Harvard. Studies of the rhetoric of figures not previously examined include Richard A. Cherwitz and James W. Hiken's essay on John Stuart Mill; Dennis R. Bormann's piece on Adam Möller; Victoria Myers's study of Coleridge's rhetorical theory; and Susan C. Jarratt's essay on Walter Pater.

Winifred Bryan Horner is doing valuable and original work on nineteenth-century Scottish rhetoric, a comparatively new area of study, and one which she terms "the missing link" in an article to appear in a forthcoming collection of essays in honor of James Kinneavy, edited by Rosalind Gabin. She has also prepared three bibliographical articles from this research, the first of which, "Nineteenth-Century Rhetoric at the University of Edinburgh with an Annotated Bibliography of Archival Materials," appeared in the *Rhetoric Society Quarterly* in the fall of 1989. Two more articles will cover similar material at the University of Glasgow and the Universities of the North: Aberdeen and St. Andrews. She has also written an account of writing instruction at the eighteenth- and nineteenth-century British universities for the spring 1990 issue of *Rhetoric Review*, and it will be reprinted in James J. Murphy's *A Short History of Writing Instruction from Ancient Greece to Twentieth-Century America*, scheduled for publication by the Hermagoras Press in 1990. Professor Horner is also under contract to the Southern Illinois University Press for a book tentatively entitled *Nineteenth-Century Scottish Rhetoric: The American Connection*.

A still existing problem for those studying major figures in nineteenth-century rhetoric is the scarcity of good editions of their work. The Southern Illinois Landmarks series is still the touchstone with its editions of Gilbert Austin, Edward Channing, Thomas De Quincey, Chauncey Allen Goodrich, and Richard Whately. Auer and Banninga's edition of John Adams's *Lectures* is the only other work of this kind on nineteenth-century figures of which I am aware.

Summing up the present state of scholarship in nineteenth-century rhetoric, we may say that while a few useful and valuable studies that attempt to generalize about the period or movements within it do exist, they represent only the vanguard of work which is yet to come. And new work is on the way. Nan Johnson promises a book by 1991 on the philosophical foundations, theoretical principles, and popular practices of the nineteenth-century tradition in North America, and Robert Connors is writing an essay on the decline of rhetoric in American colleges from 1870 to 1910.

We are still waiting for a body of scholarship to develop around figures other than Richard Whately. De Quincey seems a likely candidate, considering the work already done on him, and new interest in the rhetorical ideas of both Coleridge and Hazlitt may signal the beginning of some significant work on both figures. In addition, we need more thorough scholarly pieces on many significant minor rhetoricians—Samuel Kirkham, Henry Mandeville, William Russell, William Shedd, Ebenezer Porter, and John Witherspoon—who have either been overlooked or were only briefly noticed in the *Quarterly Journal of Speech*'s series of reviews over fifty years ago. As a matter of fact, this deficiency is now being addressed. C. Carroll Hollis's essay on Whitman's *Leaves of Grass* cites Kirkham's rhetoric text, and Thomas Miller's edition of John Witherspoon's work is scheduled for publication in the summer of 1990.

A generation ago, the only persons in English departments producing significant scholarship on nineteenth-century rhetoric were Kitzhaber and Wallace Douglas. In the last decade and a half, however, we have seen new and important work by Edward P. J. Corbett, Andrea Lunsford, Hal Weidner, Robert Connors, Leo Rockas, James Berlin, Winifred Horner, Nan Johnson, Gerald Mulderig, Stephen Judy, William Covino, Sharon Crowley, Frank D'Angelo, Richard Dillman, C. Carroll Hollis, Susan Jarratt, Marshall Kremers, Marie Secor, William Woods, and myself.

Considering the amount of scholarship in both the history and theory of rhetoric by people in English departments, one would expect to see curriculum and program modifications to accommodate this interest. It has taken longer than many of us had expected, and much remains to be done, but information about rhetoric history and theory is reaching teachers at the grass-roots level, and we can expect new attitudes gradually to filter down to a general public which has been badly educated in this area for most of the twentieth century.

Future Directions

What remains to be done? A great deal. Nineteenth-century rhetoric offers some rich opportunities for research in a number of areas. First, like the rhetoric of every other historical period, it needs to be defined. How inclusive should the term be? Broad enough to include not only the preceptive tradition but also the rhetorics of science, the feminist movement, abolition, and political and social rhetoric, both pre- and post–Civil War? Or should one narrow the definition to the preceptive tradition, as I have essentially done here, and then study the ways in which the other "rhetorics" of the period appropriated segments of the preceptive tradition? Or should one take a completely different approach, as James Berlin has done, and define the rhetoric of this or any other period in terms of its epistemological assumptions?

All of these questions lead inevitably to discussions of historiography and the rhetoric of histories of rhetoric. These issues have already been argued, to some extent, in a 1988 session of the Conference on College Composition and Communication. The remarks by the participants—James Murphy, Robert Connors, Sharon Crowley, Richard Enos, Victor Vitanza, Susan Jarratt, Nan Johnson, Jan Swearingen, and James Berlin—along with their post-conference reflections were published in *Rhetoric Review* 7 (Fall 1988): 5–49.

The 1988 CCCC panel was actually one event in a sequence reported in *Pre/Text* 8 (Spring–Summer 1987). The first was the formation of an informal group to address questions about "re/visionary" histories of rhetoric, the lack of histories of rhetoric, and the lack of rhetorics of histories of rhetoric. The second event was a 1987 CCCC panel entitled "The Forum for the Interdisciplinary Study of Rhetoric," the papers for which were published in *Pre/Text* in 1987. After the 1988 CCCC panel, the third event in the series, a subsequent meeting was planned for May 1989 at the University of Texas at Arlington. I have no report on this meeting at the time of this writing.

Much of the discussion at these meetings and in these papers is heavily influenced by postmodern critical thought (how anything can be "*post*modern" continues to baffle me except in the world of people for whom the material and conceptual facts of life are all verbal constructs, continuously adapting to their contexts and the shifting nature of language and reality), which makes the not so new or profound discovery that cultural contexts are complex and always in flux and that language which attempts to deal with this phenomenon is inadequate because also in flux.

None of the individuals involved in these "events" seems aware that in 1976 Winston Weathers described a style, Grammar B, to cope with these problems, not even Victor Vitanza, that occasional Paganini of the printed page, who employs some of the devices of Grammar B while writing deconstructed prose. They are also largely unaware of the fact that in insisting on the interdisciplinary nature of rhetoric, they are carrying out the rhetoric program developed by Fred Newton Scott at Michigan in the 1890s.

I cannot leave this subject without an additional note on style. In a number of papers which I read, increasingly under protest, I discovered authors enslaved by current literary critical jargon. It is characterized by extensive use of such terms as *privilege, reify, valorize, foreground*, and even an occasional *non-foundational* and *criteriology*. This is "lit/crit speak," a subspecies of "academic/speak," a language greatly inferior to English in both diction and syntax. I suggest that it be avoided.

The bibliographical work done to date has given us some pretty good maps of the territory, but other, more detailed bibliographies, on individuals and issues relevant to nineteenth-century rhetoric, would be welcome. These would assist scholars preparing editions and studies of both major and minor figures, which we continue to need. For example, we are still waiting for a definitive edition of Alexander Bain's work on rhetoric. Considering Bain's influence, that would appear to be a significant gap.

Essays, of the quality of Frederick Burwick's on De Quincey, on all the major figures would lay the groundwork for some profitable exchange of opinion about them. One has only to compare the quantity of literary criticism developed around comparable nineteenth-century producers of belles lettres to realize the shallowness of the intellectual soil in which we still work. Editions would serve two purposes. First, they would give us reliable texts on which to base a body of scholarship about the various figures. Second, they would make accessible a number of books that are extremely difficult to get now. The Southern Illinois University Press has shown itself to be most receptive to good proposals of this kind. Let us hope that more will be forthcoming and that the market will justify producing them.

As C. Carroll Hollis's and Richard Dillman's essays suggest, literary criticism of classic nineteenth-century American writers would be considerably enriched by studies examining the knowledge these writers had of the rhetoric of their time. This is a point at which scholars of rhetoric and literature could assist one another a great deal.

Finally, the next revision of this section on nineteenth-century rhetoric will have to include primary and secondary work by Continental European rhetoricians. The beginnings of such an effort have already been made by Don Abbott in a bibliography of eighteenth- and nineteenth-century Spanish rhetorical treatises which he published in *Rhetorica* 4 (Summer 1986): 275–92. Two excellent pieces of scholarship on German rhetoricians of the period have also come to my attention: Dennis Bormann's essay on Adam Möller, which argues that this German rhetorician was far in advance of his time, and Sander Gilman, Carole Blair, and David Parent's edition and translation of Friedrich Nietzsche's essays on rhetoric and language, which has just been published (in 1989) by Oxford University Press. They argue that Nietzsche's philosophy can be read more productively in light of his conception of language, that Nietzsche has preceded Ricoeur, Derrida, and Foucault in the movement to reverse the intellectual status of rhetoric and philosophy, and that he is a forerunner of the modern emphasis on the study of the nature of discourse. Clearly, a study of nineteenth-century German rhetoric could begin by questioning De Quincey's assertion that it did not exist.

As this material accumulates, it should lay the background for a truly comprehensive study of nineteenth-century rhetoric. Whether this is the book Nan Johnson is already writing, we will have to wait to see. If it isn't, she will surely have taken us much closer to such a work, which we can now expect to see before the turn of the century.

Bibliography

Primary Sources

Adams, John Quincy. *Lectures on Rhetoric and Oratory, Delivered to the Classes of Senior and Junior Sophisters in Harvard University.* 2 vols. Cambridge: Hilliard and Metcalf, 1810. Reprinted: J. Jeffrey Auer and Jerald L. Banninga, eds. New York: Russell and Russell, 1962.

Austin, Gilbert. *Chironomia, or a Treatise on Rhetorical Delivery.* London: T. Cadell and W. Davies, 1806. Reprinted in facsimile: Mary Margaret Robb and Lester Thonssen, eds. Southern Illinois University Press Series, Landmarks in Rhetoric and Public Address, edited by David Potter. Carbondale: Southern Illinois University Press, 1966.

Bain, Alexander. *English Composition and Rhetoric: A Manual.* London: Longmans, Green and Co., 1866.

Buck, Gertrude. *The Metaphor—A Study in the Psychology of Rhetoric.* Contributions to Rhetorical Theory, no. 5. Edited by Fred Newton Scott. Ann Arbor: Inland Press, 1899.

Channing, Edward T. *Lectures Read to the Seniors in Harvard College.* Boston: Ticknor and Fields, 1856. Reprinted: Dorothy Anderson and Waldo Braden, eds. Southern Illinois University Press Series, Landmarks in Rhetoric and Public Address, edited by David Potter. Carbondale: Southern Illinois University Press, 1968.

Day, Henry N. *The Art of Discourse.* New York: Charles Scribner and Co., 1867.

De Quincey, Thomas. *The Collected Writings of Thomas De Quincey.* Edited by David Masson. 14 vols. Edinburgh: Black, 1889–1990.

———. *De Quincey's Literary Criticism.* Edited by Helen Darbishire. London: Henry Frowde, 1909.

———. *Essays on Rhetoric.* Edited by Frederick Burwick. Southern Illinois University Press Series, Landmarks in Rhetoric and Public Address, edited by David Potter. Carbondale: Southern Illinois University Press, 1967.

Genung, John Franklin. *The Practical Elements of Rhetoric.* 2d ed. Boston: Ginn and Co., 1886.

Goodrich, Chauncey Allen. *Select British Eloquence.* New York: Harper and Brothers, 1852.

Hill, Adams Sherman. *The Principles of Rhetoric and Their Application.* 2d ed. New York: American Book Co., 1895.

Hill, David J. *The Science of Rhetoric.* New York: Sheldon and Co., 1877.

Hope, M. B. *The Princeton Text-Book in Rhetoric.* Princeton: John T. Robinson, 1859.

Jamieson, Alexander. *A Grammar of Rhetoric and Polite Literature*. First American from last London edition. New Haven: A. H. Maltby, 1820.

Lewes, G. H. *The Principles of Success in Literature*. Edited by F. N. Scott. Boston: Allyn and Bacon, 1891.

Lewis, Edwin H. *The History of the English Paragraph*. Chicago: University of Chicago Press, 1894.

Newman, Samuel P. *A Practical System of Rhetoric*. Portland: Shirley and Hyde, 1827.

Pearson, Henry G. *The Principles of Composition, with an Introduction by Arlo Bates*. Boston: D. C. Heath and Co., 1897.

Peirce, Charles Sanders. "Ideas. Stray or Stolen, About Scientific Writing, No. 1." Edited by John Michael Krois. *PR* 11 (Summer 1978): 147–55.

Rush, James. *The Philosophy of the Human Voice*. Philadelphia: J. Maxwell, 1827.

Scott, Fred Newton, and Joseph Villiers Denney. *Composition-Rhetoric, Designed for Use in Secondary Schools*. Boston: Allyn and Bacon, 1897.

———. *Paragraph-Writing*. Allyn and Bacon, 1893.

———. "Rhetoric Redivia." Edited by Donald C. Stewart. *CCC* 31 (December 1980): 413–19.

———. "Rhetoric." *New International Encyclopedia*, 763–64. New York: Dodd, Mead, 1902–1904.

[Spencer, Herbert]. "The Philosophy of Style." *Westminster Review* 114 (October 1852): 234–47.

Wendell, Barrett. *English Composition: Eight Lectures Given at the Lowell Institute*. New York: Charles Scribner's Sons, 1891.

Whately, Richard. *Elements of Rhetoric*. London, Oxford: John Murry and J. F. Parker, 1828. Reprinted: Douglas Ehninger, ed. Southern Illinois University Press Series, Landmarks in Rhetoric and Public Address, edited by David Potter. Carbondale: Southern Illinois University Press, 1963.

Secondary Sources

Anderson, Dorothy I. "Edward T. Channing's Definitions of Rhetoric." *SM* 14 (1947): 81–93.

Anderson, Floyd Douglas, and Andrew A. King. "William Hazlitt as a Critic of Parliamentary Speaking." *QJS* 67 (February 1981): 47–56.

Anderson, Robert. "James Rush—His Legacy to Interpretation." *SSJ* 33 (Fall 1967): 20–28.

Auer, J. Jeffrey, and Jerald L. Banninga. "The Genesis of John Quincy

Adams's Lectures on Rhetoric and Oratory." *QJS* 49 (April 1963): 119–32.

Baker, Virgil. "Development of Forms of Discourse in American Rhetorical Theory." *SSJ* 18 (May 1953): 207–15.

Berlin, James A. "John Genung and Contemporary Composition Theory: The Triumph of the Eighteenth Century." *RSQ* 11 (Spring 1981): 74–84.

———. "The Rhetoric of Romanticism: The Case for Coleridge." *RSQ* 10 (Spring 1980): 62–74.

———. "Rhetorics and Poetics in the English Department: Our Nineteenth-Century Inheritance." *CE* 47 (September 1985): 521–33.

———. "Richard Whately and Current-Traditional Rhetoric." *CE* 42 (September 1980): 10–17.

———. "The Transformation of Invention in Nineteenth Century American Rhetoric." *SSJ* 46 (Spring 1981): 292–304.

———. *Writing Instruction in Nineteenth-Century American Colleges.* CCCC Studies in Writing and Rhetoric. Carbondale: Southern Illinois University Press, 1984.

Block, Edward. "T. H. Huxley's Rhetoric and the Mind-Matter Debate: 1868–1874." *Prose Studies* 8 (December 1985): 21–39.

Boase, Paul H., ed. *The Rhetoric of Protest and Reform, 1878–1898.* Athens: Ohio University Press, 1980.

Bormann, Dennis R. "Adam Möller on the Dialogic Nature of Rhetoric." *QJS* 66 (April 1980): 169–81.

Braddock, Richard. "The Frequency and Placement of Topic Sentences in Expository Prose." *Research in the Teaching of English* 8 (Winter 1974): 287–302.

Braun, John Elliot. "The Philosophical Roots of the Nineteenth-Century 'Repose' in Rhetoric, with Emphasis on the Idea of Communication in the Thought of Josiah Royce." Ph.D. dissertation, University of Michigan, 1977.

———. "The 'Speculative Rhetoric' of Charles Sanders Peirce." *PR* 14 (Winter 1981): 1–15.

Brockriede, Wayne E. "Bentham's Philosophy of Rhetoric." *SM* 23 (November 1956): 235–47.

Bryan, Ferald J. "Henry Grady and Southern Ideology: An Analysis of the Texas State Fair Address." In *Rhetoric and Ideology: Compositions and Criticisms of Power*, edited by Charles W. Kneupper, 205–11. Arlington, Tex.: Rhetoric Society of America, 1989.

Burke, Rebecca J. "Gertrude Buck's Rhetorical Theory." Occasional Papers in the History and Theory of Composition, no. 1. Edited by Donald C. Stewart. Manhattan: Kansas State University, 1978.

Burwick, Frederick. "Introduction." In *Essays on Rhetoric*, by Thomas De Quincey, xi-xlviii. Southern Illinois University Press Series, Landmarks in Rhetoric and Public Address, edited by David Potter. Carbondale: Southern Illinois University Press, 1967.

Campbell, John Angus. "The Invisible Rhetorician: Charles Darwin's 'Third Party' Strategy." *Rhetorica* 7 (Winter 1989): 55–85.

———. "Scientific Revolution and the Grammar of Culture: The Case of Darwin's *Origin*." *QJS* 72 (November 1986): 351–76.

Campbell, Karlyn Kohrs. "Stanton's 'The Solitude of Self': A Rationale for Feminism." *QJS* 66 (October 1980): 304–12.

Channell, Carolyn. "Genesis and Analysis: The Role of the Essay in Nineteenth-Century Scottish Universities." *RSQ* 13 (1983): 193–200.

Cherwitz, Richard A., and James W. Hikins. "John Stuart Mill's Doctrine of Assurance as a Rhetorical Epistemology." In *Explorations in Rhetoric: Studies in Honor of Douglas Ehninger*, edited by Ray E. McKerrow, 69–84. Glenview, Ill.: Scott, Foresman & Company, 1982.

———. "John Stuart Mill's *On Liberty*: Implications for the Epistemology of the New Rhetoric." *QJS* 65 (February 1979): 12–25.

Connors, Robert. "Mechanical Correctness as a Focus in Composition Instruction." *CCC* 36 (February 1985): 61–72.

———. "The Rhetoric of Explanation: Explanatory Rhetoric from Aristotle to 1850." *WC* 1 (April 1984): 189–210.

———. "The Rhetoric of Explanation: Explanatory Rhetoric from 1850 to the Present." *WC* 2 (January 1985): 49–72.

———. "The Rise and Fall of the Modes of Discourse." *CCC* 32 (December 1981): 444–55.

———. "Textbooks and the Evolution of the Discipline." *CCC* 37 (May 1986): 178–94.

Corbett, Edward P. J. "Some Rhetorical Lessons from John Henry Newman." *CCC* 31 (December 1980): 402–12.

Covino, William. "Thomas De Quincey in a Revisionist History of Rhetoric." *Pre/Text* 4 (1984): 121–36.

Crowley, Sharon. "Invention in Nineteenth-Century Rhetoric." *CCC* 36 (February 1985): 51–60.

———. "Neo-Romanticism and the History of Rhetoric." *Pre/Text* 5 (1984): 19–37.

D'Angelo, Frank. "Nineteenth-Century Forms/Modes of Discourse: A Critical Inquiry." *CCC* 35 (February 1984): 31–42.

Denton, George R. "Herbert Spencer and the Rhetoricians." *PMLA* 34 (March 1919): 89–111.

———. "Origin and Development of Herbert Spencer's Principle of Economy." In *The Fred Newton Scott Anniversary Papers*, edited by

Clarence D. Thorpe and Charles E. Whitmore. 55–92. Chicago: University of Chicago Press, 1929.

Dillman, Richard. "Thoreau's Harvard Education in Rhetoric and Composition: 1833–1837." *Thoreau Journal Quarterly* 8 (July–October 1981): 47–62.

Douglas, Wallace. "Barrett Wendell." In *Traditions of Inquiry*, edited by John Brereton, 3–25. New York: Oxford University Press, 1985.

———. "Rhetoric for the Meritocracy." In *English in America*, edited by Richard Ohmann, 97–132. New York: Oxford University Press, 1976.

Durham, Weldon B. "The Elements of Thomas De Quincey's Rhetoric." *SM* 37 (November 1970): 240–48.

Edney, C. W. "Richard Whately on Dispositio." *SM* 21 (August 1954): 227–34.

Ehninger, Douglas. "Campbell, Blair, and Whately: Old Friends in a New Light." *WS* 19 (October 1955): 263–69.

———. "Campbell, Blair, and Whately Revisited." *SSJ* 28 (Spring 1963): 169–82. Reprinted in *Readings in Rhetoric*, edited by Lionel Crocker and Paul A. Carmack, 359–73. Springfield, Ill.: Charles C. Thomas, 1965.

———. "Introduction." In *Elements of Rhetoric*, by Richard Whately, ix–xxx. Southern Illinois University Press Series, Landmarks in Rhetoric and Public Address, edited by David Potter. Carbondale: Southern Illinois University Press, 1963.

———. "Whately on *Dispositio*." *QJS* 40 (December 1954): 439–41.

Einhorn, Lois J. "Consistency in Richard Whately: The Scope of His Rhetoric." *PR* 14 (Spring 1981): 89–99.

———. "Richard Whately's Public Persuasion: The Relationship Between His Rhetorical Theory and His Rhetorical Practice." *Rhetorica* 4 (Winter 1986): 47–65.

Ettlich, Ernest Earl. "John Franklin Genung and the Nineteenth Century Definition of Rhetoric." *CSSJ* 17 (November 1966): 283–88.

———. "Theories of Invention in Late Nineteenth Century American Rhetorics." *WS* 30 (Fall 1966): 233–41.

Gold, Ellen Reid. "The Grimke Sisters and the Emergence of the Woman's Rights Movement." *SSJ* 46 (Summer 1981): 341–60.

Gray, Giles W., and Lester Hale. "James Rush, Dramatist." *QJS* 29 (February 1943): 55–61.

Grover, David H. "Elocution at Harvard: The Saga of Jonathan Barber." *QJS* 51 (February 1965): 62–67.

Guthrie, Warren. "The Development of Rhetorical Theory in America, 1935–1850." *SM* 13 (1946): 14–22; 14 (1947): 38–54; 15 (1948): 61–71; 16 (August 1949): 98–113; 18 (March 1951): 17–30.

Haberman, Frederick. "De Quincey's Theory of Rhetoric." *Eastern Public Speaking Conference, 1940, Papers and Addresses*, 191–203. New York: H. W. Wilson Co., 1940.

———. "English Sources of American Elocution." In *A History of Speech Education in America*, edited by Karl Wallace, 105–26. New York: Appleton-Century-Crofts, 1954.

———. "John Thelwall: His Life, His School and His Theory of Elocution." *QJS* 33 (October 1947): 292–98.

Hale, Lester L. "Dr. James Rush." In *A History of Speech Education in America*, edited by Karl Wallace, 219–37. New York: Appleton-Century-Crofts, 1954. Reprinted in *Readings in Rhetoric*, edited by Lionel Crocker and Paul A. Carmack, 529–41. Springfield, Ill.: Charles C. Thomas, 1965.

———. "Dr. James Rush—Psychologist and Voice Scientist." *QJS* 35 (December 1949): 448–55.

———. "Principles of James Rush as Applied to Interpretation." *SSB* 7 (November 1941): 43–45.

Harrington, Elbert. "Rhetoric and the Scientific Method of Inquiry." *University of Colorado Studies, Series in Language and Literature* 1 (December 1948): 1–64.

Hochmuth, Marie, and Richard Murphy. "Rhetorical and Elocutionary Training in Nineteenth-Century Colleges." In *A History of Speech Education in America*, edited by Karl Wallace, 153–77. New York: Appleton-Century-Crofts, 1954.

Hollis, C. Carroll. "Rhetoric, Elocution, and Voice in *Leaves of Grass*." *Walt Whitman Quarterly Review* 2 (Fall 1984): 1–21.

Horner, Winifred. "Nineteenth-Century Rhetoric at the University of Edinburgh with an Annotated Bibliography of Archival Materials." *RSQ* 19 (Fall 1989): 365–75.

———. "The Roots of Writing Instruction: Eighteenth- and Nineteenth-Century Britain." *RR* 8 (Spring 1990): 322–45. Reprinted as "Writing Instruction in Great Britain: Eighteenth and Nineteenth Centuries" in *A Short History of Writing Instruction from Ancient Greece to Twentieth-Century America*, edited by James J. Murphy, 121–49. Davis, Calif.: Hermagoras Press, 1990.

———. "Scottish Roots for the Rhetorical Tradition." In *The Rhetorical Tradition and Modern Writing*, edited by James J. Murphy, 85–95. New York: MLA, 1982.

Hoshor, John P. "American Contributions to Rhetorical Theory and Homiletics." In *A History of Speech Education in America*, edited by Karl Wallace, 129–52. New York: Appleton-Century-Crofts, 1954.

Hostettler, Gordon F. "George Saintsbury's View of Rhetoric." *WJSC* 41 (Fall 1977): 210–20.

Howell, Wilbur S. "De Quincey on Science, Rhetoric, and Poetry." *SM* 13 (1946): 1–13.

Howes, Raymond F. "Coleridge and Rhetoric." *QJS* 12 (June 1926): 145–56.

Hudson, Hoyt. "De Quincey on Rhetoric and Public Speaking." In *Historical Studies of Rhetoric and Rhetoricians*, edited by Raymond E. Howes, 198–214. Ithaca: Cornell University Press, 1961. Reprinted in *Studies in Rhetoric and Public Speaking in Honor of James A. Winans*, 132–51. New York: Russell and Russell, 1962.

Jarratt, Susan C. "Walter Pater and the Sophistication of Rhetoric." *CE* 51 (January 1989): 73–87.

Johnson, Nan. "English Composition, Rhetoric, and English Studies in Nineteenth-Century Canadian Colleges and Universities." *English Quarterly* 20 (Winter 1987): 296–304.

————. "Innovations in Nineteenth-Century Pedagogy: The Rhetorics of Henry Day, M. B. Hope, and Franz Theremin." In *The Rhetorical Tradition and Modern Writing*, edited by James J. Murphy, 105–18. New York: MLA, 1982.

————. "Rhetoric and Belles Lettres in the Canadian Academy: An Historical Analysis." *CE* 50 (December 1988): 861–73.

Jordan, Harold M. "Rhetorical Education in American Colleges and Universities, 1850–1915." Ph.D. dissertation, Northwestern University, 1952.

Judy, Stephen. "Composition and Rhetoric in American Secondary Schools, 1840–1900." *EJ* 68 (April 1979): 34–39.

King, Andrew A. "Thomas De Quincey on Rhetoric and National Character." *CSSJ* 24 (Summer 1974): 128–34.

Kitzhaber, Albert R. "Rhetoric in American Colleges: 1850–1900." Ph.D. dissertation, University of Washington, 1953.

Kremers, Marshall. "Samuel Newman and the Reduction of Rhetoric in the Early Nineteenth-Century American Colleges." *RSQ* 13 (1983): 185–92.

Leathers, Dale G. "Whately's Logically Derived Rhetoric: A Stranger in Its Time." *WS* 33 (Winter 1969): 48–58.

Lunsford, Andrea. "Alexander Bain's Contributions to Discourse Theory." *CE* 44 (March 1982): 290–300.

————. "Essay Writing and Teachers' Responses in Nineteenth-Century Scottish Universities." *CCC* 32 (December 1981): 434–43.

McKerrow, Ray E. "Campbell and Whately on the Utility of Syllogistic Logic." *WJSC* 40 (Winter 1976): 3–13.

———. "The Ethical Implications of a Whatelian Rhetoric." *RSQ* 17 (1987): 321–27.

———. " 'Method of Composition': Whately's Earliest 'Rhetoric.' " *PR* 11 (Winter 1978): 43–58.

———. "Probable Argument and Proof in Whately's Theory of Rhetoric." *CSSJ* 36 (Winter 1975): 259–66.

———. "Richard Whately and the Revival of Logic in Nineteenth-Century England." *Rhetorica* 7 (Spring, 1987): 163–86.

———. "Richard Whately's Theory of Rhetoric." In *Explorations in Rhetoric: Studies in Honor of Douglas Ehninger*, edited by Ray E. McKerrow, 137–56. Glenview, Ill.: Scott, Foresman, & Co., 1982.

———. "Whately's Philosophy of Language." *SSJ* 53 (Spring 1988): 211–26.

Mohrmann. G. P. "The Real Chironomia." *SSJ* 34 (Fall 1968): 17–27.

Mulderig, Gerald P. "Gertrude Buck's Rhetorical Theory and Modern Composition Teaching." *RSQ* 14 (1984): 95–104.

———. "Nineteenth-Century Psychology and the Shaping of Alexander Bain's *English Composition and Rhetoric.*" In *The Rhetorical Tradition and Modern Writing*, edited by James J. Murphy, 95–104. New York: MLA, 1982.

Myers, Victoria. "Coleridge's *The Friend*: An Experiment in Rhetorical Theory." *Journal of English and Germanic Philology* 86 (January 1987): 9–32.

O'Donnell, Victoria. "The Reform of the Municipal Corporations: An Historical Case Study in the Rhetoric of Social and Political Control in England." In *Oldspeak/Newspeak Rhetorical Transformations*, edited by Charles W. Kneupper, 99–105. Arlington, Tex.: Rhetoric Society of America, 1985.

Oravec, Christine. "The Democratic Critics: An Alternative American Rhetorical Tradition in the Nineteenth Century." *Rhetorica* 4 (Autumn 1986): 395–421.

———. "John Muir, Yosemite, and the Sublime Response: A Study in the Rhetoric of Preservationism." *QJS* 67 (August 1981): 245–58.

Parrish, Wayland Maxfield. "The Tradition of Rhetoric." *QJS* 33 (December 1947): 464–67.

———. "Whately and His Rhetoric." *QJS* 15 (February 1929): 58–79. Reprinted in *Readings in Rhetoric*, edited by Lionel Crocker and Paul A. Carmack, 374–96. Springfield, Ill.: Charles C. Thomas, 1965.

———. "Whately on Elocution." In *The Rhetorical Idiom: Essays in Rhetoric, Oratory, Language, and Drama, Presented to Herbert A. Wichelns*, edited by Donald C. Bryant, 43–52. Ithaca: Cornell University Press, 1958.

Pence, Orville. "The Concept and Function of Logical Proof in the Rhetoric System of Richard Whately." *SM* 20 (March 1953): 23–39.

Pomeroy, Ralph S. "Whately's *Historic Doubts*: Argument and Origin." *QJS* 49 (February 1963): 62–74.

Rahskopf, Horace G. "John Quincy Adams: Speaker and Rhetorician." *QJS* 32 (December 1946): 435–41. Reprinted in *Readings in Rhetoric*, edited by Lionel Crocker and Paul A. Carmack, 463–73. Springfield, Ill.: Charles C. Thomas, 1965.

Ray, John W. "The Moral Rhetoric of Franz Theremin." *SSJ* 40 (Fall 1974): 33–49.

Reid, Ronald F. "The Boylston Professorship of Rhetoric and Oratory, 1806–1904: A Case Study of Changing Concepts of Rhetoric and Pedagogy." *QJS* 45 (October 1959): 239–57.

Ried, Paul E. "The Boylston Chair of Rhetoric and Oratory." *WS* 24 (Spring 1960): 83–88. Reprinted in *Readings in Rhetoric*, edited by Lionel Crocker and Paul A. Carmack, 456–62. Springfield, Ill.: Charles C. Thomas, 1965.

———. "The First and Fifth Boylston Professors: A View of Two Worlds." *QJS* 74 (May 1988): 229–40.

———. "Francis Child: The Fourth Boylston Professor of Rhetoric and Oratory." *QJS* 55 (October 1969): 268–75.

———. "Joseph McKean: The Second Boylston Professor of Rhetoric and Oratory." *QJS* 46 (April 1960): 419–24.

Robb, Mary Margaret, and Lester Thonssen. "Introduction." In *Chironomia*, by Gilbert Austin, ix–xxi. Southern Illinois University Press Series, Landmarks in Rhetoric and Public Address, edited by David Potter. Carbondale: Southern Illinois University Press, 1966.

Rockas, Leo. "The Quintilian of Amherst: John Franklin Genung." *New England Quarterly* 54 (March 1981): 54–73.

Rodgers, Paul C. "Alexander Bain and the Rise of the Organic Paragraph." *QJS* 51 (December 1965): 399–408.

Rosner, Mary. "Reflections on Cicero in Nineteenth-Century England and America." *Rhetorica* 4 (Spring 1986): 153–82.

Scott, Fred Newton. "Introduction" and "Notes." In *Essays on Style, Rhetoric, and Language*, by Thomas De Quincey, iii–v, ix–xxiv. Boston, Allyn & Bacon, 1893.

Secor, Marie J. "The Legacy of Nineteenth Century Style Theory." *RSQ* 12 (Spring 1982): 76–94.

Self, Robert T. *Barrett Wendell*. Twayne United States Authors Series, no. 261. Boston: G. K. Hall, 1975.

Shearer, Ned. "Alexander Bain and the Genesis of Paragraph Theory." *QJS* 58 (December 1972): 408–17.

———. "Alexander Bain and the Teaching of Rhetoric." *CSSJ* 23 (Spring 1973): 36–73.

Sproule, J. Michael. "The Psychological Burden of Proof: On the Development of Richard Whately's Theory of Presumption." *CM* 43 (June 1976): 115–29.

Stewart, Donald C. "The Barnyard Goose, History, and Fred Newton Scott." *EJ* 67 (November 1978): 14–17.

———. "Fred Newton Scott." In *Traditions of Inquiry*, edited by John Brereton, 26–49. New York: Oxford University Press, 1985.

———. "The Nineteenth Century." In *Historical Rhetorical: An Annotated Bibliography of Selected Sources in English*, edited by Winifred Bryan Horner, 229–69. Boston: G. K. Hall, 1980.

———. "Rediscovering Fred Newton Scott." *CE* 40 (January 1979): 539–47.

———. "The Status of Composition and Rhetoric in American Colleges, 1880–1902: An MLA Perspective." *CE* 47 (November 1985): 734–46.

———. "Two Model Teachers and the Harvardization of English Departments." In *The Rhetorical Tradition and Modern Writing*, edited by James J. Murphy, 118–30. New York: MLA, 1982.

Talley, Paul M. "De Quincey on Persuasion, Invention, and Style." *CSSJ* 16 (November 1965): 243–54.

Uhlig, Claus. "Conceptual Architecture in Nineteenth Century Writing." *Comparative Literature Studies* 23 (Fall 1986): 218–33.

Warnick, Barbara. "A Rhetorical Analysis of Episteme Shift: Darwin's *Origin of the Species*." *SSCJ* 49 (Fall 1983): 26–42.

Weidner, Hal Rivers. "Three Models of Rhetoric: Traditional, Mechanical, and Vital." Ph.D. dissertation, University of Michigan, 1975.

Wellek, Rene. "De Quincey's Status in the History of Ideas." *PQ* 23 (July 1944): 248–72.

Winans, James A. "Whately on Elocution." *QJS* 31 (February 1945): 1–8. Reprinted in *Readings in Rhetoric*, edited by Lionel Crocker and Paul A. Carmack, 397–408. Springfield, Ill.: Charles C. Thomas, 1965.

Woods, William F. "Nineteenth-Century Psychology and the Teaching of Writing." *CCC* 36 (February 1985): 20–41.

Young, Richard. "Paradigms and Problems: Needed Research in Rhetorical Invention." In *Research on Composing: Points of Departure*, edited by Charles Cooper and Lee Odell, 29–47. Urbana: National Council of Teachers of English, 1978.

CONTEMPORARY RHETORIC

James L. Kinneavy

Introduction, Definitions, and Boundaries

With the advent of the last decade of this century, a text on the status of rhetorical studies mandates a chapter on the rhetoric of the past ninety years.[1] If the rest of the work is more than antiquarianism, there ought to be a lively present state of the art in our century. And indeed there is. But sketching the picture for this century is not as easy as it may seem. Rhetoric, for various reasons, has been systematically exiled from entire disciplines in many countries until quite recently. The position of Tacitus during the reign of Domitian that rhetoric thrives under democracy and languishes under tyranny and dictatorship is also true of this century.

Even in democracies such as France, Great Britain, and many others, rhetoric has not been in the ascendancy as an academic discipline in this century. However, in countries like these, practical rhetoric has been omnipresent and pervasive. This paradox of scholarly contempt and practical fealty, unparalleled in history, has created, on the one hand, serious chasms in scholastic investigations and, on the other, unmanageable mountains of partially mapped information.

This concurrent poverty and richness almost condemns the present attempt to failure at the outset. In addition, the varied meanings of the term *rhetoric* in this century further complicate the issue. Yet the attempt must be made. There are so many important investigations

1. The following writers coauthored the indicated sections: Richard Roy Penticoff ("Introduction, Definition, and Boundaries"), Christopher Holcomb ("Situational Context"), Katherine Kane ("Communication Theory, Hermeneutics, and Pragmatism"), Jason Ball ("Dialectic, Exploration, and Epistemology"), Randi Voss ("Technical Writing, Journalism, and Information Theory"), Tim Martin and Susan Warshauer ("Propaganda, Political Rhetoric, and Commercial Advertising"), Catherine Eskin ("Religious Oratory"), Alison Regan ("Women's Studies/Gender Studies"), Claire Miller ("Self-Expression"), Laura Graglia ("Mass Media and Small Group Media"), Michael Chapski ("Semiotics and Semiology"), Bartholomew Thornton ("Rhetoric as Metaphor"), Susan Romano ("Rhetoric and the Teaching of Composition"). Hugh Burns and James W. Parlett wrote the section on "Computers and Rhetoric."

going on by large groups of scholars exploring common and overlapping areas, yet often not communicating with one another, that some endeavor must be made to bring them together, even at the risk of forgetting, neglecting, or underestimating the importance of some and overemphasizing others. And, of course, many of these groups do not consider themselves rhetoricians at all.

A brief outline of the position of rhetoric at the beginning of this century might help the reader to understand the current situation. On the Continent, rhetoric was almost totally in academic decline. The decline of rhetoric in France has been examined in some detail by Paul Ricoeur in *The Rule of Metaphor* (1977) and by Gérard Genette in *Figures III* (1972). The ambivalent attitude of nineteenth-century Germany to rhetoric and rhetoric's eventual disfavor have been chronicled by Joachim Goth in *Nietzsche und die Rhetorik* (1970). At Oxford and Cambridge, despite the continuation of the weekly or fortnightly written essays presented to the tutor, rhetoric as a subject for reading and examinations was no longer required by the end of the nineteenth century. In Belgium, rhetoric as a required reading topic in universities was discontinued in the middle of the 1920s, as Chaim Perelman tells us in *The Realm of Rhetoric* (1982).

In the United States, the academic transfers of rhetoric were both more perceptible and more dramatic than in much of Europe. With the establishment of departments of English in American universities in the latter part of the nineteenth century, the allocation of the various components of the liberal arts tradition of the trivium was an early and overriding concern. Writing in the first issue of *Publications of the Modern Language Association* in 1886, James Morgan Hart, in an article entitled "The College Course in English Literature, How It May Be Improved," illustrates the issue with disarming candor: "What does *not* rightfully pertain to English literature? Settling this preliminary question will help us greatly. The main question resolves itself into three: What are we to do with logic, with rhetoric, and with English philology (Anglo-Saxon and Early English)?" (84). Hart is here speaking of the disposition of the basic components of education in Western civilization for over two thousand years. He would like to relegate logic and rhetoric to philosophy and would retain some philology in literature departments.

The historical response to his suggestions was not long in coming. In 1914, speech teachers in English departments, dissatisfied with their inferior status, dramatically walked out of the convention of the National Council of Teachers of English and set about establishing their own departments. In effect, they took rhetoric and dialectic and elocution with them. And the systematic study of rhetoric in America till quite recently has remained the province of scholars in departments of speech communications. The same decade also saw logic disposed of. The appearance in 1910 of Alfred North Whitehead and Bertrand Russell's *Principia Mathematica* sent a clear signal to all liberal arts teachers that they were no longer experts in logic. Logic quickly found its new scholarly home in departments of philosophy or mathematics. Since neither speech nor philosophy has often been required in undergraduate programs, the demise of the core training in the liberal arts can be dated from this decade in American education.

English departments, however, were still saddled with the job of training the incoming student to write logically and persuasively, although English teachers were given no training in either logic or rhetoric as a discipline. Nor were English teachers expected to engage in rhetorical scholarship. It might be added, nevertheless, that this did not prevent English teachers from writing most of the textbooks used in composition classes for the next fifty years in America. Generally they adopted without question the modified approach to the modes of discourse derived from Alexander Bain and the paragraph approach of Barrett Wendell and others outlined by Donald Stewart in the preceding chapter.

Important exceptions to these tendencies in the first half of the century were the work of I. A. Richards, *The Philosophy of Rhetoric* (1930), his collaboration with C. K. Ogden on *The Meaning of Meaning* (1923), the work of Richard M. Weaver, probably best seen in an anthology of his materials, *Language Is Sermonic: Richard M. Weaver on the Nature of Rhetoric* (1970), Wayne C. Booth's *The Rhetoric of Fiction* (1961), and Kenneth Burke's *The Grammar of Motives* (1945) and *The Rhetoric of Motives* (1950).

Teachers in English departments awoke from their dogmatic slumbers in this regard only in the 1960s. Massive increases in college registrations brought hordes of students to composition classes, many of whom were only marginally literate. With the appearance of Edward P. J. Corbett's *Classical Rhetoric for the Modern Student* (1965), English departments can be said to have brought to life their scholarly concerns with rhetoric. Today, one of the brightest features of English departments is their concern with the many, varied scholarly and practical regions of rhetoric. It is precisely these regions that I hope to outline in the following pages.

One of these regions that has only recently elicited some systematic scholarship in English departments is the general history of rhetoric—with the major exceptions of Sister Miriam Joseph and Wilbur Samuel

Howell, whose work on Shakespeare, the Renaissance, and the eighteenth century is covered in earlier chapters. This renewed historical interest is evidenced by the present book itself, and also by Winifred Bryan Horner's companion volume, *Historical Rhetoric: An Annotated Bibliography of Selected Sources in English* (1980). On a larger scale, there has been the formation of the International Society for the History of Rhetoric, which issues a biannual journal, *Rhetorica*.

Reflecting current interest in new literary history and in historiography, a group of young scholars has focused these concerns on the history of rhetoric in a series of conferences at The University of Texas at Arlington and at Purdue and in several sessions at the annual meetings of the Conference on College Composition and Communication. The 1987 Spring/Summer issue of *Pre/Text* is devoted to "Historiography and the Histories of Rhetoric I: Revisionary Histories" and is probably a fairly accurate indicator of their concerns. Susan Jarratt's "Toward a Sophistic Historiography," John Schilb's "Differences, Displacements, and Disruptions: Toward Revisionary Histories of Rhetoric," James A. Berlin's "Revisionary History: The Dialectical Method," and Victor J. Vitanza's " 'Notes' Towards Historiographies of Rhetorics; or, Rhetoric of the Histories of Rhetorics: Traditional, Revisionary, and Sub/Versive" are the four articles in the edition; they are followed by a "Colloquy" among the four authors.

One of the four authors in this collection, James A. Berlin, has written summary histories of rhetoric in the United States in the nineteenth century and in the twentieth century. The categories used by Berlin in the latter, *Rhetoric and Reality: Writing Instruction in American Colleges, 1900–1985* (1987), have already been influential in the field. A shorter version of this book is Berlin's essay on the same topic in James J. Murphy, ed., *A Short History of Writing Instruction from Ancient Greece to Twentieth-Century America* (1990).

History, however, is not as prominent an area as some of the other contemporary interests of rhetoricians. A survey of these fields is an exciting odyssey, although limitations must be placed upon the endeavor. In the first place, the projected audience of this book consists primarily of teachers and graduate students in English and related areas. Consequently, some facets of the discipline fundamental to particular areas of rhetoric removed from the immediate concerns of such departments are not considered in this chapter. Within the English department's province, further, some areas are arbitrarily being excluded. Thus literature and literary criticism and theory, except as they overlap overtly with rhetoric, are excluded. So also are folklore, linguistics, drama, and the philosophy of language—with similar reservations. Thus, I will not consider some of the very legitimate areas of rhetoric: marketing, managerial rhetoric, discussion and debating techniques, interviewing, oral interpretation, film and radio and television production (as such), general semantics and modern linguistic semantics, narrative theory, theory of description, axiology, logic, and the philosophy of science. Finally, entire areas of modern psychology, such as learning theory and cognitive science, are also excluded.

The list of topics included will, by implication, define the areas of rhetoric that I consider promising for scholarship at the current time. The rationale for the sequence, after some initial reference materials, is based upon the semiotic model that I have elaborated in *A Theory of Discourse* (1971). First considered are a number of works emphasizing the relation of the situational context to the rhetorical text. Then material relevant to general theories of discourse or interpretation or pragmatics is considered. Then follow nine sections having to do with particular functions of discourse. The first three, informal logic, dialectic and exploration, and information theory (with short notices on journalism and technical writing), all relate to expository writing. The next four, political rhetoric and propaganda, religious oratory, rhetorical criticism (with a short notice on advertising), and women's voices, all concern persuasive discourse. The eighth section is devoted to self-expression as a rhetorical issue, and a final section is devoted to media of discourse (mass media and small group media).

These nine sections all have to do with pragmatics. Two sections are then devoted to semantic issues. The first explores semiotics and semiology, a major field of investigation at the present time. In the second, rhetoric as metaphor is considered; this is possibly the dominant view of rhetoric on the Continent at the present time and raises a critical issue in both Europe and America in this century, the epistemological basis or bases of rhetoric.

Syntactic issues currently being investigated are not considered in isolation but are examined in the sections of the book having to do with teaching composition and rhetoric.

Reference Works

Unfortunately, few general reference works are devoted specifically to rhetoric. This is partly due to the sprawling nature of the discipline; it has no major departmental base, nor is there a unifying national or international group or conference of any long standing. Nevertheless, some bibliographic works do exist as well as some indexes and some dictionaries and glosses.

The closest thing to a comprehensive annual bibliography is the coverage in the *Rhetoric Society Quarterly*. This periodical (a bargain at the price) draws its material from the *Weekly Record* listings. It is quite complete since the compilers have a very comprehensive view of rhetoric; but it is limited to American publications, an increasingly important drawback, although its frequent bibliographic surveys compensate, in part, for this deficiency. A new journal, *Rhetorik: Ein internationales Jahrbuch*, published in Stuttgart, has for the past few years given the discipline an annual bibliography supplementing that of the *Rhetoric Society Quarterly*.

A few surveys of rhetorical materials exist. In 1986 Charles W. Seefeldt published "Fifteen Years of the *Rhetoric Society Quarterly*: A Bibliography of Bibliographies," citing sixty-four bibliographies in that journal. They covered antiquity, Great Britain, America, Europe, cultural movements, rhetorical criticism, ethics and rhetoric, and reading, writing, and rhetoric. A brief survey for France was made by Michèle Lacoste in *Communications* (1970). The entire issue was devoted to rhetoric and includes Roland Barthes's summary of classical rhetoric for French readers, Gérard Genette's study of the decline of rhetoric in France (later incorporated into *Figures III*), and Franz Gunther's three-page bibliography of rhetorical research in the United States.

Indexes relating to rhetoric are also limited. However, the superb *Index to Journals in Communication Studies through 1985*, edited by Ronald J. Matlon and Peter C. Facciola, covers fourteen major American journals: *Quarterly Journal of Speech, Speech Communication Monographs, Speech Teacher, Southern Speech Communication Journal, Western Speech, Central States Speech Journal, Today's Speech, Bulletin of the Association of Departments & Administrators in Speech Communication, Philosophy and Rhetoric, Journal of Communication, Journalism Quarterly, Journal of Broadcasting, Journal of the American Forensic Association*, and *Human Communication Research*. This index is the single most valuable bibliographic tool available for twentieth-century rhetoric. Its strength, the American rhetorical scene for seventy-five years, is also its limitation: its coverage of the Continent is very spotty. All of the tables of contents of the journals are reproduced, a lengthy indexing of twelve major subjects with detailed subtopics is given, and there is an index of contributors. Three editions have appeared, the latest in 1987. All editions cover all of the periodicals since their founding (thus *Quarterly Journal of Speech* goes back to 1915).

The second most useful index, particularly to the researcher interested in teaching composition, is the monthly *Current Index to Journals in Education*, which indexes about three hundred journals across the entire field of education. By supplementing this with the monthly index of *Resources in Education*, a more practical and less research-oriented publication, one gets a fairly thorough survey of this area of rhetoric. The latter publication includes books, practicum papers, instructional materials, speeches, legal materials, audiovisual references, tests, and so on. Many of the descriptors of the thesaurus, which is periodically enlarged, relate to areas of rhetoric. Both of these publications are part of the Educational Retrieval Information Centers (ERIC).

Several of the more general citation indexes have made rhetoric and allied areas a part of their more comprehensive coverage. Thus the *Arts and Humanities Citation Index* covers 1,100 periodicals fully and an additional 5,000 selectively. As a result, for example, the May–August 1981 entries under *rhetoric, rhetorical, rhetoricity,* and so on run to 269 items. The *Social Sciences Citation Index* also covers many journals that include materials related to rhetoric; it indexes 1,500 journals fully and 2,800 selectively. Finally, the *Modern Language Association International Bibliography of Books and Articles on the Modern Languages and Literature* and the *Education Index* also index rhetorical materials.

Four dictionaries and glossaries ought to be mentioned also. Three are more historical than contemporary, but all are useful. Henri Morier, *Dictionnaire de poétique et de rhétorique* (1961), and Heinrich Lausberg, *Handbuch der literarischen Rhetorik: Eine Grundlegung der Literaturwissenschaft* (1960), are both interested in the overlap of rhetoric and literature. Both are excellent in their chosen province, the history of rhetoric. Much smaller, but handy, is Richard A. Lanham's *A Handlist of Rhetorical Terms* (1969); as in the larger works of Morier and Lausberg, Lanham's emphasis is on literary concerns. Linda Woodson, in *A Handbook of Modern Rhetorical Terms* (1979), attempts to consider more contemporary material particularly germane to the teaching of composition. In this sense her work supplements the other three. Nevertheless, it is clear that there is no work that attempts a comprehensive coverage of the many areas of contemporary rhetoric.

Some Promising Areas in Contemporary Rhetoric

Situational Context

Certainly one of the most overpowering concepts in contemporary rhetoric, obvious in many different disciplines, is the notion that a piece of discourse must be judged against the situational and cultural contexts in which it was produced and in which it is being interpreted.

Rhetoricians in different disciplines, students of classical rhetoric, some philosophers, some theologians, speech act theorists, and literary critics join together in affirming this tenet of contemporary rhetoric.

Among writers in the field of speech communication, Lloyd F. Bitzer, in "The Rhetorical Situation" (1968), almost made this notion a manifesto of the journal *Philosophy and Rhetoric* in its first issue. Bitzer's work has been supported by many others in the discipline since, and it has also been attacked on occasion. Richard Vatz, in "The Myth of the Rhetorical Situation" (1972), one of the more notable retorts, precipitated a controversy on the issue. At its extreme, the obsequiousness of text to situational context can reduce rhetoric to history and dismiss language as an insignificant echo of political or economic action. Bitzer has responded to some criticisms in "Functional Communication: A Situational Perspective" (1980).

Kenneth Burke, however, whose pentad structure of act, agent, agency, purpose, and scene is a continual assertion of the importance of the various elements of the dramatic context of discourse, maintains the central importance of man as a symbolic animal. His *A Grammar of Motives* (1945) may be his most extended statement on situational context, but his whole corpus is a commentary on the issue. Carolyn R. Miller considers Bitzer and Burke and some other contextualists in "Genre as Social Action" (1984). In English departments, tagmemicists have applied to the rhetorical process of composing Kenneth L. Pike's theory of interpreting a culture by the internal (emic) norms of the members of the culture itself. Richard E. Young, Alton L. Becker, and Kenneth L. Pike's *Rhetoric: Discovery and Change* (1970) may be the best rhetorical application of this tagmemic principle.

The classical parallel to this notion, the concept of timeliness or *kairos*, was the core of Plato's rhetorical theory (see *Phaedrus* 272a), but it was only given prominence in this century by Augusto Rostagni in "Un Nuovo capitolo nella storia della retorica della sofistica" (1922) and by Mario Untersteiner's sympathetic treatment in *The Sophists* (1954). Its application to composition can be seen in Kinneavy's "*Kairos*: A Neglected Concept in Classical Rhetoric" (1983) and "The Relation of the Whole to the Part in Composition and in Interpretation Theory" (1986). He also shows the importance of the idea in Freud and in speech act theorists, particularly in Mary Louise Pratt's *Toward a Speech Act Theory of Literary Discourse* (1977).

A strong movement in modern anthropology reflects the same concern. Ethnomethodology, the idea that the methodology of analysis of a given culture ought to be conditioned by the norms of that culture, has been a major movement in the same direction of increasing emphasis on situation and cultural context. Two summary treatments of this movement are Roy Turner, ed., *Ethnomethodology: Selected Readings* (1974) and Houston Wood and Hugh Methan, *The Reality of Ethnomethodology* (1975). An interesting application of ethnography to the gender problems in writing is Linda Brodkey's *Academic Discourse as Social Practice* (1987).

Finally, the reaction of a fair number of critical theorists against the near autonomy of the text in literary criticism in the 1950s and 1960s has resulted in different emphases on situational context by various movements in philosophical and literary criticism. Although their works were written earlier, Mikhail M. Bakhtin's *The Dialogical Imagination* (1981) and N. K. Voloshinov's *Marxism and the Philosophy of Language* (1973) made their impact on the Anglo-American rhetorical scene in the 1970s and 1980s. They clearly argued for a representation in rhetorical and literary works of the many voices in the social world. Jacques Derrida in *Dissemination* (1981), Edward W. Said in *Beginnings* (1975), the group anthologized by Josué Harari in *Textual Strategies* (1979), Stanley Fish in *Is There a Text in This Class?* (1980), and others all underscore the same motif from different perspectives.

Communication Theory, Hermeneutics, and Pragmatics

Most communication theories, theories of interpretation, and theories of general discourse also stress the critical relation of the language product to the cultures that produced and interpret it. In this sense they reinforce the emphasis of the works in the previous section; this is particularly true of theories of general interpretation and the latest theories of pragmatics.

General communication theories in this century have been derived from two major sources, in my opinion. First, many theories use the information theory structure of Claude E. Shannon and Warren Weaver, presented in *The Mathematical Theory of Communication* (1964). Influential examples of such a theory can be seen in Colin Cherry, ed., *Pragmatic Aspects of Human Communication* (1974). A more psychological view of the process can be seen in George A. Miller, *Communication, Language and Meaning* (1973). A view incorporating the influence of modern mass media can be seen in Wilbur Schramm, *Men, Messages, and Media: A Look at Human Communication* (1973). An attempt to apply pragmatic theory to rhetoric, from a somewhat different perspective, can be seen in Walter A. Beale, *A Pragmatic Theory of Rhetoric* (1987).

The second major source for general communication theories in this century has been the semiotic structure elaborated by Charles W. Morris in *Signs, Language, and Behavior* (1946). It has been used by semioticians, linguists, literary theorists, logicians, information theorists, composition theorists, and so on. We will return to this model in some detail in the section on semiotics below.

In addition to general communication theory considered under that nomenclature, a second important comprehensive view of the entire language process is that of hermeneutics. Beginning with biblical and legal theories of interpretation, the hermeneutic process was generalized to all of the humanities by Friedrich Schleiermacher and Wilhelm Dilthey in the nineteenth century. Martin Heidegger then enlarged this notion to that of philosophical hermeneutics, a view that considers all understanding at any level to be an interpretation of the world. His position is presented in *Being and Time* (1962, 182–210), in which he also considers the forestructure that anyone brings to a process of interpretation (275–77, 358–64, 370, 424, especially). This forestructure and the resulting structures of interpretation are carefully analyzed by Hans-Georg Gadamer in *Truth and Method* (1986). Rudolf Bultmann applied these notions to biblical interpretation in Hans Werner Bartsch's collection *Kerygma and Myth: A Theological Debate* (1953) and in other works. Heidegger's interpretation theories also strongly influenced such French thinkers as Paul Ricoeur, Jacques Derrida, and Jacques Lacan; the first two of these consider rhetoric at great length (see below, the section titled "Rhetoric as Metaphor").

The relation of the Heideggerian forestructure to rhetoric was already implicit in the remark of Schleiermacher that rhetoric was the obverse side of the coin from hermeneutics. And, since in Heidegger every act of intelligence is an act of interpretation, it is easy to view rhetoric as the interpretation of the world to someone who, in turn, interprets the writer's interpretation. Consequently, Heidegger's forestructure, Gadamer's "prejudices," and Bultman's "myths" become immediately relevant to the process of writing (see the section on "Rhetoric and the Teaching of Composition").

A strikingly similar position can be seen in three current theories in pragmatics. Daniel Bobrow and Donald Norman's "Some Principles of Memory Schemata" (1975), Roger Schank and Robert Abelson's "Scripts, Plans, and Knowledge" (1977), and Marvin Minsky's "A Framework for Representing Knowledge" (1975) are all quite parallel, in reading theory, to the work of the hermeneuticists in interpretation theory. All of the theories posit a background of information and prejudgments brought to the business of interpreting anything. A recent application of pragmatic theory to rhetoric, though from a different perspective, can be seen in Walter A. Beale's *A Pragmatic Theory of Rhetoric* (1987).

The pragmatic position was not arrived at immediately. There were earlier syntactic emphases by two Prague school linguists, Vilem Mathesius, "On Linguistic Characterology with Illustrations from Modern English" (published in 1964, although the work was done in the 1930s), and Frantisek Danes, "One Instance of Prague School Methodology: Functional Analysis of Utterance of Text" (1970). These were followed by semantic emphases in analyzing whole discourses. The work of Walter Kintsch (1974) and of Teun van Dijk and Kintsch (1978) is possibly some of the best in that area.

Argumentation, Informal Logic, and the Rhetoric of Science

Certainly one of the success stories of the twentieth century has been the formalization of logic, which has permitted the creation of mathematical logic and the application of logic to computers. But the very precision and rigidity of the categories of formal logic have also made quite clear that much of the logic of ordinary discourse and of some technical discourse in areas like value theory, law, ethics, and politics is not amenable to the inflexible axioms and obstinate inference patterns of formal logic. Consequently, there has been a chorus of voices in several areas speaking for an informal logic.

Possibly the most conspicuous of these voices are those of the Belgian rhetoricians Chaim Perelman and L. Olbrechts-Tyteca in *The New Rhetoric: A Treatise on Argumentation* (1969), in which they argue for a reconsideration of the topics of Aristotle in a modern way and apply this new logic to law, political reasoning, and other areas. Stephen E. Toulmin, also interested in legal reasoning, has elaborated a combination of deductive and inductive reasoning in *The Uses of Argument* (1958) and later works. His model has been heavily adopted in speech communication departments, especially because of the work of Douglas Ehninger (1974). A classical model for argumentation, based upon the status theory, stresses the type of issue that is at the center of the argument: whether it is a matter of fact, or of definition, or of value. A text (and accompanying reader) using this approach is that of Jeanne Fahnstock and Marie Secor, *A Rhetoric of Argument* (1982). On the Continent, argumentation has taken a movement similar to that taken by *topoi* analysis, that is, a consideration of the kinds of argumentation proper to specific disciplines, such as law, theology, or literary theory. An anthology typical of such work is that edited by Michael Schecker, *Theorie der Argumentation* (1982); Schecker himself considers argumentation as a type of speech act. In 1987, *Argumentation*, a journal with an international advisory board, was launched and promises to be the focus of argumentation theory in the future. An American journal emphasizing debate, *Argumentation and Advocacy*, was also inaugurated in 1988.

In a similar vein, Kurt Baier's *The Moral Point of View: A Rational Basis of Ethics* (1958) has launched in ethics and value theory the movement often called the logic of *good reasons*. He argues that in these areas we are often willing to settle for less than the ultimate and perfect axiom or reason and operate with only good reasons.

From a somewhat similar perspective, ethnomethodologists, referred to above in the section on situational context, object to the rigid imposition of an outside norm on a subculture: to understand the practical reasoning of a subculture, it is unfair to assess it by the standards of scientific reasoning. Two-thirds of Roy Turner's anthology *Ethnomethodology: Selected Readings* (1974) is devoted to this issue.

Some influential Marxists, for different reasons, question the validity of the quantification of some political and sociological concepts. Friedrich Pollock, Theodor W. Adorno, and Max Horkheimer in essays in Paul Connerton, ed., *Critical Sociology* (1976), raise these issues. Other thinkers, arguing for a *praxis*, rather than a *theoria*, approach the subject somewhat differently. Jürgen Habermas, in *Theory and Practice* (1973), analyzes the kind of thinking that eventuated in action and revolution in Hegel and Marx; and Richard J. Bernstein, in *Praxis and Action* (1971), attempts a similar analysis. A much more fundamental philosophical approach to the modern notion of the objectivity of scientific knowledge has been taken by Heidegger in "The Question Concerning Technology" (1954, 1976).

Finally, a group of cognitive psychologists has also differentiated the logic of informal discourse from that of the formal logicians. Typical of such investigations is that of Richard Nisbett and Lee Ross, *Human Inference: Strategies and Shortcomings of Social Judgment* (1980).

A third recent perspective on the logic and techniques of science is that of the rhetoric of science. Scientists in many fields publish the results of their investigations. But few scientists analyze these publications as *discourses*. Literary products are examined by literary critics, but few other discourse areas are subjected to the careful scrutiny that many novels, poems, and plays receive. Recently, however, people in several disciplines, using techniques derived from rhetorical and literary criticism, are analyzing scientific texts as discourses. The University of Wisconsin Press has already published three such studies and promises more in its series Rhetoric of the Human Sciences. The first, Donald N. McCloskey's *The Rhetoric of Economics* (1985), shows the use of traditional rhetorical techniques such as appeals to ethos, common and special topic arguments, and proof by analogy and metaphor in contexts where one would expect careful and scientific logic. He analyzes these practices as used by some of the current major figures in economics and questions the strict scientific logic of much modern science. He does not, however, denigrate the rhetoric in these works. He asks scientists to recognize its presence and its importance in the dissemination of scientific texts.

The second volume in the series is a set of twenty-two papers delivered at a meeting at the University of Iowa in 1984, titled *The Rhetoric of the Human Sciences: Language and Argument in Scholarship and Human Affairs* (1987) and edited by John S. Nelson, Allan Megill, and Donald N. McCloskey. This book extends the thesis of McCloskey's volume on economics to a number of other disciplines from anthropology to history and mathematics and law.

The third volume is Charles Bazerman's *Shaping Written Knowledge: The Genre and Activity of the Experimental Article in Science* (1988). Bazerman's book is much more in the terrain of the scientists themselves. He examines the historical development of patterns of writing or modes of exploration and proof and occasionally reaches conclusions somewhat shocking to the scientists. His study of the gradual decline of the exploratory in favor of the rigidly statistical in psychology studies stunned the psychology scholars in his audience at a presentation at the University of Texas. His work uses careful linguistic and paraliterary analysis combined with historical sampling. Recently other scholars have taken up this concern. Alan Gross has an article on "Discourse on Method: The Rhetorical Analysis of Scientific Texts" in *Pre/Text* (1988). The area is just opening up.

Dialectic, Exploration, and Epistemology

Questioning the validity of the rules of formal logic as they apply to some types of human situations is really an epistemological inquiry. So also are the major concerns of this section. Chaim Perelman has done much of his work in the periodical *Dialectica*, which is dedicated to the provisional and changing nature of knowledge. As Frédéric Gonseth said in the first issue of this periodical, "Real scientific progress is not a step from certitude to certitude, from reality to reality, it is a step from provisional and cumulative evidence to further provisional and cumulative evidence" ("L'idée de dialectique aux entretiens de Zurich," 32). The tentative, sometimes even questionable, nature of scientific knowledge is a major motif in modern thought generally. Its application to rhetoric has been made by such thinkers as Jacques Derrida in his essay "White Mythology" (1974), which I will mention again in relation to rhetoric as metaphor. Other frontal attacks on the security of scientific thought, such as those made by Karl Popper in *The Logic of Scientific Discovery* (1959) and by Paul K. Feyerabend in *Against Method: Outline of an Anarchistic Theory of Knowledge* (1978), are applied to rhetoric by disciples and practitioners. Both emphasize the negative and even mythical nature of science. An attempt to apply Feyerabend's theories to rhetoric has been made in the first volume of *Pre/Text*. The application of Popper's and Feyerabend's work may conceivably cleanse the stables of much accumulated filth. Some of our rhetorical theories are eminently falsifiable, though they may not be verifiable at all.

Popper and Feyerabend have drawn many of their conclusions from examining scientists in the process of exploring. The concept of exploration as such has proved a rich field for modern rhetoric and composition theory. Richard E. Young, Alton L. Becker, and Kenneth L. Pike, in *Rhetoric: Discovery and Change* (1970), apply their own exploratory principles (their heuristic) to the process of writing. Their heuristic is derived from scientific roots; it is not surprising, therefore, that for these three rhetoricians, rhetoric is almost reduced to a pursuit for truth, or to a dialectic.

Another heuristic of science, that of Thomas S. Kuhn, outlined in *The Structure of Scientific Revolutions* (2d ed., 1970), has also been given several adaptations to rhetoric, particularly by Kinneavy, *A Theory of Discourse*, and by several freshman textbook writers, such as Maxine Hairston and John J. Ruszkiewicz, *The Scott Foresman Handbook with Writing Guide* (1991).

Kenneth Burke's work, referred to in the section on situational context, is also a clear illustration of the application to rhetoric of a dialectic that is at least partly Hegelian in origin. Large sections of the *Grammar of Motives* are devoted explicitly to dialectic.

The dialectical importance of rhetoric is also seen in two major works from the Continent. One is Ernesto Grassi's *Rhetoric as Philosophy: The Humanist Tradition* (1980), which argues against the separation of rhetoric from philosophy and attempts to show historically how the influence of Cicero has been more important for the philosophical tradition than we now concede. Samuel Ijselling, in *Rhetoric and Philosophy in Conflict: An Historic Survey* (1976), also attempts a rapprochement between the two disciplines. These historic procedures can be profitably juxtaposed to the rather synchronic techniques of a fair number of writers in speech communication. Henry Johnstone (1969), Robert L. Scott (1976), Richard A. Cherwitz (1977, 1982), and others have attempted to move rhetoric from its traditional position as an after-the-fact deliverer of truth to a truth-generating function (they call it epistemic) in certain kinds of discourse. James Berlin has applied this to composition studies in the historic surveys of the nineteenth and twentieth centuries mentioned above (1984, 1987).

Three other areas of research in dialectic—highly promising for rhetorical implications, in my opinion—are the three approaches to the subject-object problem proposed by Martin Heidegger, Georg Lukács, and Theodor W. Adorno. Heidegger's solution to the subject-object dichotomy, presented in *Being and Time* (1962, especially 244–356), establishes a primordiality of hermeneutic thought over scientific thought; if rhetoric is included in hermeneutic thought (as poetry is), then another important epistemology of rhetoric must be examined, an epistemology that will obviously be related to the Heideggerian concept of forestructure examined above in the section on hermeneutics.

In addition, the Marxist theory of subject-object convergence in society, as presented in Lukács, *History and Class Consciousness* (1922, 1974), and the curious primacy of object in Adorno's analysis (1978) both have major rhetorical ramifications. So also does Adorno's concept of *Negative Dialectics* (1966, 1973). Both Lukács and Adorno insist that society, especially economic and industrial society, so severely conditions the "reality" of any given individual and the way in which such a "reality" is perceived that talk about simple subject and simple object is impossible. In effect, the rhetoric of capitalism must be considered in talking about knower and known, or subject and object.

Technical Writing, Journalism, and Information Theory

Three separate fields—technical writing, journalism, and information theory—can be discussed together here because all are similar types of referential discourse. Rhetorically, they are all concerned with transmitting information, though both technical writing and journalism do much more. Traditionally, the purpose of technical writing has been to present information clearly and disinterestedly—the writing itself is merely a medium for the facts, and the writer is a sort of faceless go-between, with the audience interested only in the information. The most obvious function of journalism is to produce the news story, a factual report. And information theory is concerned with the transmission of information in its electronic, its semantic, and its pragmatic dimensions.

But increasingly, following the current destabilizing of the notion of objectivity as it relates to writers, language, and even reality, these fields are, although still concentrating on the referential function of communication, giving greater attention to the two previously neglected corners of the communication triangle—the writer and the audience. They are also now more interested in problems of language.

In technical writing, recent leading scholarship reflects these trends. Mary Coney, for example, in "Contemporary Views of Audience Theory: A Rhetorical Perspective" (1989), calls for a reappraisal of conceptions of audience suitable to new ideas about the writing process, invention, language, and knowledge itself. James Zappen goes back to the classical tradition to point out the probabilistic, political, and ethical dimensions of rhetoric in "Historical Studies in the Rhetoric of Science and Technology" (1987). David Dobrin questions the very concept of objectivity in "Is Technical Writing Particularly Objective?" (1985). Taken together these works indicate the need for a theory that would encompass the changes in the field, but such a theory has not yet been forthcoming. Books in this field are still limited to guides, manuals, and textbooks that traverse well-worn paths. Most are rule oriented and not up-to-date in recent composition or rhetorical theory.

There are two recent book-length surveys of technical writing, one edited by Sarojini Balachandran (1977) and the other by Gerald J. Alred, Diana C. Reep, and Mohan R. Limaye (1981). The first is restricted to books and articles since 1965 related to engineers and scientists. It is an excellent annotated bibliography about such topics as encouraging engineers to write, training engineers and scientists to write, manual writing, the impact of computers and word processors on writing, and so on. The second is a larger historical view and a larger conceptual definition of technical writing, particularly because it encompasses business writing.

A short notice must also be given to journalism. An influential book outlining different views of the functions of journalism is Frederick S. Siebert, Wilbur Schramm, et al., *Four Theories of the Press: The Authoritarian, Libertarian, Social Responsibility, and Soviet Communist Concepts of What the Press Should Be and Do* (1956). Two journeyman introductions to the business of reporting are Curtis MacDougall's *Interpretive Reporting* (1977) and Mitchell V. and Blair Charnley's *Reporting* (1979). A more technical book is that of Philip Meyer, *Precision Journalism: A Reporter's Introduction to Social Science Methods* (1979). A book questioning the capitalistic and totalitarian control of news channels is Herbert I. Schiller's *Communication and Cultural Domination* (1976).

Journalism, however, is also trying to break new ground using old theories. Books in the field assume that the referent, for them "the news," is a recognizable, unambiguous entity, but then devote hundreds of pages to the complex problems of finding it, interpreting it, and presenting it. Much discussion is also devoted to the problem of subjectivity and the relation of the journalist to the "facts," and to the problem of audience. But these problems have not yet been incorporated into a more comprehensive new theory.

The most interesting rhetorical work in journalism is being done in ethics; scholars in this area are beginning to recognize the contingent nature of "the news" and to see ethical problems as an inevitable result of there being as many versions of an event as there are interested witnesses to it. Although ethics is not new to journalism, there certainly is a revival of interest in journalistic ethics. Tom Goldstein, in *Killing the Messenger: 100 Years of Media Criticism* (1989), has collected fifteen essays from the past century that he considers self-critical, although he acknowledges that such work is largely lacking in contemporary journalism. John Merrill in *The Dialectic in Journalism: Toward a Responsible Use of Press Freedom* (1989) and Edmund Lambeth in *Committed Journalism: An Ethic for the Profession* (1986) both draw on the classical traditions of dialectic and ethics to help solve modern moral issues in journalism.

Unlike journalism, and like the work in pragmatics discussed above, the movement in information theory in rhetoric has moved from the syntactic to the semantic to the pragmatic. Claude E. Shannon and Warren Weaver's *The Mathematical Theory of Communication* (1964) inaugurated the syntactic phase in this country and, as we have seen, influenced theories of communication. With the important application of this theory to the semantic level by Yehoshua Bar-Hillel in *Language and Information: Selected Essays on Their Theory and Application* (1964), it became possible to make rhetorical applications at particular discourse levels. Rulon S. Wells made the move to pragmatics in "A Measure of Subjective Information" (1961). A much more extensive application to informative discourse as such was made by James L. Kinneavy in *A Theory of Discourse* (1971, 1980), using Bar-Hillel and Carnap's theories. A recent book attempting to make the connection between informative discourse and mathematics is that of Rudy Rucker, *Mind Tools: The Five Levels of Mathematical Reality* (1987).

Propaganda, Political Rhetoric, and Commercial Advertising

The next four sections generally relate to what I have called *persuasive* discourse. Sometimes, particularly in "Rhetorical Criticism" and "Women's Studies/Gender Studies," items mentioned relate to more than one area (for example, some items are relevant to both scientific and literary discourse). Because of the increasing importance of mass media in our society, persuasive discourse has penetrated almost every aspect of our lives. Indeed, it may be that the twentieth century is the most persuasive of all centuries. It is indeed possible that human beings have been manipulated by verbal techniques more in our era than at any other time in history. Yet this aspect of language is often almost totally ignored by entire departments of English, French, Spanish, Russian, and so on.

One person who for decades has studied political propaganda is Harold D. Lasswell. Possibly his best theoretical book on the subject is *Language of Politics* (1949), written in conjunction with several of his associates. His *Propaganda and Promotional Activities: An Annotated Bibliography*, reprinted in 1969, is still a major work. Another important voice has been that of Leonard Doob, *Public Opinion and Propaganda* (1966). A European analysis of Nazi propaganda is Eugen Hadsmovsky's *Propaganda and National Power: The Organization of Public Opinion for National Politics* (1972). Most of the works mentioned so far in this section are earlier studies of propaganda in World Wars I and II. A more recent study of Russian propaganda is that of Frederick C. Barghoorn, *Soviet Union Propaganda* (1964). Undoubtedly, with the recent developments in Eastern Europe, there will soon be searching studies of propaganda in many countries that have until recently not permitted such investigations. One recent survey of research into propaganda is Garth S. Jowett's "Propaganda and Communication: The Re-Emergence of a Research Tradition" (1987), which discusses fourteen new books that signal a revival of interest in the role of propaganda as a tool of mass persuasion and examines modern concerns about public opinion and advertising.

Some of the best analyses of American domestic and foreign political rhetoric have been made by writers in speech communication. The *Index to Journals in Communication Studies through 1985*, cited above, for instance, lists many specific entries under different American presidents from Roosevelt through Reagan. It also includes analyses of regional American, as well as British and European, political rhetoric. Some of the better practical analysts are also good theorists. A few of these, for whom both a theoretical and an analytical entry are listed in the bibliography, are L. W. Rosenfield (1968, 1976), Bruce E. Gronbeck (1975, 1978), David L. Swanson (1977, 1978), and Walter R. Fisher (1973, 1980).

A fascinating article on political rhetoric by Hans-Jochen Schild, "Political Rhetoric: A Potential Threat to Democracy; Questions Concerning the Study of Political Rhetoric" (1988), discusses the danger to democracies of political rhetoric without an accompanying analysis of language control. A particular form of political rhetoric is the selective reporting of news. An article by Edward S. Herman, "Diversity of News: 'Marginilizing' the Opposition" (1985), examines this technique as it was used in the coverage of events in Cambodia, East Timor, El Salvador, and Nicaragua.

Political rhetoric is also a major concern of the Frankfurt Marxists, but they examine the influence of political propaganda on the economic scene in a different way than do any of the studies hitherto presented. Consequently their works are an excellent bridge between politics and advertising. Theodor W. Adorno's *Introduction to the Sociology of Music* (1976), Jürgen Habermas's *Communication and the Evolution of Society* (1979), Max Horkheimer's *Critical Theory* (1972), and Herbert Marcuse's *One-Dimensional Man* (1972) are a few of the important works in this area.

In advertising, which has been looked at more constructively than critically, a few major works present a good background to the subject. A recent poll indicates that the most widely read book in advertising is not a scholarly work at all, but a biographical report by David Ogilvy, *Confessions of an Advertising Man* (1983). Two recent books on advertising are Michael L. Rothschild's *Advertising: From Fundamentals to Strategies* (1987) and Dorothy Cohen's *Advertising* (1988). The traditional periodical in the field has been *Advertising Age*, but *Adweek* (1979–) is a recent competitor; it also has five regional editions: East, Southeast, Midwest, West, and Southwest. *The International Encyclopedia of Communication* (1989), edited by Erik Barnouw, is a new addition to materials on advertising and communication generally.

Two analytical works on advertising, influential in several university departments, are Erving Goffman, *Gender Advertisements* (1979), and the earlier study of Marshall McLuhan, *The Gutenberg Galaxy* (1962).

Religious Oratory

The scholarship in religious oratory is not nearly as interesting, in my opinion, as that in political or commercial rhetoric. However, at least two interesting intersections—those of preaching with mass media and of preaching with modern theology—show some rhetorical potential.

Probably the most thorough coverage of the history of preaching written in this century is Yngve Brilioth's *A Brief History of Preaching* (1965). This work, however, covers only the first half of this century, since it first appeared in 1945. An exhaustive bibliographical collection of American materials by William Thompson and William Toohey is *Recent Homiletical Thought: A Bibliography, 1935–65* (1967). Thompson, a Baptist, and Toohey, a Catholic, coedited the book-review section of *Preaching*, a periodical that attempts to cover the current scene. Harry Caplan and Henry H. King, in a series of monographs between 1949 and 1956, have compiled bibliographies on preaching for Italian, Spanish, Scandinavian, Dutch, English, German, and French. Karl Rahner has edited *The Renewal of Preaching: Theory and Practice* (1968), an attempt at a coverage of preaching in ten different countries, which has much bibliographic material (nearly all Catholic). John A. Melloh has a more recent review of preaching materials, "Publish or Perish: A Review of Preaching Literature, 1981–1986" (1988), and so does Richard Lischer, "Recent Books on Preaching" (1987).

Three important influences can be seen in American preaching in this century. First there is the overpowering influence of the nineteenth-century masterpiece by John Broadus, *On the Preparation and Delivery of Sermons*, a book in its twenty-ninth edition in 1944 since its appearance in 1870. This text's sources were not limited to Baptist ministers, possibly because of its deep roots in classical rhetorical theory. Broadus says, quite candidly, "The author's chief indebtedness for help has been to Aristotle, Cicero, and Quintilian, and to Whately and Vinet. The last two (together with Ripley) had been his textbooks" (xiii). These rhetorical, rather than doctrinal, sources are evident in the organization of the text—a quite basic arrangement of argument, style, and delivery—and in the virtues of style—clarity, energy, elegance.

The second overpowering influence in American preaching has been that of Harry Emerson Fosdick. Fosdick's famous statement on preaching, "What is the Matter with Preaching?," first published in 1928, became a manifesto for much of the pulpit practice in America for the next fifty years. His charge to ministers to address a problem that their listeners could see as relevant to their lives has moved sermons away from the exegesis of Scripture to the exploratory and the topical. He has been held responsible even for some of the current tendencies in television oratory by such figures as Jerry Falwell and for the techniques of such mass media performers as Billy Graham. In this general area, Bruce A. Rosenberg's *The Art of the American Folk Preacher* (1970) should also be mentioned.

Theology, thirdly, has made some impressive marks on preaching in this century, mostly in the latter half of the century. Rudolf Bultmann, arguably the single most dominant theologian of the last fifty years, by emphasizing the message of the gospel, the proclamation function of the minister, and the necessity of presenting the biblical message in modern terms (demythologized from the biblical presentations), heavily influenced Christian preaching theory and practice in both Protestant and Catholic circles. In particular his premise that the biblical message must be separated from the myths of the first century A.D. necessitated a new view of pulpit practice. Dietrich Ritschl's *A Theology of Proclamation* (1960), Otto Semmelroth's *The Preaching Word: On the Theology of Proclamation* (1965), and the work of Rahner mentioned above, *The Renewal of Preaching*, clearly show this legacy.

Rhetorical Criticism

In a generic sense, of course, most of the critical essays referred to throughout this essay constitute rhetorical criticism. However, the term has taken on a particular meaning for a large group of writers, mostly in departments of speech communication, in the past half-century. The meaning was wrestled with in a seminal book edited by Lloyd F. Bitzer and Edwin Black, *The Prospect of Rhetoric: Report of the National Developmental Project* (1971). Many of the major names in the field are included in this collection, and it represents some of the major motifs of the movement, such as criticism of the rhetorical tradition, the movement to empirical research, and the incorporation of models from the social sciences.

The attack on traditional, but especially neo-Aristotelian, rhetoric came, however, in a full blast from Edwin Black's *Rhetorical Criticism: A Study in Method* (1965), an influential text. Herbert W. Simons, *Persuasion: Understanding, Practice, and Analysis* (1976), has given new directions to the study of persuasion. Donald Bryant's "Rhetoric: Its Function and Its Scope" (1953) and A. Craig Baird's *Rhetoric: A Philosophical Inquiry* (1965) were both influential in asking questions, the answers to which constitute rhetorical criticism today. They inquired about the scope of rhetoric, the epistemology of rhetoric, its relation to philosophy, and so on.

Some of the important names in the field have already been mentioned in other contexts and are included in the bibliography under the sections indicated: Lloyd Bitzer in considering situational context (section III); L. W. Rosenfield, Bruce E. Gronbeck, David L. Swanson, and Walter R. Fisher under political rhetoric (section VIII); Henry W. Johnstone, Robert L. Scott, and Richard A. Cherwitz under epistemological problems (section VI); Lionel Crocker and Harry Caplan and Henry H. King under religious rhetoric (section IX).

One severe qualification must be made about putting some of these writers under *persuasion* as a concept distinguished from referential discourse. Particularly the writers connected with the epistemic nature of rhetoric would not want their work to exclude what I have called exploratory or scientific discourse—and I do not intend such an exclusion here.

Women's Studies/Gender Studies

Interest in gender and rhetoric has emerged from the studies of gender and literature and gender and language that were instituted by feminist scholars in the 1970s. What is known as "gender studies" today started as "women's studies" two decades ago. While there is little feminist work that labels itself "rhetorical," there is a mass of work devoted to studying the influence of gender on rhetorical situations.

In 1971, the National Council of Teachers of English published *A Case for Equity*, a collection of essays that explored, as the editor, Susan McAllester, put it, the "Puzzling . . . dilemma of American women in 1971 as encountered by college teachers and students" (p. vii), especially in departments of English. This publication was followed by an issue of *College English* edited by Elaine Hedges and entitled "Women Writing and Teaching" (1972), which again addressed the status of women in universities. This work paved the way to works like *Gendered Subjects* (1986), edited by Margo Culley and Catherine Portuges, that examine the issues of feminist pedagogy.

The holistic or synthesizing tendency of feminist analysis has been sustained and encouraged by two interdisciplinary publications that remain central to ongoing study: *Feminist Studies*, founded by Ann Howard Calderwood in 1969 and first published in 1972, and *Signs: Journal of Women in Culture and Society*, established in 1975 under the editorship of Catherine R. Stimpson. Special issues of other journals concerned with the theory and analysis of textual interpretation have been devoted to feminist theory. Of note here is an issue of *Critical Inquiry* on "Writing and Sexual Difference" (1981).

In one of the seminal works of feminist theory, *The Second Sex* (1953), Simone de Beauvoir defined the idea of woman as Other. This concept has formed the basis for a great deal of feminist work. Much of the original feminist work in discourse analysis was done in English departments by women who sought to isolate "female" qualities in women's writings and to distinguish feminine rhetorical and discursive practices from their masculine counterparts. First with their book *The Madwoman in the Attic* (1979), and more recently with their two-volume *No-Man's Land—The Place of the Woman Writer in the Twentieth Century* (1988–1989), Sandra M. Gilbert and Susan Gubar have contributed to the theory and analysis of discourse within the framework of literary analysis. While Gilbert and Gubar examine writers, *Gender and Reading: Essays on Readers, Texts, and Contexts* (1986), edited by Elizabeth A. Flynn and Patrocinio P. Schweickart, focuses on reader response.

Some scholars have recognized different kinds of "otherness." They have given attention to marginalized literatures and have examined the ways in which race, ethnicity, social class, and sexual preference also affect rhetorical and discursive practices. *But Some of Us Are Brave: Black Women's Studies* (1982), edited by Gloria T. Hull, Patricia Bell Scott, and Barbara Smith, and *This Bridge Called My Back: Writings by Radical*

Women of Color (1983), edited by Gloria Anzaldua and Cherrie Moraga, both offer good overviews of interdisciplinary minority women's studies, and both have comprehensive bibliographies.

Another area of current interest is the interpretation and use of European discourse theory, especially French feminist theory, which often has its roots in psychoanalytical and post-structuralist theories. *New French Feminism* (1980), edited by Elaine Marks and Isabelle de Courtivron, and *Sexual/Textual Politics* (1985) by Torril Moi both offer the American reader a sampling of French feminist theory along with thorough bibliographies. Moi's book and *The Future of Difference* (1980), a collection of essays edited by Hester Eisenstein and Alice Jardine, attempt to bring together American and Continental feminist concerns. *Gender & Theory* (1989), edited by Linda Kauffman, addresses the relationships of post-structuralist, Marxist, and psychoanalytical theory to feminism.

Finally, a practical note: recognizing that linguistic usage both reflects and affects social attitudes, scholars have studied sexism in language and have published guidelines for nondiscriminatory usage. *Language, Gender, and Professional Writing: Theoretical Approaches and Guidelines for Nonsexist Usage* (1989), by Francine Wattman Frank et al., gives an overview of research on sexism in language and suggests alternatives to sexist usage.

Self-Expression

A last type of rhetorical genre that has, in a sense, only come into its own in this century, is that in which the expression of the speaker assumes dominance in the text, oral or written, with the consequence that the persuasive appeal, or the literary art, or the scientific or explanatory is reduced to a secondary or tertiary role. Cursing, some prayer, manifestos, gripe sessions, some contracts, and personal journals are forms that can take on this major role. Interest in this type of discourse is found usually among people professionally concerned with psychological counseling, education, composition training, or philosophical wholeness of personality.

I will arbitrarily limit my coverage to the latter two categories. In the training for composition teaching, three names have come to the fore, insisting that one of the best ways to get students to write in any genre is to let them express themselves freely. Afterward, with some minimal scribal fluency, the students can move on to expository writing, or literary creations, with more ease. Ken Macrorie's *Uptaught* (1970), Peter Elbow's *Writing without Teachers* (1973), and Lou Kelley's *From Dialogue to Discourse* (1972) were among the early books that presented this viewpoint convincingly. They have affected the structure of textbooks from elementary school through freshman college English since that time. In the 1980s, expressive discourse has been also found to be quite useful in teaching technical writing and writing across the curriculum, as will be seen in the section on "Rhetoric and the Teaching of Composition."

But expressive discourse need not be restricted to the schoolroom in order to justify its existence. It may be regarded as the most fundamental of all language experiences. This issue is addressed by a philosophical tradition deriving originally from Hegel's *The Phenomenology of Mind* and transmitted through Martin Heidegger's *Being and Time,* Jean-Paul Sartre's *Being and Nothingness,* Maurice Merleau-Ponty's *The Primacy of Perception* and *Phenomenology of Perception,* and Georges Gusdorf's *Speaking (La Parole).* The last mentioned is the most explicit statement of the position insofar as discourse explicitly is concerned. The tradition of Sartre, Merleau-Ponty, and Gusdorf has been put to theoretical use by James L. Kinneavy in *A Theory of Discourse.*

Until quite recently, as can be seen from the preceding paragraphs, philosophers, English teachers interested in writing, and psychologists have been those mainly concerned with this area of discourse study. Scholars in speech communications have lately evinced an interest in this field. Typical of such articles is Isaac E. Catt's "Rhetoric and Narcissism: A Critique of Ideological Selfism" and Harold Barrett's "Narcissism and Rhetorical Maturity," both published in 1986.

Mass Media and Small Group Media

With the advent of contemporary mass media, the channel of communication has become virtually as central as the message; indeed, in the phrase of Marshall McLuhan, the medium is the message. McLuhan's most extensive analysis of this phenomenon is his *Understanding Media: The Extensions of Man* (1964). Earlier, Walter J. Ong, in *Ramus, Method, and the Decay of Dialogue* (1958), had chronicled the move from an oral to a visual universe in media.

Today, no one interested in rhetoric can ignore the importance, even for the written word, of film, television, radio, and even the modern magazine itself. At the present time the most dominating influences in theory are probably structuralism and Marxism, though some thinkers not affiliated with either school have done excellent work. The members of the Frankfurt school, mentioned above under political and commercial rhetoric, must also be mentioned in this connection. A somewhat similar approach to the problem of the influence of mass media on the populace is the work of Michael Real, whose latest book is

Supermedia: A Cultural Approach (1989). Herbert J. Gans, in *Popular Culture and High Culture* (1968), questions the legitimacy of looking upon certain types of cultural genres as superior to the mass media genres. John G. Cawelti, in *Adventure, Mystery, and Romance* (1976), examines such popular genres as the detective story, the western, and the social melodramatic novel. Martin J. Medhurst and Thomas W. Benson, in *Rhetorical Dimensions in Media: A Critical Casebook* (1984), also examine the rhetoric of these media and include a fine bibliography.

In the field of television, Raymond Williams, *Television: Technology and Cultural Form* (1975), and John Fiske, *Television Culture* (1987), are excellent. The first is an intelligent Marxist reading, and the second is a semiotic study of television and society. Horace Newcomb's anthology, *Television: The Critical View*, in its fourth edition, offers various perspectives on the medium. For the cinema, Thomas Schatz's *Hollywood Film Genres* (1981) uses Continental and structuralist techniques to investigate the movies.

Both film and television pose the question of the rhetoric of the visual image. Some excellent work has been done in this area. Roland Barthes in *Mythologies* (1972) and in *Image—Music—Text* (1978) pioneered in this area. Bill Nichols's *Ideology and the Image* (1981) continues this trend.

A fine new journal has come on the scene since the first edition of this book. *Critical Studies in Mass Communication*, started in 1984, has already made a major impact on the field. And the *Journal of Broadcasting and Electronic Media* since 1985 has enlarged its domain to include all electronic media.

Mass media are not the only media that have been subjected to careful analysis in this century. In the field of small group media at least a few of the important studies ought to be mentioned, particularly as they relate to family relationships. Some of these are: Harold H. Kelley, *Personal Relationships: Their Structures and Processes* (1979); Harold H. Kelley and John N. Thibaut, *Interpersonal Relations: A Theory of Interdependence* (1978); Murray S. Davis, *Intimate Relations* (1973); and Mark L. Knapp, *Interpersonal Communication and Human Relationships* (1984). An anthology in this area is edited by Robert T. Graig and Karen Tracy, *Conversational Coherence: Form, Structure, and Strategy* (1983).

Semiotics and Semiology

It could be argued, with some plausibility, that the most pervasive structure of American and European discourse analysis has been provided by the semiotic framework of "syntactics, semantics, pragmatics," which has also provided the structure of this essay and has been adopted by logicians, linguists (structural or transformational), discourse analysts, rhetoricians, literary theorists, information theorists, and semioticians themselves. I have referred above to the semiotic influence, precisely because of its pervasiveness. When the triad is translated into discourse terms, such as *text* (referend, syntactic), *subject matter* (referent, semantic), and *sender* and *receiver* (pragmatic), it becomes the familiar communication triangle at the base of much contemporary rhetorical thinking.

Although semiotics, in a formal sense, is almost totally a twentieth-century discipline, its early history in the work of Charles Sanders Peirce reaches back into the nineteenth century and earlier. Achim Eschbach and Jurgen Trabant, in *History of Semiotics* (1983), have given us the first full history of the subject. For a geography of the subject, one can consult the entries in *Semiotics 1984* (1985), edited by John Deely. The topics range from the semiotics of literature through visual arts, film, music, law, architecture, philosophy, linguistics, and some issues in the history of semiotic inquiry. Another excellent anthology, edited by Robert E. Innis, *Semiotics: An Introductory Anthology* (1985), has chapters by Charles S. Peirce, Ferdinand de Saussure, V. N. Voloshinov, Karl Bühler, Susanne K. Langer, Claude Lévi-Straus, Gregory Bateson, Roman Jakobson, Charles Morris, Roland Barthes, Meyer Shapiro, Emile Beneviste, Umberto Eco, René Thom, and Thomas A. Sebeok—a roll call of important names in the field. A European two-volume anthology, *Aims and Prospects of Semiotics* (1985), edited by Herman Parret and Hans-Georg Ruprecht, rivals the 1985 Deely anthology mentioned above for range and comprehensiveness.

Any work on semiotics must begin with and continue to consult *The Collected Papers of Charles Sanders Peirce* (1960–1966). A long section in volume 1, paragraphs 219–307, is almost the beginning of the modern discipline. In volume 1, paragraphs 300–417, he applies his triad to phenomenology and metaphysics; in volume 2, paragraphs 100–104, he applies it to logic, in paragraphs 105–10 to "speculative rhetoric," and so on. These should be supplemented with *Semiotics and Significs: The Correspondence between Charles S. Peirce and Lady Victoria Welby*, edited by C. S. Hardwick and J. Cook (1973). The most useful secondary work on Peirce, for me, is that of Murray G. Murphey, *The Development of Peirce's Philosophy* (1961).

Much of the terminology and many of the concepts of modern semiotics derive from Charles William Morris's *Signs, Language, and Behavior* (1946, 1955). He systematically applied the ideas of Peirce and others to discourse theory. His earlier *Foundations of the Theory of Signs* (1938) was part of a concerted attempt by a number of major modern philosophers and scientists to make semiotics the foundation of an international view of sciences and philosophy. The first comprehensive encyclopedia has been edited by Thomas A. Sebeok, *Encyclopedic Dictionary of Semiotics* (1986). It is in three volumes, with the third volume being a bibliography.

In France, undoubtedly the most significant figure in semiology (an attempt to apply semiotics to entire cultural systems of meanings) has been Roland Barthes. In his *Mythologies* (1972) he analyzes many modern cultural forms (sports, striptease, and so forth) and then in the last chapter erects a theory of these cultural systems of "myth." A more theoretical treatment is to be found in his *Elements of Semiology* (1968). One of his most fascinating analyses is *The Fashion System* (1983), a semantic investigation of the world of dress and fashions. The most recent translation of Barthes's work into English is *The Semiotic Challenge* (1988). The book includes a short history of rhetoric, a theory of narrative, and applications of semiotics to medicine, sociology, urbanism, advertising, biblical passages, and a tale of Poe.

In Italy certainly the most vocal authority has been Umberto Eco in *A Theory of Semiotics* (1976), *The Role of the Reader* (1979), and *Semiotics and the Philosophy of Language* (1984). In the first he erects a major alternative theory to that of Morris; in the second he applies his system to particular texts and takes cognizance of the reader, a component of meaning he had systematically ignored in his first book; in the third he considers the deconstruction of the sign and analyzes metaphor, symbol, code, and other types of signs.

Rhetoric as Metaphor

As was pointed out in the first part of this chapter, rhetoric in Europe in the nineteenth and twentieth centuries has often been simply equated with figures of speech. And this notion persists in some areas, but with a particular twist deriving mainly from Nietzsche. With the publication of some of Nietzsche's lectures on rhetoric in the Musarion edition, *Gesammelte Werke, Fünfter Band: Vorlesungen 1872–1876* (1922), scholars have seen the importance of his treatment of metaphor from an epistemological standpoint. If all of language is metaphorical and, consequently, only a partial and inaccurate rendition of reality, even science and philosophy are condemned to metaphor and rhetoric in their reports of the world, according to Nietzsche. Jacques Derrida takes up this theme, using Nietzsche, and applies this theory to all discourse, including science and literary criticism. His treatment, "White Mythology," first appeared in French in *Poétique* (1971), in an edition that also included a translation into French of much of the

Nietzsche material from the Musarion edition, as well as several articles on Nietzsche's views on rhetoric.

In this article, Derrida also reviewed the work of Gaston Bachelard, *La Formation de l'esprit scientifique* (1938), and G. Canguilhem, *Etudes d'histoire et de la philosophie des sciences* (1973), both of whom had studied the use of metaphor by scientists in great detail. Derrida finally rejected Bachelard's thesis that it is possible to erect science and a literary criticism on language which has metaphor as its base. Bachelard's thesis was also defended in a lengthy reply by Paul Ricoeur, in *The Role of Metaphor* (1977). Derrida responded with "The Retrait of Metaphor" (1978).

Both Gérard Genette in *Figures of Literary Discourse* (1982) and Roland Barthes in "The Old Rhetoric: An Aide Mémoire," *The Semiotic Challenge* (1988), regret the narrowing of rhetoric to this figural view. However, a Belgian group of rhetoricians, the Groupe Mu, has made this concept the basis for its *Rhétorique générale* (1971), edited by Jacques Dubois and others. It is probably significant that the work has also been translated into Spanish.

An important collection of essays, *On Metaphor* (1979), edited by Sheldon Sachs, includes three essays relating metaphor to rhetoric: one by Wayne Booth, "Metaphor as Rhetoric"; one by Paul de Man, "The Epistemology of Rhetoric"; and one by Paul Ricoeur, "The Metaphorical Process of Cognition, Imagination, and Feelings."

De Man's *Allegories of Reading: Figural Language in Rousseau, Nietzsche, Rilke, and Proust* (1979) is probably the most influential work in the Nietzsche-Derrida tradition at the present time. De Man does consider "persuasion" an alternative to a figural notion of rhetoric, but he questions whether the two may not be the same thing in the long run.

The most thorough application of a topical way of reading to a whole discipline is no doubt Hayden White's *Metahistory: The Historical Imagination in Nineteenth-Century Europe* (1973). He uses the four master tropes of metaphor, synecdoche, metonymy, and irony to analyze four historians and four philosophers of history to show that each thinks in a basic figural way. Two write history through the lenses of metaphor, two through those of the synecdochic part-whole relationship, two as causally determined metonymically, and two ironically.

Rhetoric and the Teaching of Composition

Most of the interest in the contemporary study of rhetoric in departments of English has come about because of the "literacy crisis," as it is called, in our schools and universities. There is much evidence that, for a number of reasons, students cannot write as well as they used to thirty or forty years ago. Yet high school and college graduates still must write in their subsequent careers—more, in fact, than most of them imagine. The business of teaching students to write in a culture that is, on the surface at least, more dominated by television and radio than by the written media has become a major preoccupation of English and other departments. Indeed, it is this aspect of rhetoric that, probably more than any other, has inspired this book and that is the major professional commitment of most of the authors of the chapters.

Consequently, it is fitting that the volume should include as one of its major sections some of the exciting work underway in this area. Most of it, it must be admitted, is of fairly recent date; there has probably been more written in this area in the past thirty years than in the previous three centuries. It is difficult, therefore, to limit the coverage of this area, just as it has been difficult to limit the coverage of all of the concerns of this chapter.

After some bibliographic and general material, I will try to follow the traditional rhetorical order of invention, organization, and style. Consequently I will next give some theories on invention and process, then some approaches to arrangement, a few modern views of revision, some concerns with student dialects, some pedagogical approaches, and finally a word about the subject matter of students' writing.

The most thorough bibliographic survey of material in this field is by Gary Tate, editor of *Teaching Composition: 12 Bibliographic Essays* (2d ed., 1987). The topics covered are invention (Richard E. Young); structure in nonnarrative form (Richard L. Larson); style (Edward P. J. Corbett); aims, modes, and forms of discourse (Frank D'Angelo); writing tests (Richard Lloyd-Jones); basic writing (Mina P. Shaugnessy); basic writing update (Andrea Lunsford); language varieties and composition (Jennifer M. Giannasi); literacy, linguistics, and rhetoric (W. Ross Winterowd); literary theory and composition (Joseph J. Comprone); rhetoric and literature (Jim W. Corder); writing across the curriculum (James L. Kinneavy); and computers and composition (Hugh Burns).

Another excellent bibliographic survey is that by George Hillocks, Jr., *Research in Written Composition: New Directions for Teaching* (1986). This work updates the work of the same scope by Richard Braddock, Richard Lloyd-Jones, and Lowell Schoer in 1963 and attempts to validate the usefulness of experimental and empirical studies in composition study. Two earlier works in this area are *Perspectives on Recent Research and Scholarship in Composition* (1985), edited by Ben W. McClelland and Timothy R. Donovan, and *New Directions in Composition Research* (1984), edited by Richard Beach and Linda S. Bridwell. "Heuristic Procedures and the Composing Process: A Selected Bibliography" (1982), by Richard Leo Enos et al., is almost as extensive in coverage as the Tate volume.

In addition to the annual updates to the general field of rhetoric mentioned early in this essay, an important recent addition focuses on the particular area of this section. Erika Lindemann has prepared two bibliographies covering materials since 1984 in the projected annual *Longman Bibliography of Composition and Rhetoric* (1987, 1989). The first two books have been exemplary in their coverage; none of the other general bibliographies equals their comprehensiveness or depth for this area.

Several useful anthologies can serve as an introduction to the teaching of composition. Edward P. J. Corbett and Gary Tate, in *The Writing Teacher's Sourcebook* (1988), have assembled articles or chapters of books on most of the issues treated in this section and have additional bibliographic recommendations. In addition, Donald McQuade has edited a fine collection of more scholarly works in *The Territory of Language: Linguistics, Stylistics, and the Teaching of Composition* (2d ed., 1986). Somewhat more limited in scope, but exhaustive for its field, is *Sentence Combining: A Rhetorical Perspective* (1985), edited by Donald A. Daiker, Andrew Kerek, and Max Morenberg.

The periodical most dedicated to the teaching of composition for many years is *College Composition and Communication*. Other periodicals that frequently treat composition issues are *College English* and *English Journal* (for secondary schools). In the area of research, *Research in the Teaching of English* publishes empirically based scholarship on composition. More recent journals include the *Rhetoric Review*, the *Journal of Basic Writing*, the *Journal of Advanced Composition*, *Journal of Teaching Writing*, and *Composition Chronicle*.

The dominant theoretical view of the field of composition for the first half of the century was based on what were at the time usually called the forms of discourse and have now come to be called the modes of discourse: narration, description, exposition, and argumentation. These were generally derived from the faculty psychology of Alexander Bain, a Scottish rhetorician of the nineteenth century. In the 1940s and 1950s his approach was displaced at the high school by what was called the language arts and at the college level by the communication arts of reading, writing, speaking, and listening. But this approach did not basically affect the curriculum or the textbook offerings. These came to be crystallized in the trilogy of literature, writing, and grammar both in high schools and in colleges (though grammar was renamed linguistics in the colleges).

With the revival of classical rhetoric described above, and with infiltrations from literary theory and psychology, rhetoricians began to evolve various theoretical approaches as a base on which to build the massive writing instruction going on in English departments. James Moffett, *Teaching the Universe of Discourse* (1968, 1983), has a theory with roots in Piaget and general semantics. James N. Britton's *The Development of Writing Abilities (11–18)* (1975) centers on the functions of language and bases its developmental orientation on Piaget. James L. Kinneavy's *A Theory of Discourse* is also based on the functions or aims of discourse and draws heavily from semiotics and the history of the liberal arts tradition. Frank J. D'Angelo's *A Conceptual Theory of Rhetoric* (1975) draws heavily from the historical topics of rhetoric and also from the master tropes in the rhetorical tradition. Richard E. Young, Alton L. Becker, and Kenneth L. Pike, in *Rhetoric: Discovery and Change* (1970), use a tagmemic approach to composition drawn from linguistics.

The last fifteen years have seen the rise of an emphasis on process in composition teaching, with a consequent deemphasis on the concept of simply being satisfied with the end product. The results have been pedagogical, psychological, and rhetorical. One of the early voices in this area was Gordon R. Rohman, whose "Pre-Writing: The Stage of Discovery in the Writing Process" (1966) was an important statement of the movement. Young, Becker, and Pike's book mentioned in the preceding paragraph was also influential, as was Janice Lauer's "Heuristics and Composition" (1970). The psychological aspect of the movement can be seen particularly in the work of Linda S. Flower and John R. Hayes; two of their important essays are "The Cognition of Discovery: Defining a Rhetorical Problem" (1980) and "The Dynamics of Composing: Making Plans and Juggling Constraints" (1980). Janet Emig, in *The Composing Processes of Twelfth Graders* (1971), also presents a psychological study of the writing process. Some recent reservations about the process approach have been voiced by Lester Faigley in "Competing Theories of Process: A Critique and a Proposal" (1986).

Some scholars who emphasize process have recently joined with the philosophical movement of the social construction of meaning, particularly as exemplified by Richard Rorty, *Philosophy and the Mirror of Nature* (1979), and Peter L. Berger and Thomas Luckman, *The Social Construction of Reality: A Treatise in the Sociology of Knowledge* (1967). The idea that notions of reality are socially constructed neatly corresponded to a pedagogy of members of peer groups helping each other write. The champion of this view of collaborative learning in writing has been Kenneth Bruffee, who has written two influential articles, "Collaborative Learning and the Conversation of Mankind" (1984) and "Social Construction, Language, and the Authority of Knowledge: A

Bibliographical Essay" (1986). An important book on these cluster groups is Ann Ruggles Gere's *Writing Groups: History, Theory, and Implications* (1987). This notion was given further rhetorical impetus by Karen Burke Le Fevre's *Invention as a Social Act* (1987).

Another fairly recent movement in composition theory is what might be called an anti-theory trend. One of the more vocal and strident books advocating this position is that of C. H. Knoblauch and Lil Brannon, *Rhetorical Traditions and the Teaching of Writing* (1984). It largely repudiates the classical rhetorical tradition, the use of rhetorical genres, the teaching of logical or invention skills, and the like. Despite the fact that reviews of the book were almost universally negative, it continues to have some currency. Stephen M. North in *The Making of Knowledge in Composition: Portrait of an Emerging Field* (1987) turns to the kind of knowledge that practitioners of the teaching of composition have, which he calls lore and distinguishes from formal theory.

James L. Kinneavy makes a similar distinction but adds the kind of practical knowledge made in moral and political acts to recall the long tradition of *theoria-praxis-poiesis* that runs from Aristotle through the Middle Ages and the Renaissance (in Hobbes, for instance) into the three critiques of Kant, and in Marxist theories of knowledge and action (see "Thinkings and Writings," 1989). Kinneavy, however, does not move in the direction of an opposition to theory.

While still discussing the level of the whole composition, we must add a new section to the earlier edition. In the past fifteen years the movement called "writing across the curriculum" has been the most impressive. This movement has been adopted, in one form or another, by half of the colleges surveyed by the Modern Language Association in 1983. Griffin, in a 1984 survey published as "Programs for Writing across the Curriculum" (1985), found that 66 percent of his respondents had some form of writing across the curriculum.

At the secondary level the movement had come from the influence of the book by Britton and his associates mentioned above. At the college level, one of the most influential programs was that initiated at Michigan in 1981, requiring each student to take a course in the student's major field with a substantial writing component. The departments included all of those in the College of Literature, Science, and the Arts. Another influential program was that initiated throughout Beaver College in 1977. Both of these programs had teachers in the various disciplines handling the courses. A different type of course, taught in the English department but requiring students to write papers having to do with their major fields, was first offered at Brigham Young University, then at Maryland, Texas, and other institutions. These programs are described and analyzed at some length in Kinneavy, "Writing across the Curriculum" (1983).

Some excellent anthologies describing particular programs and providing bibliographies exist for writing-across-the-curriculum programs. Toby Fulwiler and Art Young, the founders of the fine program at Michigan Technological University, have edited *Language Connections: Writing and Reading across the Curriculum* (1982). Another fine collection, with course descriptions from many different disciplines, is that edited by Anne Ruggles Gere, *Roots in the Sawdust: Writing to Learn across the Disciplines* (1985). Similar descriptions of courses in the Michigan program can be seen in *Forum: Essays on Theory and Practice in the Teaching of Writing* (1983), edited by Patricia Stock.

The Britton report (1975), undoubtedly the most influential study in writing across the curriculum in the last fifteen years, articulated some of the major motifs that currently preoccupy such programs in English-speaking countries—the concern with writing in all departments of a school, the attention given to the various purposes of writing, the distinguishing of different audiences in writing, and the care for using language as a learning device. These emphases have been found in both high school and college programs in writing across the curriculum.

The fourth emphasis, using writing as a way to learn the subject matter, has been the focus of some important articles. Janet Emig's "Writing as a Mode of Learning" (1977) is one of the earliest and one of the best. Another frequently cited article is that by Anne J. Herrington, "Writing to Learn: Writing across the Disciplines" (1981). A third fine article is David Hamilton's "Interdisciplinary Writing" (1980). This emphasis has been operative in four of the influential programs mentioned above, those at Michigan, Beaver College, Michigan Tech, and Maryland.

The many programs in writing across the curriculum clearly represent a concern for subject matter in writing courses. Another statement of the concern for subject matter in writing courses came from a different direction. In 1987 E. D. Hirsch, Jr., published a best-seller called *Cultural Literacy*. In his earlier work in composition Hirsch had been concerned with measuring the readability of student prose. But the more Hirsch became concerned with writing problems, the more he became convinced that many students simply did not have the cultural background to enable them to engage in intelligent prose about many matters. This problem he referred to as the issue of cultural literacy. Hirsch's book has engendered much debate in the past few years.

The study of the organization of the parts of a discourse insofar as they relate to the teaching of composition has not been nearly as interesting a field as either general composition theory or invention and process. However, a few studies ought to be mentioned. Richard L. Larson's bibliographical essay in the Tate volume (1987), mentioned earlier, is a survey of much of the material available. Herbert A. Simon, in *The Sciences of the Artificial* (1981), addresses the problem of creating the structures of the artificial but does not go into rhetorical concerns in any depth. At the level of the sentence, Ross Winterowd's "The Grammar of Coherence" (1970) attempts to isolate the possible ways of combining sentence concepts. Another approach to combining parts of a discourse has been the recent work of some scholars in what has come to be called coherence and cohesion. One of the better studies in this area is that of Stephen P. Witte and Lester Faigley, "Coherence, Cohesion, and Writing Quality" (1981).

At the sentence and the paragraph level, the twentieth century has seen some interesting developments. Francis Christensen, in *Notes toward a New Rhetoric* (1967, 1978), elaborated a new theory of paragraph development, largely based upon his research on Hemingway's writing style. Kenneth L. Pike, in "A Linguistic Contribution to Composition" (1964), applied tagmemic theory to composition, as did A. L. Becker in "A Tagmemic Approach to Paragraph Analysis" (1965). Paul Rodgers, Jr., in "A Discourse-Centered Rhetoric of the Paragraph" (1966), argued for a more holistic view of the paragraph in its relation to the entire theme.

Certainly the most spectacular and interesting work on the sentence in teaching composition has been that of the sentence combiners, some following the work of Christensen and some following the lead of Kellog Hunt, who has shown that the sentence complexity of the student develops systematically from the lower grammar grades through college. His most influential report was *Grammatical Structures Written at Three Grade Levels* (1965). John C. Mellon (1969), Frank O'Hare (1973), and Donald Daiker et al. (1985) have made experimental studies using the sentence-combining techniques in high school and freshman college composition classes, in all three cases with significant results compared to traditional techniques. Joseph M. Williams, in *Style: Ten Lessons in Clarity & Grace* (1984), has made an excellent combination of linguistics and rhetoric in studying problems of sentence structure and punctuation. He is not a sentence combiner, but he has learned from the movement.

Syntax and vocabulary were both an issue in a heated controversy in the sixties (somewhat abated, but not solved today) about the use of nonstandard and minority dialects in the teaching of composition. Certainly the most stimulating articles on this subject came from the pen of James H. Sledd, whose "Bi-Dialectalism: The Linguistics of White Supremacy" (1969) and "Doublespeak: Dialectology in the Service of Big Brother" (1972) both aroused considerable controversy. Geneva Smitherman's "English Teacher, Why You Be Doing the Thangs You Don't Do?" (1972) focused the issue in an article written in black dialect. In 1974, the National Council of Teachers of English and the Conference on College Composition and Communication both approved a statement on "Students' Rights to Their Own Language."

Possibly the most telling empirical finding of this century in composition research relating to grammar has been the accumulated evidence that the isolated teaching of formal grammatical skills (traditional, structural, or transformational) cannot be shown to bring any significant improvement in writing, reading, or speaking skills. Ingrid Strom in "Research in Grammar and Usage and Its Implications for Teaching Writing" (1960) and Richard Braddock, Richard Lloyd-Jones, and Lowell Schoer in *Research in Written Composition* (1963) summarize sixty years of research on the topic. George Hillocks, Jr., in *Research in Written Composition: New Directions for Teaching* (1986) adds twenty-three years more of accumulated evidence.

Another important field of concern having to do with mechanical problems was examined by Mina P. Shaughnessy in a masterful piece of research. *Errors and Expectations* (1977) analyzes thousands of essays by students entering into the CUNY schools in New York and systematizes their errors into intelligible and finite patterns. She also points out how important these errors seem to these students. Her study has been one of the foundations of work in basic writing since that time.

Some worthwhile work in revision as a process in teaching composition has also challenged traditional notions. Braddock and his associates in the book just mentioned had summarized early work on the subject. Nancy I. Sommers in "Revision Strategies of Student Writers and Experienced Adult Writers" (1980) has emphasized the danger of letting revision degenerate into a concern for mechanics. Ellen W. Nold, in *Re-vising: Toward a Theory* (1979), attempts to put what we currently know into a manageable synthesis that the teacher can use in teaching revising.

Another area in which empirical research has come a long way is that of assessing student papers. Early criticisms of subjectivity in grading criteria and lack of agreement on the part of graders have been carefully met by rigorous and tested research methods. It is now possible, by means of training sessions, to arrive at better than 90 percent agreement among graders. Sometimes the papers are graded by a reading that gives only a summary "holistic" grade, as it is called. Sometimes there is an analysis of different elements. A good summary of existing knowledge in this field can be seen in Stephen P. Witte and Lester Faigley, *Evaluating College Writing* (1983).

Computers and Rhetoric

Computers have become commonplace tools for writers, scholars, teachers, researchers, information managers, and even mere rhetoricians, so it is not surprising that advances in computer technology affect contemporary rhetorical issues. Nor is it particularly novel that while critical views of how knowledge is constructed or deconstructed, used or abused, shared or not shared often differ widely, rhetoricians still require tools for validating theories of discourse, context, hermeneutics, dialectic, propaganda, and semiotics, among others. Such rhetorical concerns are extensive and complex. What is controversial is that the computer may be too much help, may be too smart. Herein lies the debate: how intelligent will these machines become? In the last edition of this volume, the computer was described as a "medium already affecting secretarial practice and methods of teaching composition." Obviously, much has happened in less than eight years. Suffice it to say that, as a major instrument of the information age, the computer with its electronic interactivity has opened new ways for investigating the classical rhetorical canon—invention, arrangement, style, memory, and delivery. Although much of the activity has centered on composition and the teaching of composition, the newest generation of computer software will be explored more as a medium in its own right, comparable to books, film, and television.

Where does one begin to grapple with the literature? Helen J. Schwartz's and Lillian S. Bridwell-Bowles's "A Selected Bibliography on Computers in Composition" (1984) and the "Update" (1987) are fine starting places, for each provides a list of articles, books, and software on computer-assisted instruction in composition. These articles are especially thorough for composition programs based on word processing. Solveig Olsen as editor of *Computer-Assisted Instruction in the Humanities* (1985) reports the findings of the Modern Language Association's conference on the instructional uses of computers in the high school and undergraduate humanities curriculum. A cautious optimism is reflected in the twelve essays in the first part of the volume, and the second part is an invaluable list of "Sources and Resources," including people, programs, and print sources. Hugh Burns's "Computers and Composition" (1987) is another good starting point. In his bibliographical essay, he reviews the historical context from the mid-1960s through the late 1980s. He also summarizes the state-of-the-art computer-assisted instruction (CAI) in teaching composition and foreshadows future intellectual and practical issues of using computers to teach writing. Paula R. Feldman and Buford Norman's *The Word-worthy Computer: Classroom and Research in Applications in Language and Literature* (1987) is another comprehensive overview with an excellent bibliography, well worth reading and using.

Jeanne W. Halpern and Sarah Liggett in *Computers and Composing: How the New Technologies Are Changing Writing* (1984) discuss how word processing, interactive television, audio mail, electronic mail, and dictating equipment are changing the way writers write. Specifically, they focus on how dictation/word processing systems have affected business writing and argue that composition teachers should establish better connections between the classroom and the business world through an understanding of the technological work setting. William Wresch's *The Computer in Composition Instruction: A Writer's Tool* (1984) was the first collection—thirteen essays—by composition teachers who had attempted to harness computers to their own purposes: prewriting, editing and grammar instruction, word processing research, and integrated writing processors. Wresch's volume emphasizes software design, development, and classroom applications. In the same vein, James L. Collins and Elizabeth A. Sommers in *Writing On-Line: Using Computers in the Teaching of Writing* (1985) collected practical essays on teaching writing with word processors. William Zinsser's *Writing with a Word Processor* (1983) depicts how useful computers can be after one breaks through the fear and trembling Ellen Nold (1975) warned humanists about in her early call for research. If word processors are servants, they can help writers achieve clarity, simplicity, and humanity.

The computer has made many rhetoricians more active in pursuing the technological promise. Cynthia L. Selfe in *Computer-Assisted Instruction in Composition: Create Your Own!* (1986) describes the process of creating computer-assisted instruction: identifying assumptions about writing, selecting topics, planning the interaction, designing, developing lessons, giving appropriate feedback, designing screen displays, making field tests, and communicating the results. Helen J. Schwartz's *Interactive Writing: Composing with a Word Processor* (1985) was the first textbook to keep the rhetorical strategies center stage, letting the word processor stay in the tactical background. More recently, William V. Costanzo in *The Electronic Text: Learning to Read and Reason with Computers* (1989) brings developments in cognitive psychology and advanced computing techniques to reading and writing issues.

As our theories and practices in rhetoric account for the advantages and disadvantages of a dynamic text, contemporary rhetorical scholarship will find itself deeply concerned with examining text as a means of representing knowledge and with investigating the nature of rhetorical processing itself. Invention scholarship, for example, has already been exciting. Ellen McDaniel's "A Comparative Study of First-Generation Invention Software" (1986) is a good place to start. Philip D. Gillis's "Using Computer Technology to Teach and Evaluate Prewriting" (1987) and Dawn Rodrigues and Raymond J. Rodrigues's "Computer-Based Invention: Its Place and Potential" (1984) are also important for establishing a foundation. In terms of text dynamics, Edward Barrett's *Text, Context, and Hypertext* (1988) presents twenty articles on new paradigms for writing and rhetorical studies with a special emphasis on new concepts such as hypertext, hypermedia, and automated publishing—an intriguing examination of computers in the corporate culture. The impact in such settings is only beginning to be discussed in rhetorical circles; studies such as Terry Winograd and Fernando Flores's *Understanding Computers and Cognition: A New Foundation for Design* (1986) and Shoshana Zuboff's *In the Age of the Smart Machine: The Future of Work and Power* (1988) present many dilemmas of transforming information models to knowledge models—in the human mind as well as at the workplace. Such radical new paradigms invite more in the way of critical perspectives on the composition classroom, as can be found in Gail E. Hawisher and Cynthia L. Selfe's *Critical Perspectives on Computers and Composition Instruction* (1989).

Often a "machine-in-the-garden" motif occurs in this literature as a sign that the focus of our scholarship is on puzzling out a figure-ground relationship between human and computer—sometimes one sees the machine, sometimes one sees the human. What needs to be understood are the dynamic computer-human interactions. Seeing both is important. Douglas R. Hofstadter in *Godel, Escher, Bach: An Eternal Golden Braid* (1980) presents "a metaphorical fugue on minds and machines in the spirit of Lewis Carroll," and he won the 1980 Pulitzer Prize for his labors. Hofstadter explores on several levels how our minds develop formal systems of explanation, only to realize that the system cannot explain itself. Sherry Turkle in *The Second Self: Computers and the Human Spirit* (1984) presents a fascinating account of how computers are affecting culture. She argues that the computer is a psychological machine because it makes a person think about his or her own processes; a computer becomes a second self. Seymour Papert in *Mindstorms: Children, Computers, and Powerful Ideas* (1980) views computers in education as having tremendous power to stimulate ideas, as tools for discovery and self-enrichment. Upbeat about human-computer communication as a natural process, he tells the story of the LOGO environment, the computer language that gave us the "turtle—a computer object to think with." Colette Daiute's *Writing and Computers* (1985) stimulates us to think about computers and writing in fresh ways because she stresses the social, physical, and cognitive processes of computer-assisted writing. Roger C. Schank and Peter G. Childers in *The Cognitive Computer: On Language, Learning, and Artificial Intelligence* (1984) probe the basic issues of linguistics, learning, and even philosophy in artificial intelligence research. They also explore the implications of computer literacy and natural language understanding for using computers in schools. Hugh Burns in "The Promise of Artificial Intelligence Research for Composition" (1985) defines such research as a way to investigate how we operate as writers, thinkers, arrangers, and editors. He introduces expert systems and speculates about intelligent computer-assisted instruction in the composition classroom. The future promises more interdisciplinary research among cognitive scientists, linguists, computer scientists, educators, and rhetoricians as "intelligent" software is designed, developed, evaluated, and used.

A number of professional journals are publishing articles on computers and rhetoric. Three are regularly dedicated to such topics: *Computers and Composition, Computers in the Humanities,* and *Computational Linguistics*. Other journals now exploring issues related to computers and rhetoric are *College Composition and Communication, College English, Research in the Teaching of English, Journal of Advanced Composition, Journal of Basic Writing, Educational Technology, The Computing Teacher, Classroom Computing, T.H.E. Journal, Academic Computing*. Tracking the technology itself as the electronic capabilities improve year by year is also a good practice. Some of the more widely available journals are *Byte, Personal Computing, AI Magazine,* and *Infoworld*.

Experts may continue to disagree about the extent to which information technology will be useful in contemporary rhetoric, but coming to terms with innovation, with ideas, with inference, with uncertainty, with consequences of action, with human understanding in a complex world, with self-expression—such "topoi" have long presented a challenge and an opportunity for rhetoricians no matter what century they lived in. Our century just happens to have a knowledge machine in the garden.

Bibliography

The sections in the bibliography correspond to the sections in the text of the chapter. Readers are advised to check all sections related to their interests for works that overlap.

I. Introduction, Definition, and Boundaries

Applebee, Arthur N. *Tradition and Reform in the Teaching of English*. Urbana, Ill.: National Council of Teachers of English, 1974.

Berlin, James A. "Revisionary History: The Dialectical Method." *Pre/Text* 8 (Spring/Summer 1987): 47–61.

———. *Rhetoric and Reality: Writing Instruction in American Colleges, 1900–1985*. Carbondale: University of Southern Illinois Press, 1987.

———. "Writing Instruction in School and College English, 1890–1985." In *A Short History of Writing Instruction from Ancient Greece to Twentieth-Century America*, edited by James J. Murphy, 183–220. Davis, Calif.: Hermagoras Press, 1990.

Berlin, James A., and Robert P. Inkster. "Current-Traditional Rhetoric Paradigm and Practice." *Freshman English News* 8 (Winter 1980): 1–4, 13–14.

Bitzer, Lloyd F., and Edwin Black, eds. *The Prospect of Rhetoric: Report of the National Developmental Project*. Sponsored by Speech Communication Association. Englewood Cliffs, N.J.: Prentice-Hall, 1971.

Booth, Wayne C. *The Rhetoric of Fiction*. Chicago: University of Chicago Press, 1961, 1982.

Burke, Kenneth. *The Grammar of Motives*. Berkeley: University of California Press, 1945, 1969.

———. *The Rhetoric of Motives*. Berkeley: University of California Press, 1950, 1969.

Corbett, Edward P. J. *Classical Rhetoric for the Modern Student*. 1965. 2d ed. New York: Oxford University Press, 1971.

Genette, Gérard. "La Rhétorique restreinte." *Figures III*. Paris: Editions du Seuil, 1972.

Goth, Joachim. *Nietzsche und die Rhetorik: Untersuchungen zur deutschen Literaturgeschichte*. Tübingen: Max Niemeyer Verlag, 1970.

Hairston, Maxine. "The Winds of Change: Thomas Kuhn and the Revolution in the Teaching of Writing." *CCC* 33, no. 1 (February 1982): 76–82.

Hart, James Morgan, J.U.D. "The College Course in English Literature, How It May Be Improved." *PMLA* 1 (1886): 84–94.

Horner, Winifred Bryan. *Historical Rhetoric: An Annotated Bibliography of Selected Sources in English*. Boston: G. K. Hall, 1980.

Jarrat, Susan. "Toward a Sophistic Historiography." *Pre/Text* 8 (Spring/Summer 1987): 9–26.

Kinneavy, James L. *A Theory of Discourse*. New York: W. W. Norton & Co., 1971, 1980.

Murphy, James J., ed. *The Rhetorical Tradition and Modern Writing*. New York: MLA, 1982.

———. *A Short History of Writing Instruction from Ancient Greece to Twentieth-Century America*. Davis, Calif.: Hermagoras Press, 1990.

Perelman, Chaim. *The Realm of Rhetoric*. Translated by William Kluback. Notre Dame: University of Notre Dame Press, 1982.

Richards, I. A. *The Philosophy of Rhetoric*. New York: Oxford University Press, 1936.

Richards, I. A., and C. K. Ogden. *The Meaning of Meaning*. New York: Harcourt, Brace, and World, 1923.

Ricoeur, Paul. *The Rule of Metaphor: Multidisciplinary Studies of the Creation of Meaning in Language*. Translated by Robert Czerny. Toronto: University of Toronto Press, 1977.

Schilb, John. "Differences, Displacements, and Disruptions: Toward Revisionary Histories of Rhetoric." *Pre/Text* 8 (Spring/Summer 1987): 47–61.

Vitanza, Victor J. " 'Notes' Towards Historiographies of Rhetorics; or, Rhetoric of the Histories of Rhetorics: Traditional, Revisionary, and Sub/Versive." *Pre/Text* 8 (Spring/Summer 1987): 63–125.

Weaver, Richard M. *Language Is Sermonic: Richard M. Weaver on the Nature of Rhetoric*. Edited by Richard L. Johannesen, Bernard Strickland, and Ralph T. Eubanks. Baton Rouge: Louisiana State University Press, 1970.

Young, Richard E. "Paradigms and Problems: Needed Research in Rhetorical Invention." In *Research in Composing*, edited by Charles Cooper and Lee Odell, 29–47. Urbana, Ill.: National Council of Teachers of English, 1978.

II. Reference Works

Arts and Humanities Citation Index (1976–). Philadelphia: Institute for Scientific Information.

Barthes, Roland. "L'Ancienne rhétorique—aide-mémoire." *Communications* 16 (1970): 172–229.

Current Index to Journals in Education (1969–). Phoenix: Oryx Press.

Dyck, Joachim. "Rhetorical Studies in West Germany 1971–1973: A Bibliography." *RSQ* 8 (Spring 1978): 77–81.

———. With addenda by Peter Jehn. "Rhetorical Studies in West Germany 1974–1976: A Bibliography." *RSQ* 7 (Winter 1977): 1–19.

Education Index (1929–). New York: H. W. Wilson Co.

Gunther, Franz. "La Recherche rhétorique aux Etats-Unis." *Communications* 16 (1970): 235–37.

Lacoste, Michèle. "Choix bibliographique." *Communications* 16 (1970): 230–35.

Lanham, Richard A. *A Handlist of Rhetorical Terms: A Guide for Students of English Literature*. Berkeley: University of California Press, 1969.

Lausberg, Heinrich. *Handbuch der literarischen Rhetorik: Eine Grundlegung der Literaturwissenschaft*. 2 vols. Munich: Max Heuber Verlag, 1960.

Matlon, Ronald J., and Peter C. Facciola, eds. *Index to Journals in Communication Studies through 1985*. Falls Church, Va.: Speech Communication Association, 1987.

MLA International Bibliography of Books and Articles on the Modern Languages and Literatures (1886–). New York: MLA.

Morier, Henri. *Dictionnaire de poétique et de rhétorique*. Paris: Presses Universitaires de France, 1961.

Pike, Kenneth L. *Language in Relation to a Unified Theory of the Structure of Human Behavior*. 3 vols. Glendale, Calif.: Summer Institute of Linguistics, 1960.

Resources in Education (1974–). Washington, D.C.: U.S. Government Printing Office.

Rhetoric Society Quarterly (1969–). St. Cloud, Minn.: Rhetoric Society of America.

Rhetorik: Ein internationales Jahrbuch (1980–). Stuttgart: Fromman-Holzboog.

Seefeldt, Charles W. "Fifteen Years of the *Rhetoric Society Quarterly*: A Bibliography of Bibliographies." *RSQ* 16, nos. 1–2 (1986): 99–105.

Social Sciences Citation Index (1969–). Philadelphia: Institute for Scientific Information.

Woodson, Linda. *A Handbook of Modern Rhetorical Terms*. Urbana, Ill.: National Council of Teachers of English, 1979.

III. Situational Context

Bakhtin, Mikhail M. *The Dialogical Imagination: Four Essays*. Edited by Michael Holquist. Translated by Caryl Emerson and Michael Holquist. Austin: University of Texas Press, 1981.

Bitzer, Lloyd F. "Functional Communication: A Situational Perspective." In *Rhetoric in Transition*, edited by Eugene White, 21–38. University Park: Pennsylvania State University Press.

———. "The Rhetorical Situation." *PR* 1 (1968): 1–14.

Brodkey, Linda. *Academic Writing as Social Practice*. Philadelphia: Temple University Press, 1987.

Burke, Kenneth. *A Grammar of Motives*. Berkeley: University of California Press, 1945, 1969.

Derrida, Jacques. *Dissemination*. Translated by Barbara Johnson. Chicago: University of Chicago Press, 1981.

Fish, Stanley. *Is There a Text in This Class? The Authority of Interpretive Communities*. Ithaca: Cornell University Press, 1980.

Harari, Josué, ed. *Text Strategies: Perspectives in Post-Structuralist Criticism*. Ithaca: Cornell University Press, 1979.

Kinneavy, James L. "*Kairos*: A Neglected Concept in Classical Rhetoric." In *Rhetoric and Praxis: The Contribution of Classical Rhetoric to Practical Reasoning*, edited by Jean Dietz Moss, 79–105. Washington, D.C.: Catholic University of America Press, 1983.

———. "The Relation of the Whole to the Part in Composition and in Interpretation Theory." In *The Territory of Language: Linguistics, Stylistics, and the Teaching of Composition*, edited by Donald McQuade, 292–312. Carbondale: Southern Illinois University Press, 1986.

Miller, Carolyn R. "Genre as Social Action." *QJS* 22, no. 2 (May 1984): 151–67.

Pratt, Mary Louise. *Toward a Speech Act Theory of Literary Discourse*. Bloomington: Indiana University Press, 1977.

Rostagni, Augusto. "Un Nuovo capitolo nella storia della retorica e della sofistica." *Studi italiani di filologia classica*, n.s. 2 (1922): 148–201.

Said, Edward W. *Beginnings: Intention and Method*. Baltimore: Johns Hopkins University Press, 1975.

Turner, Roy, ed. *Ethnomethodology: Selected Readings*. Baltimore: Penguin Books, 1974.

Untersteiner, Mario. *The Sophists*. Translated by Kathleen Freeman. Oxford: Basil Blackwell, 1954.

Vatz, Richard. "The Myth of the Rhetorical Situation." *PR* 6 (Summer 1972): 154–61.

Voloshinov, V. N. *Marxism and the Philosophy of Language*. Translated by Ladislav Matejka and I. R. Titunik. New York: Seminar Press, 1973.

Wood, Houston, and Hugh Mehan. *The Reality of Ethnomethodology*. New York: John Wiley & Sons, 1975.

Young, Richard E., Alton L. Becker, and Kenneth L. Pike. *Rhetoric: Discovery and Change*. New York: Harcourt, Brace and World, 1970.

IV. Communication Theory, Hermeneutics, and Pragmatics

Beale, Walter A. *A Pragmatic Theory of Rhetoric*. Carbondale: Southern Illinois University Press, 1987.

Bobrow, Daniel, and Donald Norman. "Some Principles of Memory Schemata." In *Representation and Understanding: Studies in Cognitive Science*, edited by Daniel Bobrow and Allen M. Collins, 131–50. New York: Academic Press, 1975.

Bultmann, Rudolf. "New Testament and Mythology." In *Kerygma and Myth: A Theological Debate*, edited by Hans Werner Bartsch, translated by Reginald H. Fuller, 1–45. London: S.P.C.K., 1953.

Cherry, Colin, ed. *Pragmatic Aspects of Human Communication*. Theory and Decision, no. 4. Hingman, Mass.: Kluwer Boston, 1974.

Danes, Frantisek. "One Instance of Prague School Methodology: Functional Analysis of Utterance of Text." In *Methods and Theory in Linguistics*, edited by Paul Garvin, 132–46. The Hague: Mouton, 1970.

Gadamer, Hans-Georg. *Truth and Method*. Translated by G. Barden and J. Cumming. New York: Seabury Press, 1986.

Heidegger, Martin. *Being and Time*. Translated by John Macquarrie and Edward Robinson. New York: Harper & Row, 1962.

Journal of Communication (1951–). Philadelphia: Annenberg School of Communication, University of Pennsylvania.

Journal of Pragmatics (1977–). Amsterdam: North-Holland.

Kintsch, Walter. *The Representation of Meaning in Memory*. Hillsdale, N.J.: Erlbaum, 1974.

Mathesius, Vilem. "On Linguistic Characterology with Illustrations from Modern English." In *A Prague School of Linguistics*, edited by Josef Vachek, 59–67. Bloomington: Indiana University Press, 1964.

Miller, George A. *Communication, Language, and Meaning: Psychological Perspectives*. New York: Basic Books, 1973.

Minsky, Marvin. "A Framework for Representing Knowledge." In *The Psychology of Computer Vision*, edited by Patrick H. Winston, 211–75. New York: McGraw-Hill, 1975.

Morris, Charles W. *Signs, Language, and Behavior*. Englewood Cliffs, N.J.: Prentice-Hall, 1946.

Schank, Roger, and Robert Abelson. "Scripts, Plans, and Knowledge." In *Thinking: Readings in Cognitive Science*, edited by Philip N. Johnson-Laird and Peter C. Wason, 421–32. New York: Cambridge University Press, 1977.

Schramm, Wilbur. *Men, Messages, and Media: A Look at Human Communication*. New York: Harper and Row, 1973.

Shannon, Claude E., and Warren Weaver. *The Mathematical Theory of Communication*. Urbana: University of Illinois Press, 1964.

Van Dijk, Teun, and Walter Kintsch. "Toward a Model of Text Comprehension and Production." *Psychological Review* 85 (September 1978): 363–94.

V. Argumentation, Informal Logic, and the Rhetoric of Science

Adorno, Theodor W. "Sociology and Empirical Research." In *Critical Sociology*, edited by Paul Connerton, 237–57. New York: Penguin Books, 1976.

Baier, Kurt. *The Moral Point of View: A Rational Basis of Ethics*. Ithaca: Cornell University Press, 1958.

Bazerman, Charles. *Shaping Written Knowledge: The Genre and Activity of the Experimental Article in Science*. Rhetoric of the Human Sciences, 3. Madison: University of Wisconsin Press, 1988.

Bernstein, Richard J. *Praxis and Action: Contemporary Philosophies of Human Activity*. Philadelphia: University of Pennsylvania Press, 1971.

Connerton, Paul, ed. *Critical Sociology*. New York: Penguin Books, 1976.

Ehninger, Douglas. *Influence, Belief, and Argument: An Introduction to Responsible Persuasion*. Glenview, Ill.: Scott, Foresman and Co., 1974.

Fahnstock, Jeanne, and Marie Secor. *A Rhetoric of Argument*. New York: Random House, 1982.

Gross, Alan. "Discourse on Method: The Rhetorical Analysis of Scientific Texts." *Pre/Text* 9 (Fall/Winter 1988): 169–85.

Habermas, Jürgen. *Theory and Practice*. Translated by John Virtel. Boston: Beacon Press, 1973.

Heidegger, Martin. "The Question Concerning Technology." *Basic Writings, from Being and Time (1927) to the Task of Thinking (1964)*, edited by David Farrell Krell, 283–317. 1954. Translated by William Lovitt. New York: Harper and Row, 1976.

Horkheimer, Max. "Traditional and Critical Theory." In *Critical Sociology*, edited by Paul Connerton, 206–24. Translated by J. O. Connell et al. New York: Penguin Books, 1976.

McCloskey, Donald N. *The Rhetoric of Economics*. Rhetoric of the Human Sciences, 1. Madison: University of Wisconsin Press, 1985.

Nelson, John S., Allan Megill, and Donald N. McCloskey, eds. *The Rhetoric of the Human Sciences: Language and Argument in Scholarship and Human Affairs*. Rhetoric of the Human Sciences, 2. Madison: University of Wisconsin Press, 1987.

Nisbett, Richard, and Lee Ross. *Human Inference: Strategies and Short-comings of Social Judgment.* Century Psychology Series. Englewood Cliffs, N.J.: Prentice-Hall, 1980.

Perelman, Chaim, and L. Olbrechts-Tyteca. *The New Rhetoric: A Treatise on Argumentation.* Translated by John Wilkinson and Purcell Weaver. Notre Dame: University of Notre Dame Press, 1969.

Pollock, Friedrich. "Empirical Research into Public Opinion." In *Critical Sociology,* edited by Paul Connerton, 225–36. Translated by Thomas Hall. New York: Penguin Books, 1976.

Schecker, Michael, ed. *Theorie der Argumentation.* Tübingen: TB-Verlag Narr, 1977.

Toulmin, Stephen E. *The Uses of Argument.* Cambridge: Cambridge University Press, 1958.

Turner, Roy (see III, *supra*).

VI. Dialectic, Exploration, and Epistemology

Adorno, Theodor W. *Negative Dialectics.* 1966. Translated by E. B. Ashton. New York: Continuum, 1973.

———. "Subject and Object." In *The Essential Frankfurt School Reader,* edited by Andrew Arato and Eikr Gebhardt, 497–511. New York: Urizen Books, 1978.

Berlin, James A. (see I, *supra*).

Burke, Kenneth (see III, *supra*).

Cherwitz, Richard A. "Rhetoric as 'A Way of Knowing': An Attenuation of the Epistemological Claims of the 'New Rhetoric'." *SSJ* 42 (Spring 1977): 207–19.

———. "Toward a Rhetorical Epistemology." *SSCJ* 47 (1982), 135–62.

Derrida, Jacques. "White Mythology: Metaphor in the Text of Philosophy." Translated by F. C. T. Moore. *NLH* 6 (Autumn 1974): 5–74.

Dialectica (1947–). Neuchâtel, Switzerland: Société Dialectica.

Feyerabend, Paul K. *Against Method: Outline of an Anarchistic Theory of Knowledge.* London: Verso, 1978.

Gonseth, Frederic. "L'Idée de dialectique aux entretiens de Zurich." *Dialectica* 1 (1947): 21–37.

Grassi, Ernesto. *Rhetoric as Philosophy: The Humanist Tradition.* Translated by John Michael Krois and Azizeh Azodi. University Park: Pennsylvania State University Press, 1980.

Hairston, Maxine, and John Ruszkiewicz. *The Scott Foresman Handbook with Writing Guide.* Glenview, Ill.: Scott, Foresman and Co., 1991.

Heidegger, Martin (see IV, *supra*).

Ijselling, Samuel. *Rhetoric and Philosophy in Conflict: An Historic Survey.* Translated by Paul Dunphy. The Hague: M. Nijhoff, 1976.

Johnstone, Henry W. "Truth Communication and Rhetoric in Philosophy." *Revue Internationale de Philosophie* 25 (1969): 405–6.

———. *Validity and Rhetoric in Philosophical Argument: An Outlook in Transition.* University Park, Pa.: Dialogue Press of Man and World, 1978.

Kinneavy, James L. (see I, *supra*).

Kuhn, Thomas S. *The Structure of Scientific Revolutions.* 2d ed. Chicago: University of Chicago Press, 1970.

Lukács, Georg. *History and Class Consciousness: Studies in Marxist Dialectics.* 1922. Translated by Rodney Livingstone. London: Merlin Press, 1974.

Popper, Karl. *The Logic of Scientific Discovery.* Translated by Julius and Lan V. Fried. London: Hutchinson & Co., 1959.

Ruszkiewicz, John J. *Well-Bound Words: A Rhetoric.* Glenview, Ill: Scott, Foresman and Co., 1981.

Scott, Robert L. "On Viewing Rhetoric as Epistemic: Ten Years Later." *CSSJ* 27 (Winter 1976): 258–66.

Young, Richard E., Alton L. Becker, and Kenneth L. Pike (see III, *supra*).

VII. Technical Writing, Journalism, and Information Theory

Alred, Gerald J., Diana C. Reep, Mohan R. Limaye, with the assistance of Michael A. Mikolajczak. *Business and Technical Writing: An Annotated Bibliography of Books, 1880–1980.* Metuchen, N.J.: Scarecrow Press, 1981.

Balachandran, Sarojini, ed. *Technical Writing: A Bibliography.* Urbana, Ill., and Washington, D.C.: American Business Communication Association and Society for Technical Communication, 1977.

Bar-Hillel, Yehoshua. *Language and Information: Selected Essays on Their Theory and Application.* Reading, Mass.: Addison-Wesley, 1964.

Charnley, Mitchell V., and Blair Charnley. *Reporting.* New York: Holt, Rinehart and Winston, 1979.

Charrow, Veda R. *Linguistic Theory and the Study of Legal and Bureaucratic Language.* Washington, D.C.: Document Design Project, 1981.

Coney, Mary. "Contemporary Views of Audience Theory: A Rhetorical Perspective." *Technical Writing Teacher* 14 (Fall 1989): 319–36.

Dobrin, David. "Is Technical Writing Particularly Objective?" *CE* 47 (March 1985): 237–51.

Goldstein, Tom. *Killing the Messenger: 100 Years of Media Criticism.* New York: Columbia University Press, 1989.

Information Sciences (1968–). New York: Elsevier North-Holland.

Lambeth, Edmund. *Committed Journalism: An Ethic for the Profession.* Bloomington: Indiana University Press, 1986.

Kinneavy, James L. (see I, *supra*).

MacDougall, Curtis. *Interpretive Reporting.* New York: Macmillan, 1977.

Merrill, John. *The Dialectic of Journalism: Toward a Responsible Use of Press Freedom.* Baton Rouge: Louisiana State University Press, 1989.

Meyer, Philip. *Precision Journalism: A Reporter's Introduction to Social Science Methods.* Bloomington: Indiana University Press, 1979.

Mills, Gordon H., and John A. Walter. *Technical Writing.* 4th ed. New York: Holt, Rinehart and Winston, 1978.

Racker, Joseph. *Technical Writing: Techniques for Engineers.* Englewood Cliffs, N.J.: Prentice-Hall, 1960.

Redish, Janice C. *The Language of the Bureaucracy.* Washington, D.C.: Document Design Project, 1981.

Rucker, Rudy. *Mind Tools: The Five Levels of Mathematical Reality.* Boston: Houghton Mifflin Co., 1987.

Schiller, Herbert I. *Communication and Cultural Domination.* White Plains, N.Y.: International Arts and Sciences Press, 1976.

Shannon, Claude E., and Warren Weaver (see IV, *supra*).

Siebert, Frederick S., Wilbur Schramm, et al. *Four Theories of the Press: The Authoritarian, Libertarian, Social Responsibility, and Soviet Communist Concepts of What the Press Should Be and Do.* Urbana: University of Illinois Press, 1956.

Wells, Rulon S. "A Measure of Subjective Information." In *Twelfth Symposium in Applied Mathematics,* edited by Roman Jakobson, 237–44. Providence, R.I.: American Mathematical Society, 1961.

Zappen, James. "Historical Studies in the Rhetoric of Science and Technology." *Technical Writing Teacher* 14 (Fall 1987): 285–98.

VIII. Propaganda, Political Rhetoric, and Commercial Advertising

Adorno, Theodor W. *Introduction to the Sociology of Music.* Translated by E. B. Ashton. New York: Continuum, 1976.

Advertising Age (1930–). Chicago: Crain Communications.

Barghoorn, Frederick C. *Soviet Union Propaganda.* Princeton: Princeton University Press, 1964.

Barnouw, Erik, ed. *The International Encyclopedia of Communication.* 4 vols. New York: Oxford University Press and Annenberg School of Communication, University of Pennsylvania, 1989.

Cohen, Dorothy. *Advertising.* Glenview, Ill.: Scott, Foresman and Co., 1988.

Doob, Leonard. *Public Opinion and Propaganda*. 2d ed. Hamden, Conn.: Shoe String Press, 1966.

Fisher, Walter R. "Genre: Concepts and Applications in Rhetorical Criticism." *WS* 44 (1980): 288–99.

———. "Reaffirmation and Subversion of the American Dream." *QJS* 59 (1973): 260–67.

Goffman, Erving. *Gender Advertisements*. New York: Harper & Row, 1979.

Gronbeck, Bruce E. "Rhetorical History and Rhetorical Criticism: A Distinction." *Speech Teacher* 24 (November 1975): 309–20.

———. "The Rhetoric of Political Corruption: Sociolinguistic, Dialectical, and Ceremonial Processes." *QJS* 64 (1978): 145–72.

Habermas, Jürgen. *Communication and the Evolution of Society*. Translated by Thomas McCarthy. Boston: Beacon Press, 1979.

———. "On Systematically Distorted Communication." *Inquiry* 13 (1970): 205–18.

Hadsmovsky, Eugen. *Propaganda and National Power: The Organization of Public Opinion for National Politics*. Translated by Alice Mavrogordato and De Witt Mavrogordato. New York: Arno Press, 1972.

Herman, Edward S. "Diversity of News: 'Marginilizing' the Opposition." *Journal of Communication* 35 (1985): 135–46.

Horkheimer, Max. *Critical Theory: Selected Essays*. Translated by Matthew J. O'Connell and others. New York: Herder and Herder, 1972.

Journal of Advertising (1972–). Lawrence, Kans.: School of Journalism.

Journal of Advertising Research (1960–). New York: Advertising Research Foundation.

Jowett, Garth S. "Propaganda and Communication: The Re-Emergence of a Research Tradition." *Journal of Communication* 37, no. 1 (1987): 97–114.

Lasswell, Harold D., Nathan Leites, and Associates. *Language of Politics: Studies in Quantitative Semantics*. 1949. New York: C. W. Stewart, 1965.

Lasswell, Harold D., et al. *Propaganda and Promotional Activities: An Annotated Bibliography*. Chicago: University of Chicago Press, 1969.

McLuhan, Marshall. *The Gutenberg Galaxy: The Makings of Typographical Man*. Toronto: University of Toronto Press, 1962.

Marcuse, Herbert. *One-Dimensional Man: Studies in the Ideology of Advanced Industrial Society*. Boston: Beacon Press, 1972.

Ogilvy, David. *Confessions of an Advertising Man*. New York: Atheneum, 1983.

———. *Ogilvy on Advertising*. New York: Vintage Books, 1985.

Public Opinion Quarterly (1937–). New York: Elsevier North-Holland.

Quarterly Journal of Speech (1915–). Annandale, Va.: Speech Communication Association.

Rosenfield, L. W. "August 9, 1974: The Victimage of Richard Nixon." *CQ* 24 (1976): 19–23.

———. "A Case Study in Speech Criticism: The Nixon-Truman Analog." *CM* 35 (1968): 435–50.

Rothschild, Michael L. *Advertising: From Fundamentals to Strategies.* Lexington, Mass.: D. C. Heath, 1987.

Schild, Hans-Jochen. "Political Rhetoric: A Potential Threat to Democracy; Questions Concerning the Study of Political Rhetoric." *Rhetorik: Ein internationales Jahrbuch* 7 (1988): 13–24.

Swanson, David L. "The Requirements of Critical Justifications." *CM* 44 (1977): 306–20.

Swanson, David L., and Linda L. Swanson. "The Agenda-Setting Function of the Ford-Carter Debate." *CM* 45 (1978): 347–58.

IX. Religious Oratory

Brilioth, Yngve. *A Brief History of Preaching.* Translated by Karl E. Mattson. Philadelphia: Fortress Press, 1965.

Broadus, John A. *On the Preparation and Delivery of Sermons.* Rev. ed., edited by Jesse Burton Weatherspoon. New York: Harper & Brothers, 1944.

Caplan, Harry, and Henry H. King. "Italian Treatises on Preaching: A Book-List." *SM* 16 (1949): 243–52. Others in the series in the same periodical are the following: for Spanish, 17 (June 1950): 161–70; for Scandinavian, 21 (March 1954): 1–9; for Dutch, 21 (November 1954): 235–47; for English, 22 (1955): 1–159, special issue; for German, 23 (1956): 5–106; the second in the series, for French, appeared in *QJS* 36 (October 1950): 196–325.

Crocker, Lionel, ed. *Harry Emerson Fosdick's Art of Preaching: An Anthology.* Springfield, Ill.: Charles C. Thomas, 1971.

Fosdick, Harry Emerson. "What Is the Matter with Preaching?" In *Harry Emerson Fosdick's Art of Preaching: An Anthology*, edited by Lionel Crocker, 27–41. Springfield, Ill.: Charles C. Thomas, 1971.

Lischer, Richard. "Recent Books on Preaching." *Word & World: Theology for Christian Ministry* 7 (1987): 41–98.

Melloh, John A. "Publish or Perish: A Review of Preaching Literature, 1981–1986." *Worship* 62 (November 1988): 497–514.

Preaching Today (1966–). St. Louis: The Christian Preaching Conference (originally *Preaching*, 1966–1970).

Rahner, Karl, S.J., ed. *The Renewal of Preaching: Theory and Practice.*

Concilium, Theology in the Age of Renewal, vol. 33. New York: Paulist Press, 1968.

Ritschl, Dietrich. *A Theology of Proclamation*. Richmond, Va.: John Knox Press, 1960.

Rosenberg, Bruce A. *The Art of the American Folk Preacher*. New York: Oxford University Press, 1970.

Semmelroth, Otto. *The Preaching Word: On the Theology of Proclamation*. New York: Herder and Herder, 1965.

Thompson, William, and William Toohey, eds. *Recent Homiletical Thought: A Bibliography, 1935-65*. Nashville: Abingdon Press, 1967.

X. Rhetorical Criticism

Baird, A. Craig. *Rhetoric: A Philosophical Inquiry*. New York: Ronald Press Co., 1965.

Bitzer, Lloyd F. (see III, *supra*).

Bitzer, Lloyd F., and Edwin Black (see I, *supra*).

Black, Edwin. *Rhetorical Criticism: A Study in Method*. New York: Macmillan Co., 1965.

Bryant, Donald. "Rhetoric: Its Function and Its Scope." *QJS* 39 (December 1953): 401–4.

Communication Monographs (1934–). Annandale, Va.: Speech Communication Association (originally *Speech Monographs*).

Simons, Herbert W. *Persuasion: Understanding, Practice and Analysis*. Reading, Mass.: Addison-Wesley Publishing Co., 1976.

XI. Women's Studies/Gender Studies

Anzaldua, Gloria, and Cherrie Moraga, eds. *This Bridge Called My Back: Writings by Radical Women of Color*. New York: Kitchen Table Press, 1983.

Beauvoir, Simone de. *The Second Sex*. New York: Knopf, 1953.

Culley, Margo, and Catherine Portuges, eds. *Gendered Subjects: The Dynamics of Feminist Teaching*. Boston: Routledge & Kegan Paul, 1985.

Eisenstein, Hester, and Alice Jardine, eds. *The Future of Difference*. Boston: G. K. Hall, 1980.

Feminist Studies (1972–). College Park, Md.: Feminist Studies.

Flynn, Elizabeth A., and Patrocinio P. Schweikart, eds. *Gender and Reading: Essays on Readers, Texts, and Contexts*. Baltimore: John Hopkins University Press, 1986.

Frank, Francine Wattman, et al. *Language, Gender, and Professional Writ-*

ing: Theoretical Approaches and Guidelines for Nonsexist Usage. New York: MLA, 1989.

Gilbert, Sandra M., and Susan Gubar. *The Madwoman in the Attic: The Woman Writer and the Nineteenth-Century Imagination.* New Haven: Yale University Press, 1979.

————. *No Man's Land—The Place of the Woman Writer in the Twentieth Century.* Vol. 1, *The War of the Words.* New Haven: Yale University Press, 1988. Vol. 2, *Sex Changes.* New Haven: Yale University Press, 1989.

Hedges, Elaine, ed. "Women Writing and Teaching." *CE* 34 (October 1972): 1–106, special issue.

Hull, Gloria T., Patricia Bell Scott, and Barbara Smith. *But Some of Us Are Brave: Black Women's Studies.* Old Westbury, N.Y.: Feminist Press, 1982.

Kauffman, Linda, ed. *Gender & Theory: Dialogues on Feminist Criticism.* New York: Basil Blackwell, 1989.

McAllester, Susan, ed. *A Case for Equity.* Urbana, Ill.: National Council of Teachers of English, 1971.

Marks, Elaine, and Isabelle de Courtivron, eds. *New French Feminism.* Amherst: University of Massachusetts Press, 1980.

Moi, Torril. *Sexual/Textual Politics.* London: Methuen, 1985.

Signs: Journal of Woman in Culture and Society (1975–). Chicago: University of Chicago Press.

XII. Self-Expression

Barrett, Harold. "Narcissism and Rhetorical Maturity." *WJSC* 50, no. 3 (1986): 254–68.

Catt, Isaac E. "Rhetoric and Narcissism: A Critique of Ideological Selfism." *WJSC* 50, no. 3 (1986): 242–53.

Elbow, Peter. *Writing without Teachers.* New York: Oxford University Press, 1973.

Gusdorf, Georges. *Speaking (La Parole).* Translated by Paul T. Brockelman. Evanston: Northwestern University Press, 1965.

Hegel, G. W. F. *The Phenomenology of Mind.* Translated by J. B. Baillie. New York: Harper & Row, 1967.

Heidegger, Martin (see IV, *supra*).

Kelley, Lou. *From Dialogue to Discourse: An Open Approach to Competence and Creativity.* Glenview, Ill.: Scott, Foresman and Co., 1972.

Kinneavy, James L. (see I, *supra*).

Macrorie, Ken. *Uptaught.* Rochelle Park, N.J.: Hayden Book Co., 1970.

Merleau-Ponty, Maurice. *Phenomenology of Perception*. Translated by Colin Smith. New York: Humanities Press, 1962.
———. *The Primacy of Perception*. Translated by James Edel. Evanston: Northwestern University Press, 1964.
Sartre, Jean-Paul. *Being and Nothingness: An Essay on Phenomenological Ontology*. Translated by Hazel Barnes. New York: Washington Square Press, 1953.

XIII. Mass Media and Small Group Media

Barthes, Roland. *Image—Music—Text*. Translated by Stephen Heath. New York: Hill and Wang, 1978.
———. *Mythologies*. Translated by Annette Lavers. New York: Hill and Wang, 1972.
Critical Studies in Mass Communication (1984–). Annandale, Md.: Speech Communication Association.
Cawelti, John G. *Adventure, Mystery, and Romance: Formula Stories in Art and Popular Culture*. Chicago: University of Chicago Press, 1976.
Davis, Murray S. *Intimate Relations*. New York: Free Press, 1973.
Fiske, John. *Television Culture*. New York: Methuen, 1987.
Fiske, John, and John Hartley. *Reading Television*. New York: Methuen, 1978.
Gans, Herbert J. *Popular Culture and High Culture: An Analysis and Evaluation of Taste*. New York: Basic Books, 1968.
Graig, Robert T., and Karen Tracy, eds. *Conversational Coherence: Form, Structure, and Strategy*. Beverly Hills: Sage, 1983.
Human Communication Research (1974–). New Brunswick, N.J.: International Communication Association.
Journal of Broadcasting and Electronic Media (1956–). Athens, Ga.: Broadcast Education Association (formerly *Journal of Broadcasting*, 1956–1985).
Journal of Popular Culture (1967–). Bowling Green, Ohio: Popular Culture Association.
Journal of Popular Film and Television (1972–). Bowling Green, Ohio: Bowling Green State University.
Kelley, Harold H. *Personal Relationships: Their Structures and Processes*. New York: Halsted Press, John Wiley & Sons, 1979.
Kelley, Harold H., and John N. Thibaut. *Interpersonal Relations: A Theory of Interdependence*. New York: John Wiley & Sons, 1978.
Knapp, Mark L. *Interpersonal Communication and Human Relationships*. Boston: Allyn and Bacon, 1984.

McLuhan, Marshall. *Understanding Media: The Extensions of Man*. New York: McGraw-Hill, 1964.

Medhurst, Martin J., and Thomas W. Benson. *Rhetorical Dimensions in Media: A Critical Casebook*. Dubuque, Ia.: Kendall/Hunt, 1984.

Newcomb, Horace, ed. *Television: The Critical View*. 4th ed. New York: Oxford University Press, 1987.

Nichols, Bill. *Ideology and the Image: Social Representation in the Cinema and Other Media*. Bloomington: Indiana University Press, 1981.

Ong, Walter J., S.J. *The Presence of the Word: Some Prolegomena for Cultural and Religious History*. New York: Simon and Shuster, 1970.

———. *Ramus, Method, and the Decay of Dialogue: From the Art of Discourse to the Art of Reason*. Cambridge: Harvard University Press, 1958.

Real, Michael. *Supermedia: A Cultural Approach*. Newbury Park, Calif.: Sage, 1989.

Schatz, Thomas. *Hollywood Film Genres*. New York: Random House, 1981.

Social Text (1979–). Madison, Wis.: Coda Press.

Williams, Raymond. *Television: Technology and Cultural Form*. New York: Schocken Books, 1975.

XIV. Semiotics and Semiology

Barthes, Roland (see XIII, *supra*).

———. *Elements of Semiology*. Translated by Annette Lavers and Colin Smith. New York: Hill and Wang, 1968.

———. *The Fashion System*. Translated by Matthew Ward and Richard Howard. New York: Hill and Wang, 1983.

———. *The Semiotic Challenge*. Translated by Richard Howard. New York: Hill and Wang, 1988.

Deely, John, ed. *Semiotics 1984*. Lanham, Md.: University Press of America, 1985.

Eco, Umberto. *The Role of the Reader: Explorations in the Semiotics of Texts*. Bloomington: Indiana University Press, 1979.

———. *Semiotics and the Philosophy of Language*. Bloomington: Indiana University Press, 1984.

———. *A Theory of Semiotics*. Bloomington: Indiana University Press, 1976.

Eschbach, Achim, and Jurgen Trabant. *History of Semiotics*. Amsterdam: John Benjamins, 1983.

Innis, Robert E., ed. *Semiotics: An Introductory Anthology*. Bloomington: Indiana University Press, 1985.

Jakobson, Roman. *Coup d'oeil sur le développement de la sémiotique.* Studies in Semiotics, 3. Bloomington: Indiana University Press, 1975.

Morris, Charles William. *Foundations of the Theory of Signs.* Chicago: University of Chicago Press, 1938.

———. *Signs, Language, and Behavior.* New York: George Braziller, 1955.

Murphey, Murray G. *The Development of Peirce's Philosophy.* 1946. Cambridge: Harvard University Press, 1961.

Parret, Herman, and Hans-George Ruprecht. *Aims and Prospects of Semiotics: Essays in Honor of Agirdas Julien Greimas.* Amsterdam: John Benjamins, 1985.

Peirce, Charles Sanders. *The Collected Papers of Charles Sanders Peirce.* Volumes 1–6 edited by Charles Hartshorne and Paul Weiss; volumes 7–8 edited by Arthur Burks. Cambridge: Harvard University Press, 1960–1966.

———. *Semiotics and Significs: The Correspondence between Charles S. Peirce and Lady Victoria Welby.* Edited by C. S. Hardwick and J. Cook. Bloomington: Indiana University Press, 1973.

Sebeok, Thomas A. *Encyclopedic Dictionary of Semiotics.* 3 vols. The Hague: Mouton, 1986.

Semiotica (1969–). The Hague: Mouton.

XV. Rhetoric as Metaphor

Bachelard, Gaston. *La Formation de l'esprit scientifique.* 9th ed. Paris: Vrin, 1975.

Barthes, Roland (see II, *supra*).

Canguilhem, G. *Etudes d'histoire et de la philosophie des sciences.* Paris: Vrin, 1973.

De Man, Paul. *Allegories of Reading: Figural Language in Rousseau, Nietzsche, Rilke, and Proust.* New Haven: Yale University Press, 1979.

Derrida, Jacques (see VI, *supra*).

———. "The Retrait of Metaphor." *Enclitic* 2 (Fall 1978): 5–33.

Dubois, Jacques, et al. *Rhétorique générale.* Paris: Librairie Larousse, 1971.

Genette, Gérard (see I, *supra*).

———. *Figures of Literary Discourse.* Translated by Alan Sheridan. New York: Columbia University Press, 1982.

Nietzsche, Friedrich. *Gesammelte Werke. Fünfter Band: Vorlesungen 1872–1876,* 287–319. Munich: Musarion Verlag, 1922.

———. "[Rhétorique et langage: Textes traduits, présentés et annotés par Philippe Lacoue-Labarthe et Jean-Luc Nancy]." *Poétique* 5 (1971): 99–143.

Ricoeur, Paul (see I, *supra*).

Sachs, Sheldon, ed. *On Metaphor*. Chicago: University of Chicago Press, 1979.

White, Hayden. *Metahistory: The Historical Imagination in Nineteenth-Century Europe*. Baltimore: Johns Hopkins University Press, 1973.

XVI. Rhetoric and the Teaching of Composition

Beach, Richard, and Linda S. Bridwell. *New Directions in Composition Research*. New York: Guilford, 1984.

Becker, A. L. "A Tagmemic Approach to Paragraph Analysis." *CCC* 16 (December 1965): 237–41.

Braddock, Richard, Richard Lloyd-Jones, and Lowell Schoer. *Research in Written Composition*. Urbana, Ill.: National Council of Teachers of English, 1963.

Britton, James N., et al. *The Development of Writing Abilities (11–18)*. London: Macmillan Education, 1975.

Bruffee, Kenneth. "Collaborative Learning and the Conversation of Mankind." *CE* 46 (1984): 635–42.

———. "Social Construction, Language, and the Authority of Knowledge." *CE* 48 (1986): 773–90.

Berger, Peter L., and Thomas Luckman. *The Social Construction of Reality: A Treatise in the Sociology of Knowledge*. New York: Anchor Press, Doubleday, 1967.

Burke, Kenneth (see III, *supra*).

Christensen, Francis, and Bonniejean Christensen. *Notes toward a New Rhetoric: 9 Essays for Teachers*. 2d ed. New York: Harper & Row, 1978.

College Composition and Communication (1949–). Chicago: National Council of Teachers of English.

College English (1939–). Chicago: National Council of Teachers of English (formerly *English Journal, College Edition*).

Composition Chronicle (1988–). Livonia, N.Y.: Viceroy Publications.

Corbett, Edward P. J., and Gary Tate, eds. *The Writing Teacher's Sourcebook*. 2d ed. New York: Oxford University Press, 1988.

Daiker, Donald A., Andrew Kerek, and Max Morenberg. *Sentence Combining: A Rhetorical Perspective*. 2d ed. Carbondale: Southern Illinois University Press, 1985.

D'Angelo, Frank J. *A Conceptual Theory of Rhetoric*. Cambridge, Mass.: Winthrop Publishers, 1975.

———. *Process and Thought in Composition*. 2d ed. Cambridge, Mass.: Winthrop Publishers, 1980.

Emig, Janet. *The Composing Processes of Twelfth Graders*. Research Project no. 13. Urbana, Ill.: National Council of Teachers of English, 1971.

―――. "Writing as a Mode of Learning." *CCC* 28 (May 1977): 122–28.

English Journal (1912–). Chicago: National Council of Teachers of English.

Enos, Richard Leo, et al. "Heuristic Procedures and the Composing Process: A Selected Bibliography." *RSQ*, Special Issue no. 1 (1982).

Faigley, Lester. "Competing Theories of Process: A Critique and a Proposal." *CCC* 48, no. 6 (October 1986): 527–42.

Flower, Linda S., and John R. Hayes. "The Cognition of Discovery: Defining a Rhetorical Problem." *CCC* 31 (February 1980): 21–32.

―――. "The Dynamics of Composing: Making Plans and Juggling Constraints." In *Cognitive Processes in Writing*, edited by Lee Gregg and Erwin Steinberg, 3–30. Hillsdale, N.J.: Lawrence Erlbaum, 1980.

Fulwiler, Toby, and Art Young, eds. *Language Connections: Writing and Reading across the Curriculum*. Urbana, Ill.: National Council of Teachers of English, 1982.

Gere, Anne Ruggles. *Writing Groups: History, Theory, and Implications*. Carbondale: Southern Illinois University Press, 1987.

Gere, Anne Ruggles, ed. *Roots in the Sawdust: Writing to Learn across the Disciplines*. Urbana, Ill.: National Council of Teachers of English, 1985.

Graves, Donald. *Rhetoric and Composition: A Sourcebook for Teachers of English*. New York: Hayden Book Co. 1976.

Griffin, C. W. "Programs for Writing across the Curriculum: A Report." *CCC* 36 (1985): 398–403.

Halliday, M. A., and Ruqaiya Hasan. *Cohesion in English*. New York: Longman's, 1976.

Hamilton, David. "Interdisciplinary Writing." *CE* 41 (March 1980): 780–96.

Herrington, Anne J. "Writing to Learn: Writing across the Disciplines." *CE* 43 (April 1981): 379–87.

Hillocks, George, Jr. *Research in Written Composition: New Directions for Teaching*. Urbana, Ill.: National Council of Teachers of English, 1986.

Hirsch, E. D., Jr. *Cultural Literacy: What Every American Needs to Know*. New York: Vintage Books, 1988.

Hunt, Kellog W. *Grammatical Structures at Three Grade Levels*. Research Report no. 3. Urbana, Ill.: National Council of Teachers of English, 1965.

Journal of Advanced Composition (1981–). Tampa: Association of Teachers of Advanced Composition, University of South Florida.

Journal of Basic Writing (1975–). New York: Department of English, City College of New York.

Journal of Teaching Writing (1982–). Indianapolis: Indiana Teachers of Writing.

Kinneavy, James L. (see I, *supra*).

——. "Thinkings and Writings: The Classical Tradition." In *Thinking, Reasoning, and Writing*, edited by Elaine Maimon, Barbara F. Nodine, and Finbarr W. O'Connor, 169–83. New York: Longman, 1989.

——. "Writing across the Curriculum." *ADE [Association of Departments of English] Bulletin* 76 (Winter 1983): 7–14.

Knoblauch, C. H., and Lil Brannon. *Rhetorical Traditions and the Teaching of Writing*. Upper Montclair, N.J.: Boynton/Cook 1984.

Larson, Richard L. "Structure and Form in Non-Narrative Prose." In *Teaching Composition: 12 Bibliographical Essays*, edited by Gary Tate, 39–82. Fort Worth: Texas Christian University Press, 1987.

Lauer, Janice. "Heuristics and Composition." *CCC* 21 (December 1970): 398–404.

Le Fevre, Karen Burke. *Invention as a Social Act*. Carbondale: Southern Illinois University Press, 1987.

Lindemann, Erika. *Longman Bibliography of Composition and Rhetoric*. Vol. I: 1984–1985. Vol. II: 1986. New York: Longman, 1987, 1989.

McClelland, Ben W., and Timothy R. Donovan, eds. *Perspectives on Recent Research and Scholarship in Composition*. New York: MLA, 1985.

McQuade, Donald A., ed. *The Territory of Language: Linguistics, Stylistics, and the Teaching of Composition*. 2d ed. Carbondale: Southern Illinois University Press, 1986.

Maimon, Elaine P., Barbara F. Nodine, and Finbarr W. O'Connor, eds. *Thinking, Reasoning, and Writing*. New York: Longman, 1989.

——. *Writing in the Arts and Sciences*. Cambridge, Mass.: Winthrop Publishers, 1981.

Mellon, John C. *Transformational Sentence-Combining: A Method for Enhancing the Development of Syntactic Fluency in English Composition*. Research Report no. 10. Urbana, Ill.: National Council of Teachers of English, 1969.

Moffett, James. *Teaching the Universe of Discourse*. Portsmouth, N.H.: Boynton/Cook Publishers, 1983.

Nold, Ellen W. *Re-vising: Toward a Theory*. ERIC Report ED 172 212. Bethesda, Md.: Educational Resources Information Center, 1979.

North, Stephen M. *The Making of Knowledge in Composition: Portrait of an Emerging Field*. Upper Montclair, N.J.: Boynton/Cook, 1987.

O'Hare, Frank. *Sentence-Combining: Improving Student Writing without Formal Grammar Instruction*. Research Report no. 15. Urbana, Ill.: National Council of Teachers of English, 1973.

Pike, Kenneth L. "A Linguistic Contribution to Composition." *CCC* 15 (May 1964): 81–89.

Research in the Teaching of English (1967–). Urbana, Ill.: National Council of Teachers of English.

Rhetoric Review (1982–). Tucson, Ariz.: Rhetoric Review.

Rodgers, Paul, Jr. "A Discourse-Centered Rhetoric of the Paragraph." *CCC* 17 (February 1966): 2–11.

Rohman, Gordon R. "Pre-Writing: The Stage of Discovery in the Writing Process." *CCC* 16 (May 1966): 106–12.

Rorty, Richard. *Philosophy and the Mirror of Nature*. Princeton: Princeton University Press, 1979.

Shaughnessy, Mina P. *Errors and Expectations*. New York: Oxford University Press, 1977.

Simon, Herbert A. *The Sciences of the Artificial*. 2d ed. Cambridge: MIT Press, 1981.

Sledd, James H. "Bi-Dialectalism: The Linguistics of White Supremacy." *EJ* 58 (December 1969): 1307–15.

———. "Doublespeak: Dialectology in the Service of Big Brother." *CE* 33 (January 1972): 439–57.

Smitherman, Geneva. "English Teacher, Why You Be Doing the Thangs You Don't Do?" *EJ* 61 (January 1972): 59–65.

Sommers, Nancy. "Revision Strategies of Student Writers and Experienced Adult Writers." *CCC* 31 (December 1980): 378–88.

Stock, Patricia, ed. *Forum: Essays on Theory and Practice in the Teaching of Writing*. Upper Montclair, N.J.: Boynton/Cook, 1983.

Strom, Ingrid. "Research in Grammar and Usage and Its Implications for Teaching Writing." *Bulletin of the School of Education, Indiana University* (1960).

"Students' Rights to Their Own Language." *CCC* Special Issue (October 1974).

Tate, Gary, ed. *Teaching Composition: 12 Bibliographical Essays*. 2d ed. Fort Worth: Texas Christian University Press, 1987.

Tate, Gary, and E. P. J. Corbett, eds. *The Writing Teacher's Sourcebook*. New York: Oxford University Press, 1988.

Vitanza, Victor. " 'Notes' Towards Historiographies of Rhetorics; or the Rhetorics of the Histories of Rhetorics: Traditional, Revisionary, and Sub/Versive." *Pre/Text* 8 (Spring/Summer 1987): 63–125.

Williams, Joseph M. *Style: Ten Lessons in Clarity & Grace*. Glenview, Ill.: Scott, Foresman and Co., 1984.

Winterowd, W. Ross. "The Grammar of Coherence." *CE* 31 (May 1970): 828–35.

———. "Topics and Levels in the Composition Press." *CE* 34 (February 1975): 701–9.

Witte, Stephen P., and Lester Faigley. "Coherence, Cohesion, and Writing Quality." *CCC* 32 (May 1981): 189–204.

———. *Evaluating College Writing*. Carbondale: Southern Illinois University Press, 1983.

Young, Richard E., Alton L. Becker, and Kenneth L. Pike (see III, *supra*).

XVII. Computers and Rhetoric

Barrett, Edward, ed. *Text, Context, and Hypertext: Writing with and for the Computer*. Cambridge: MIT Press, 1988.

Burns, Hugh. "Computers and Composition." In *Teaching Composition: 12 Bibliographical Essays*, edited by Gary Tate, 378–400. Fort Worth: Texas Christian University Press, 1987.

———. "The Promise of Artificial Intelligence Research for Composition." In *Perspectives on Research and Scholarship in Composition*, edited by Ben W. McClelland and Timothy R. Donovan. New York: MLA, 1985.

Collins, James L., and Elizabeth A. Sommers, eds. *Writing On-Line: Using Computers in the Teaching of Writing*. Upper Montclair, N.J.: Boynton/Cook, 1985.

Computers and Composition (1983–). Houghton: Department of Humanities, Michigan Technological University.

Computers and the Humanities (1966–). Dordrecht, Netherlands: Kluwer Academic Publishers.

Computational Linguistics (1974–). Yorktown Heights, N.Y.: Association for Computational Linguistics.

Costanzo, William V. *The Electronic Text: Learning to Read and Reason with Computers*. Englewood Cliffs, N.J.: Educational Technology, 1989.

Daiute, Colette. *Writing and Computers*. Reading, Mass.: Addison-Wesley Publishing Co., 1985.

Feldman, Paula R., and Buford Norman. *The Wordworthy Computer: Classroom and Research in Applications in Language and Literature*. New York: Random House, 1987.

Gillis, Philip D. "Using Computer Technology to Teach and Evaluate Prewriting." *Computers and the Humanities* 21 (1987): 3–19.

Halpern, Jeanne W., and Sarah Liggett. *Computers and Composing: How the New Technologies Are Changing Writing*. Carbondale: Southern Illinois University Press, 1984.

Hawisher, Gail E., and Cynthia L. Selfe, eds. *Critical Perspectives on

Computers and Composition Instruction. New York: Teachers College Press, 1989.

Hofstadter, Douglas R. *Godel, Escher, Bach: An Eternal Golden Braid*. New York: Vintage Books, 1980.

McDaniel, Ellen. "A Comparative Study of First-Generation Invention Software." *Computers and Composition* 3 (1986): 7–21.

Nold, Ellen. "Fear and Trembling: The Humanist Approaches the Computer." *CCC* 26 (1975): 269–73.

Olsen, Solveig, ed. *Computer-Assisted Instruction in the Humanities*. New York: MLA, 1985.

Papert, Seymour. *Mindstorms: Children, Computers, and Powerful Ideas*. New York: Basic Books, 1980.

Rodrigues, Dawn, and Raymond J. Rodrigues. "Computer-Based Invention: Its Place and Potential." *CCC* 35 (1984): 78–87.

Schank, Roger C., with Peter G. Childers. *The Cognitive Computer: On Language, Learning, and Artificial Intelligence*. Reading, Mass.: Addison-Wesley, 1984.

Schwartz, Helen J. *Interactive Writing: Composing with a Word Processor*. New York: Holt, Rinehart, and Winston, 1985.

Schwartz, Helen J., and Lillian S. Bridwell-Bowles. "A Selected Bibliography on Computers in Composition." *CCC* 35 (1984): 71–77.

———. "A Selected Bibliography on Computers in Composition: An Update." *CCC* 38 (1987): 453–57.

Selfe, Cynthia L. *Computer-Assisted Instruction in Composition: Create Your Own!* Urbana, Ill.: National Council of Teachers of English, 1986.

Turkle, Sherry. *The Second Self: Computers and the Human Spirit*. New York: Simon and Schuster, 1984.

Winograd, Terry, and Fernando Flores. *Understanding Computers and Cognition: A New Foundation for Design*. Norwood, N.J.: Ablex, 1986.

Wresch, William, ed. *The Computer in Composition Instruction: A Writer's Tool*. Urbana, Ill.: National Council of Teachers of English, 1984.

Zinsser, William. *Writing with a Word Processor*. New York: Harper and Row, 1983.

Zuboff, Shoshana. *In the Age of the Smart Machine: The Future of Work and Power*. New York: Basic Books, 1988.

About the Contributors

Don Paul Abbott is Associate Professor of Rhetoric and Communication at the University of California, Davis. His recent works on Renaissance rhetoric include "Rhetoric and Writing in Renaissance Europe and England," in *A Short History of Writing Instruction from Ancient Greece to Twentieth-Century America*, edited by James J. Murphy (1990), and "Aztecs and Orators: Rhetoric in New Spain," in *Texte: Revue de Critique et de Théorie Littéraire* (1990).

Kerri Morris Barton is an Assistant Professor at the University of Tennessee and teaches courses in rhetoric and writing.

Ann Blakeslee is a Ph.D. student in Rhetoric at Carnegie-Mellon University. She is studying the history of scientific rhetoric and is working with scientists to identify relevant social and cultural forces that have influenced the structure of communication in various scientific disciplines.

Martin Camargo is Associate Professor of English at the University of Missouri–Columbia. His articles and monographs on medieval rhetoric have appeared in *Speculum, Viator, Rhetorica*, and other journals and collections.

Richard Leo Enos is Associate Professor of Rhetoric in the Department of English at Carnegie-Mellon University and current President of the Rhetoric Society of America. His research emphasis is in the history of rhetoric with a specialization in classical rhetoric. He has received support for the study of ancient rhetoric from the National Endowment for the Humanities and has done research on Hellenic rhetoric in Greece through the American School of Classical Studies at Athens under the auspices of the Greek Ministry of Science and Culture.

Winifred Bryan Horner is Professor of English and Radford Chair of Rhetoric and Composition at Texas Christian University. Her publications include *Rhetoric in the Classical Tradition* (1988), *Composition and Rhetoric: Bridging the Gap* (1983), and *Historical Rhetoric: An Annotated Bibliography of Selected Sources in English* (1980), as well as numerous articles on composition and rhetoric. She is past president of the Rhetoric Society of America and the National Council of Writing Program Administrators.

247

James L. Kinneavy teaches in the department of English at the University of Texas at Austin. He is the author of *A Theory of Discourse* (1971, 1980) and other books and articles on rhetoric. His most recent book is *Greek Rhetorical Origins of Christian Faith: An Inquiry* (1987).

James J. Murphy is a Professor in the department of rhetoric as well as a Professor in the separate department of English at the University of California, Davis. His many works include *Rhetoric in the Middle Ages: A History of Rhetorical Theory from Saint Augustine to the Renaissance* (1974) and *Medieval Rhetoric: A Select Bibliography* (1971; 2d ed., 1989). In addition, he was the founding editor of *Rhetorica: A Journal of the History of Rhetoric*, which began publication in 1983.

Donald C. Stewart is Professor of English at Kansas State University. The author of textbooks (*The Authentic Voice*, 1972; *The Versatile Writer*, 1986); numerous articles and chapters in books on composition history and theory ("Fred Newton Scott" in *Traditions of Inquiry*, 1985; "What Is an English Major, and What Should It Be?" 1989); and nonacademic publications (*My Yellowstone Years*, 1989), he was the Chair of the Conference on College Composition and Communication in 1983.

Index

256 / Index